CASA "MIGUEL HEREDIA C." - Macerando Sombreros

a Crespo

Bodegas de Sombreros.

CASA "MIGUEL HEREDIA C." - Departamento de Empaques

Panama
a legendary hat

© Éditions Assouline, Paris, 1995.

All Rights Reserved. No part of this publication may be reproduced or transmitted in any form or by any means, electronic or mechanical, including photocopy, recording or any other information storage and retrieval system, without prior permission in writing from the publisher.

ISBN : 2 908228 36 X

Photoengraved by Gravor (Switzerland)
Printed by Artegrafica (Italy)

First edition

Panama
a legendary hat

Text by Martine Buchet

Photographs by Laziz Hamani

Translated by John Doherty and Bernard Hœpffner

EDICIONES LIBRI MUNDI
ENRIQUE GROSSE-LUEMERN

Contents

Chapter 1
Four hundred years of panamas

Chapter 2
The Myth of the "montecristi"

Chapter 3
Cuenca :
the Andes around a hat

Chapter 4
Guayaquil :
the port of the panama

Preface

I was tired. I had journeyed nearly 7,000 miles, from Honolulu to a tiny town in Ecuador, for the privilege of viewing a genuine "montecristi fino". As I weighed it in my hands and held it to the light to study the impossibly fine weave, felt its suppleness between my fingers and listened to an old weaver lament the impending extinction of this centuries-old art, I knew my life had found its mission.

I was tortured by the likelihood that in a generation, or less, the art of weaving the most exquisitely crafted hats in the history of the world would be no more. I believed then, as I believed now, that the only way to save the art is to create a greater demand for it. And for the past eight years, creating that demand has been the consuming passion of my life. So much so that the distinctive, somewhat pungent odour of fresh *toquilla* straw and sulphur-based bleaching powder pounded into the hats by the weavers has become for my young daughter "the Daddy smell".

Perhaps it is not too late. Perhaps another generation, or two, or more, will be able to know hats as breathtaking as the one that rekindles my passion every time I see or hold it. The older weavers tell me that it is indeed a beautiful hat, but oh, by far, not as beautiful as they used to weave them forty or fifty years ago. I cannot conceive of hat – made of straw, woven by the hand of a man – more beautiful than this one. I hold it in my hands now, still in awe of its maker. Before the ribbon and leather sweatband were added, it weighed less than a letter on my stationery. I feel the brim between thumb and forefinger. I've turned book pages thicker than this. The weave itself can barely be distinguished, even by sharp-eyed sceptics who scoff that no mere hat could be worth more than a well-tailored suit. Perhaps not, if the suit were woven by hand. In fact, the feel of the hat is more akin to cloth than to straw. I have a pair of linen trousers that are not as finely woven by far.

It is unimaginable to me that this hat was crafted by human hands. With my reading glasses on, placed under a strong light, I admire row after row after row after row the tiny, even, overlapping threads of straw. The colour is that of old, well-cared-for ivory. Hold it to the light and it glows, seemingly translucent. It is truly a work of art.

Yet this incredibly exquisite hat has but one flaw. A serious flaw. A flaw I cannot forgive. It is not my size.

Brent Black[*]

[*] Journalist-writer and panama specialist in the United States.

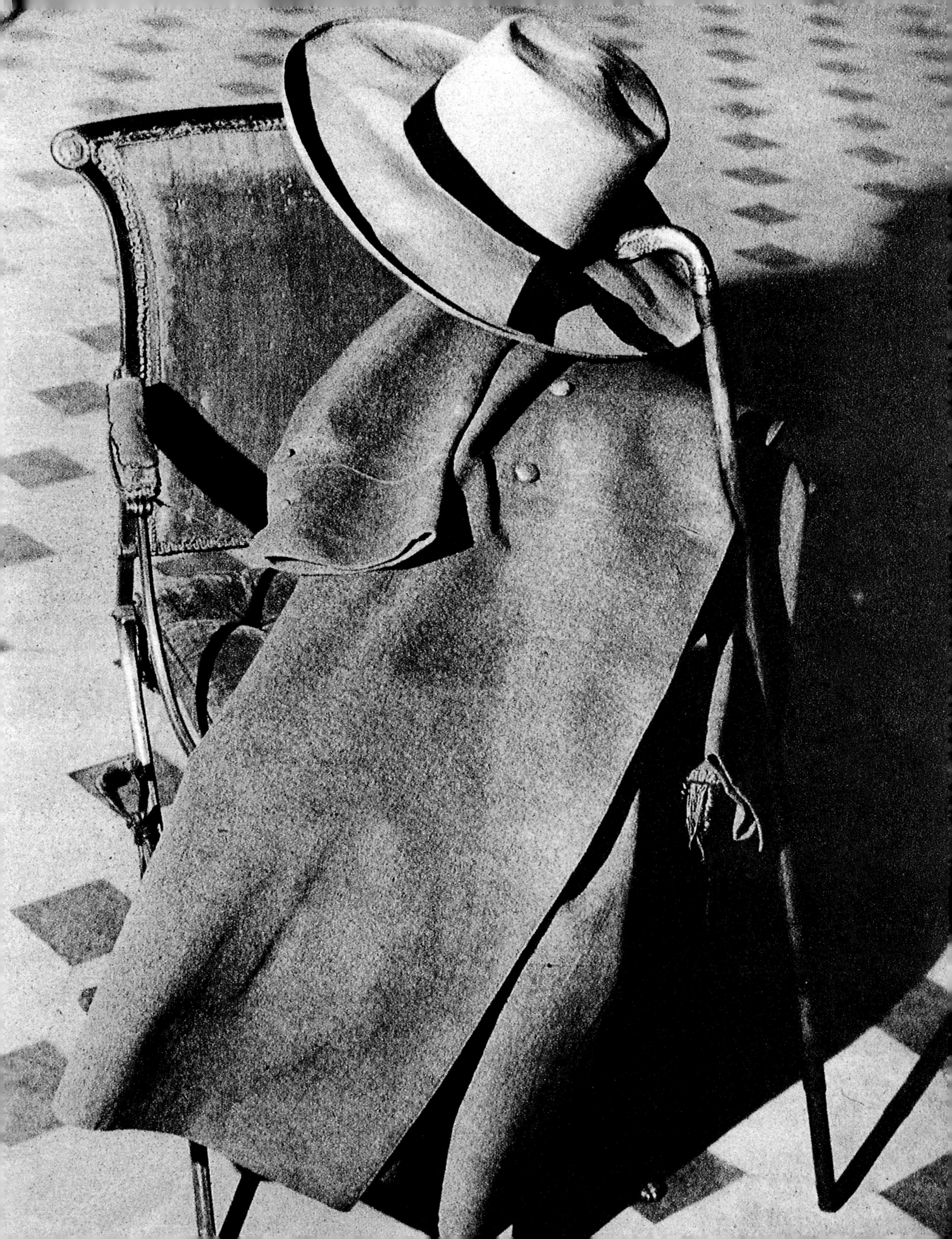

1

Four hundred years of panamas

The history of the 16th century records the fact that, after taking possession of the isthmus of Panama, the Spaniards heard about the riches of the south, and decided on a rapid extension of their conquest.

These proud, ambitious conquistadors, led by Francisco Pizarro and Diego de Almagro, reached the lands of present-day Ecuador in 1526, and some years later, in 1534, founded the Royal Audience of Quito.

The Spanish colonial empire was then set up, crushing forever Atahualpa's fabulous Inca empire. A thirst for adventure and gold drew innumerable colonists from the Iberian peninsula. They seized the land and the power in the name of their triumphant Catholicism, driven by an unchallengeable sentiment of superiority over the indigenous race which had welcomed them, and founded a society which set the seal on illegality.

In this brutal confrontation of cultures, the Spaniards and the native people discovered a great many improbable things. And if history has identified the Spanish conquest with its introduction of the horse into South America, legend, for its part, has taken hold of a curious story about hats.

The story is that the first Spaniards, discovering strange headgear being worn by some of the natives, took this light, translucent material for vampire skin. For a people who were already subjugated by these proud invaders, it was an amusing revenge to deceive them with such beliefs. Archaeological discoveries of ceramic figures wearing curious hats have been made on the Ecuadorian coast; these have contributed to the persistence of the curious anecdote. Whether it be a real fact or a native belief, this story already provided a legendary role for what was later to be known as the panama hat.

No further trace of it is to be found until a century later, in the provinces of Guayas and Manabí, which are coastal regions of Ecuador. The year 1630 saw the start of the artisanal production of this straw hat, which is unique in the world.

Francisco Delgado, a Creole of intuition and passion, now makes his entry into the legend. This talented weaver owes his place in history to the official registers. To recognise him is also to become aware of the cultural and commercial importance of a singular product which was to change the economic life of the coast for several decades. In effect, the second half of the 17th century saw the start of a notable development of this artisanate, which really took off in the 18th century.

At that time, the hat bore several names. It was called "jipijapa", from the name of a small town of Manabí which was supposed to be its traditional origin, or again, already, "montecristi", a name it still goes by today among the specialists of quality panamas.

Montecristi is a small town built on the side of a desert hill, near the large port of Manta. It dates from the 18th century, and had its hour of glory at the time of General Eloy Alfaro, an Ecuadorian hero who was born in Montecristi and spent his youth there. It owes its fame, however, to the fact that it is the home of the world's best weavers of straw hats.

The "jipijapa", or "montecristi" has also been called "toquilla", a popular name which has remained attached to it. The word is a derivative of "toque", which is the name of the hats that the Spaniards wore at the time of the conquest.

This toquilla straw, which continues today to provide a livelihood for some thousands of Ecuadorians, came into its own at the end of the 18th century, when José Pavon and Hipolito Ruiz, who were botanists at the royal gardens in Madrid, were sent to South America by King Charles IV to catalogue the flora there. The "toquilla" received the fine name of "Carludovica palmata" in honour of the king and his wife Luisa, and thus it was that it made its entry into the botany texts.

The century of the Enlightenment will never cease to be a subject of curiosity. After the conquistadors came the scholars, who crossed the seas to explore the new continent. It was at this time that France sent an expedition of three scientists – Louis Godin, Pierre Bouguer and Charles-Marie de La Condamine – to Ecuador to determine the true shape and size of the earth. Arriving in Quito in May 1736, they stayed there for nine years, calculating the length of a degree of the meridian in the neighbourhood of the equator, and extended their studies to the volcanic activity of the Andes, which was particularly intense in the 18th century.

Their visit left an indelible mark on the country, since, almost a century later, in May 1830, the first Constitutional Assembly, which was given the responsibility of

Previous page
Panama hat, cane and frock-coat, the property of Napoleon Bonaparte during his exile in Saint Helena.
Opposite page
The first panama hat. A ceramic figure, 5 cm high. Valdivia culture, 4,000 B.C.

finding a name for the newly-independent state, reached an agreement to call it as the three scientists had, all those years before, by reason of the line of equinox: the country of the Equator.

In nine years, La Condamine and his friends acquainted themselves fully with this South American land – the immense Andean mountain chain, which crosses it from one end to the other, bearing some of its towns up into the clouds, including Quito itself, the capital, which is perched at an altitude of 2,800 metres; its high, silent plateaus, which separate snow-covered mountains and volcanoes; its interminable tropical coast, turned towards the Pacific, majestic and disturbing when, each evening, it offers up its sunset; its other ocean; its green and humid jungle, called the "Oriente", which is traversed by long watercourses; its innumerable churches, as well as its colonial squares and proud haciendas.

The three scientists criss-crossed the country a number of times, attaching themselves here and there to the life of a house or a family that invited them in. This was the case with the Marqués de Maenza, who had them to stay on several occasions in his hacienda, "La Cienega", around sixty kilometres from Quito, one of the oldest estates in Ecuador and certainly one of the most beautiful. It had eight thousand hectares of crops and livestock. Its great white house, its shady patio and its little chapel, cool and luminous, were in the spirit of the few haciendas that existed at the time. La Condamine stayed there several times, on the handy pretext of carrying out volcanic studies; and indeed the imposing volcano of Cotopaxi was not all that far away.

> 4,000 B.C.: the panama's ancestor makes a first appearance in Latin American culture.

At the time, three regions, or rather three towns, were jostling for pre-eminence. They had all sprung up in the colonial 16th century: Cuenca and Quito were borne up by the Andes, while the port of Guayaquil was spread out languidly on the Pacific coast.

In this country of endless contrast, where coast and sierra seem to ignore each other, to turn their backs on each other, the toquilla straw hat had already established itself. And in the prevailing rivalry, it first chose Guayaquil, which, being entirely turned towards other worlds, could not but fascinate. Ships laden with gold, then sugar, coffee or cacao, set sail for the isthmus of Panama, which gradually, with time, became the primary trading centre of South America. From there, the merchandise made its way to Europe, or North America. And the first "montecristis" no doubt followed this route in the baggage of traders, scientists and sea-captains making their way home.

It was during the 18th century that the toquilla crossed its first oceans, proud to have conquered a number of these adventurers of the new world. Legend has forgotten the names of these first voyagers, like that of the donor of the gift made to the emperor Napoleon during his exile. And yet, during his long sojourn in Saint Helena, Napoleon exchanged the black hat of the conqueror for the striking whiteness of a magnificent "montecristi", which he never parted with thereafter.

Already, another century was under way in this new world, which was seeking an identity. At Guayaquil, the boats were unloading merchandise and revolutionary ideas from the old continent. South America was star-

Following pages
Left : Franciscan books, 15th century.
Right : Franciscan on the road
to Santo Domingo. The panama was an indispensable
companion of the voyager.

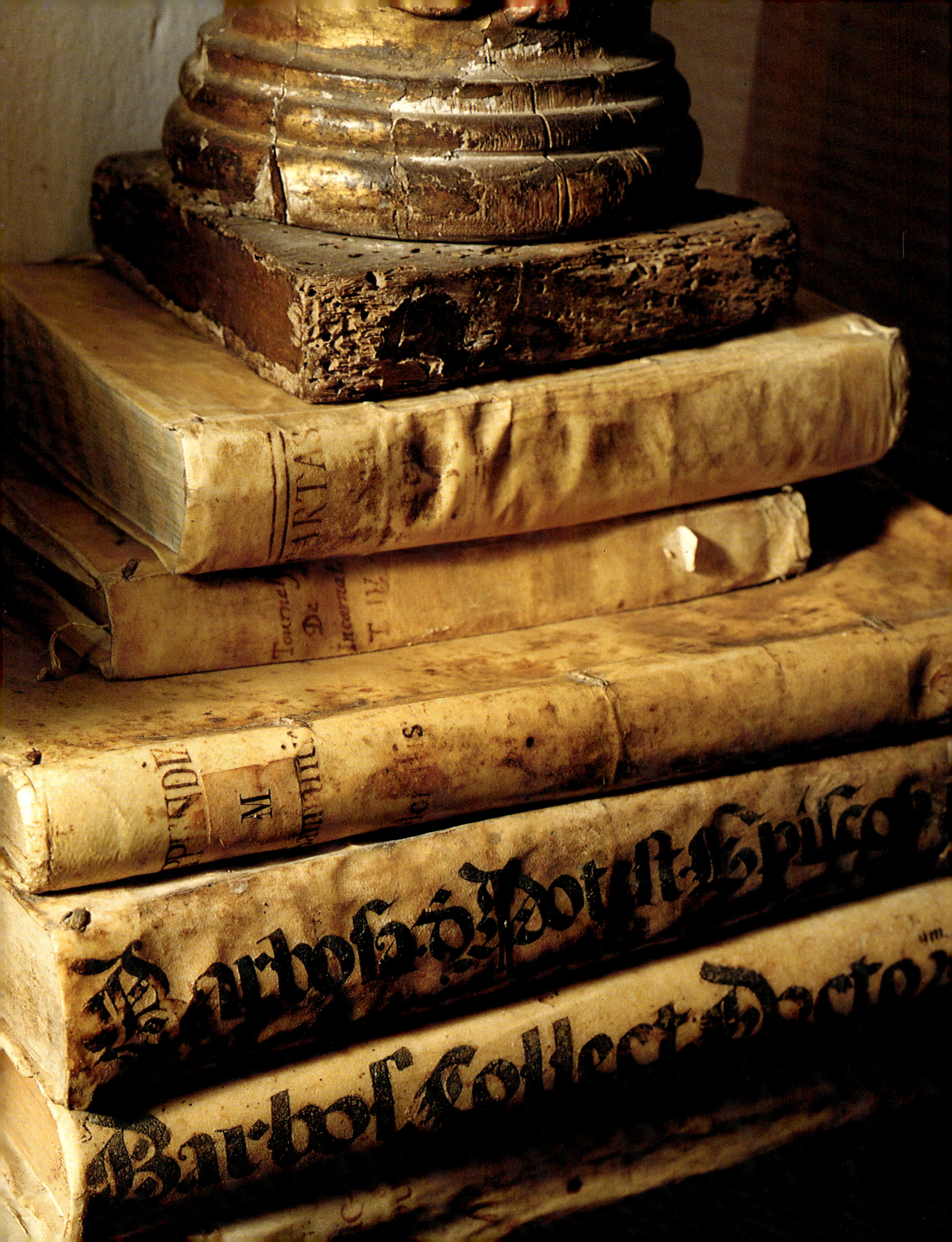

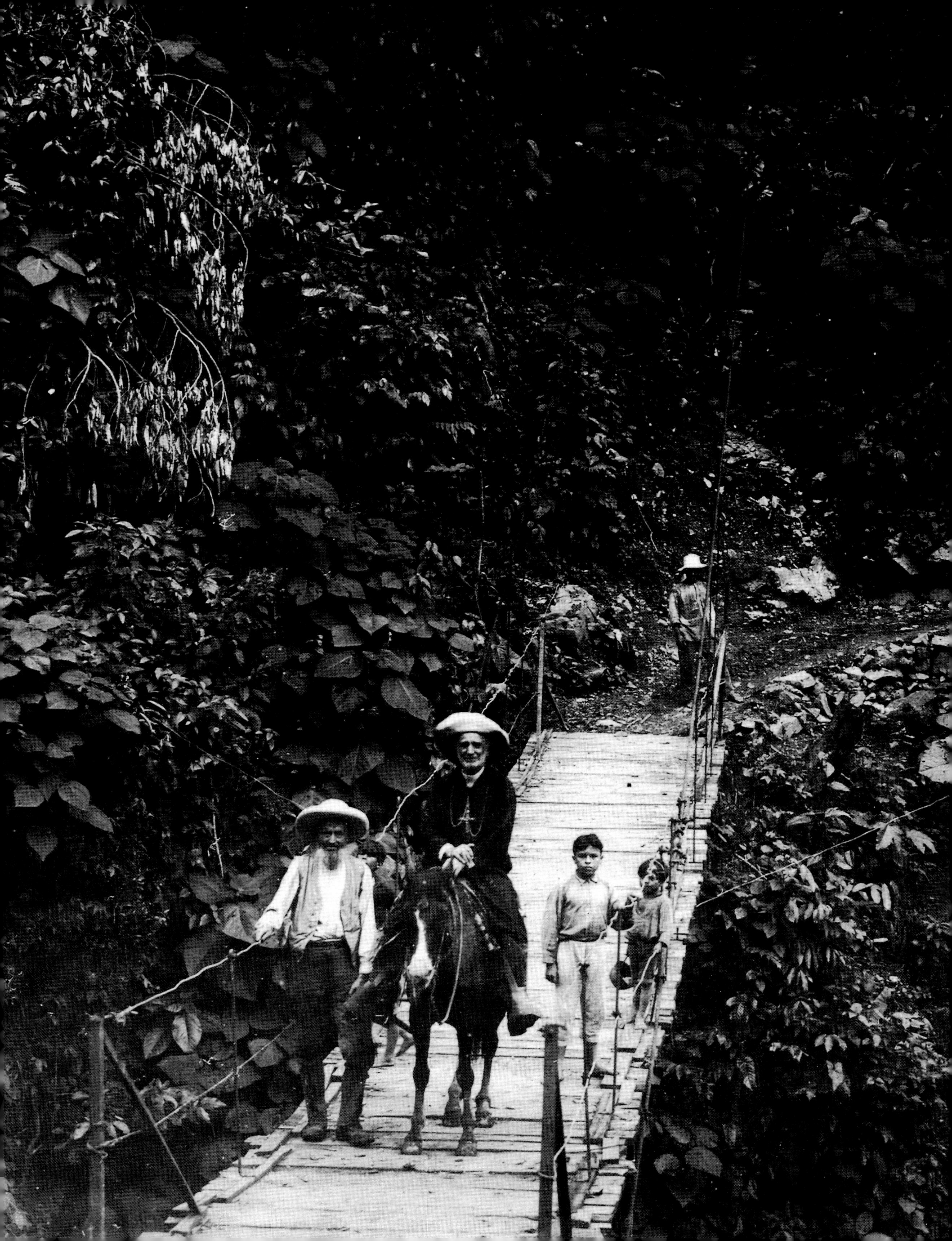

*Town hall of Jipijapa (Manabí province)
in 1912.*

ting out on its march towards independence, with, at its head, Generals Bolívar and San Martín, who placed Ecuador in the hands of Marshal Sucre. Liberated from the heavy hand of Spanish tutelage, the economic life of the country underwent a gigantic process of evolution. It was the great age of cacao. But it was equally to be that of the panama hat!

With the "jipijapa" and the "montecristi", the province of Manabí was at the centre of this activity. From now on, the toquilla hat was an integral feature of life all along the Ecuadorian coast. Light and flexible, as well as extremely strong, it became an indispensable accessory for the great "latifundistas", as well as for the plantation workers. The artisanate became organised, and the talent of certain "maestros", recognised master weavers, imposed a hierarchy of the hat, allowing it to penetrate the closed circles of sartorial snobbery, at the same time as more popular habits were developing.

The straw hat trade became more clearly defined, and more intensive. But it was not until 1835, with the arrival of Manuel Alfaro, that it made a breakthrough in other countries. When he disembarked in Guayaquil, this audacious Spanish entrepreneur decided to stay and make his fortune in Ecuador. He did not take long to spot a suitable line of business. Having settled down in the heart of Montecristi, the little town on the hill caressed by the ocean breezes, he turned to the straw hat trade with a single objective: exportation. He set up his own circuits of weavers, and perfected a system for ensuring a smooth flow of production. Very soon, the cargo ships of Guayaquil, as well as those of Manta, which was just a few kilometres from Montecristi, were being filled with his merchandise for their journey to the gulf of Panama. There, he opened a commercial centre where he also traded in cacao and pearls. History aided him in his projects, with the first tremors of gold fever. To get to the Californian Eldorado, the route frequently passed through Panama. More and more prospectors started to arrive, and the omnipresent sun made it necessary to provide oneself with a hat for the long road.

*Family of weavers in Montecristi,
in 1912.*

It was thanks to the gold-diggers that the straw hat began its conquest of the United States. In 1850, the American giant was already buying up more than two hundred and twenty thousand of them, and seven of the prospectors posed with their hats and bags of nuggets before the Mint, in Philadelphia, for a woodcut that became famous. The same year saw the inauguration of Ecuador's first railway line, which facilitated the development of the "toquilla" trade. By now, Alfaro was no longer the only person to be exporting hats, and the coming of the train gradually encouraged the emergence of increasing competition.

In response to the economic problems which afflicted certain provinces, the authorities of Cuenca, in the province of Azuay, decided, in 1836, to open a hat factory, and, some years later, they set up a workshop both for manufacture and for training.

In 1845, Don Bartolomé Serrano, a prominent citizen of the little town of Azogues, speeded up the movement by bringing in all the constituents which had made hat-making successful on the coast.

The straw of Manglar Alto, as well as the forms, bleaching processes and other indispensable expertise and instruments, took the road for Cuenca, accompanied by some weaving maestros who were given the task of passing on their art. Apprenticeship became compulsory throughout the Azuay province, for adults as well as for children, on pain of sanctions which could be as much as several days' prison! With the pace of this development, the straw hat business rapidly became one of the most profitable economic activities of the region. The art of weaving was perfected, and, in keeping with the given hierarchical structures, the little district of Biblián was

Following pages
*Left : Franciscan saint in polychrome wood.
Right : Part of the choir in the church of the monastery of San Francisco (1534).
Chapel of the "La Cienega" hacienda (17th century).*

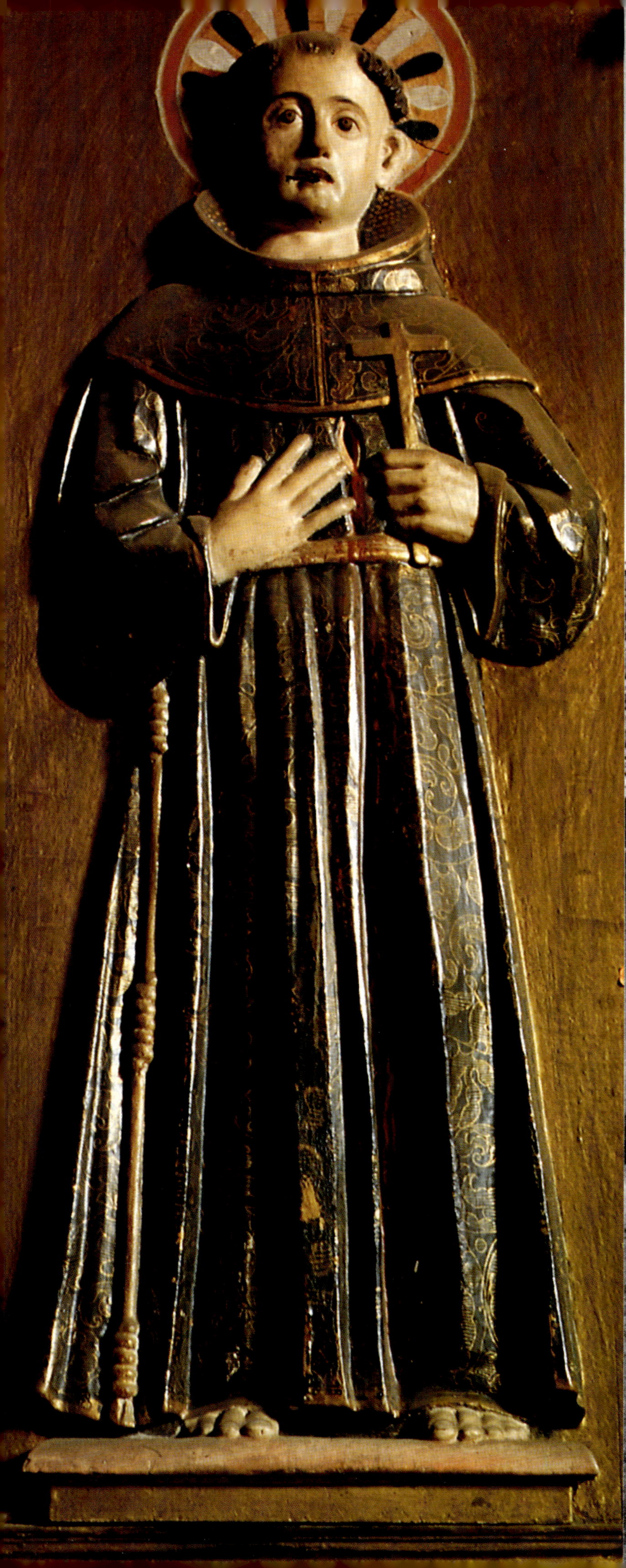
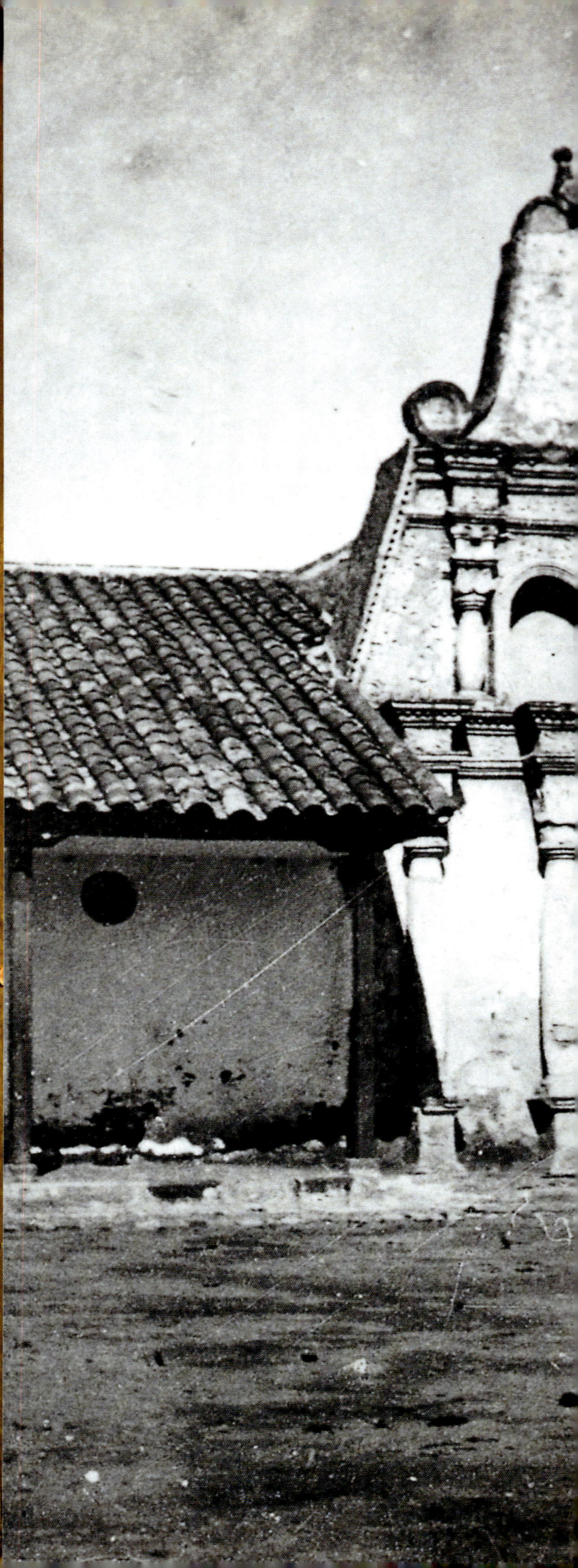

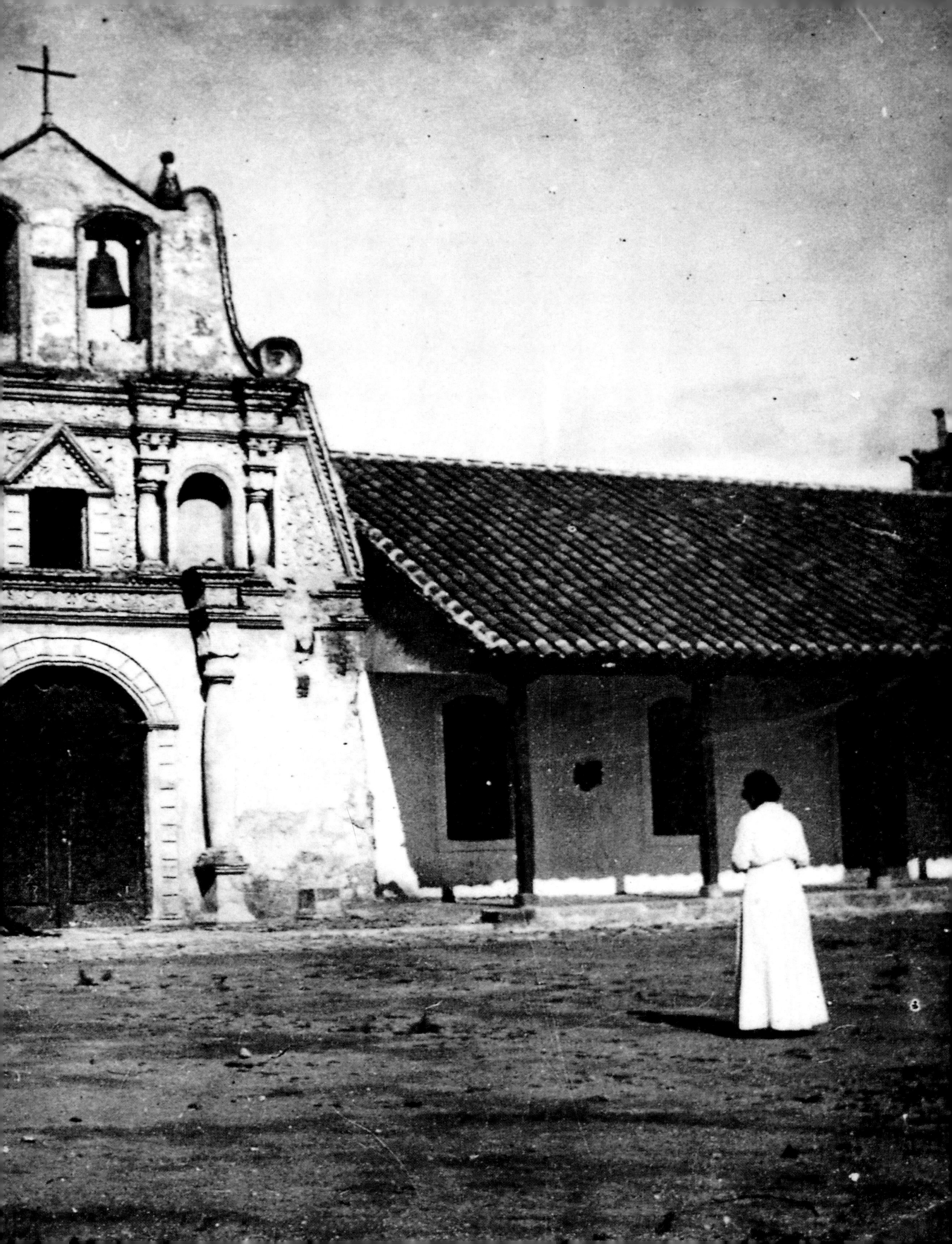

Cacao trees in the "Levante" hacienda, which belonged to Juan Polit, 1912. Chone (Manabí province).

pre-eminent in the finest types of weaving, to the extent of competing with certain "montecristis" and "jipijapas"! From that point on, the "cuenca" was a force to be reckoned with. Involved as it was in the hat trade for purely economic reasons, the region organised and developed its production according to the markets that were to be conquered, little by little outstripping the Manabí region, which leant more towards defending the perfection of the traditional craft, which it maintained with the proud knowledge of never being equalled.

In the middle of the 19th century, the success of the straw hat was such that the statistics of the National Academy of Ecuador put forward the figure, for 1863, of five hundred thousand articles originating from several regions of the country, and ready for export via Guayaquil. It is true that, in terms of markets, Europe had now become a destination, along with the United States and the neighbouring South American countries.

In 1855, Paris discovered this unrivalled straw hat during the World Fair. The catalogue did not even mention Ecuador as a participating country, and it was in the space reserved for "diverse countries" that the Frenchman Philippe Raimondi, arriving from Panama, where he lived, presented the "toquilla" hat in France for the first time. Despite quite a large stock, the young man could not satisfy the immense demand which he had created. The fineness of the texture of the hat did not cease to impress the Parisians, despite their reputation as demanding customers, and the catalogue of the World Fair mentioned a hat in "straw cloth"!

A "montecristi fino" was presented to Napoleon III, and Paris launched the fashion. The hat was quite naturally christened "panama", as the result of a confusion between the port of origin and the original provenance, as had already been the case with the Americans. Soon, the fame of the "panama" was such that the Ecuadorian authorities could do nothing to change the name of this distinctive product, which was unique in the world; it had slipped through their fingers, and was promoting the image of another country, which was being talked

*Transport of straw and sugar cane in 1915
(Guayas province).*

about more and more! And in fact, this final phase of the century marked the beginning of a gigantic project: the construction of the Panama canal by Ferdinand de Lesseps, who had been given the task of linking up the world's two greatest oceans. The newspapers of the period were very attentive to this part of the globe. The very idea – to cut a continent in two! The task was long and Herculean. Millions of cubic metres of earth had to be moved. Assistance poured in from every side, and there was certainly no lack of work.

The heat and the sun made the use of the straw hat more or less obligatory. It was extremely light, airy and protective, thanks to its broad brim. It was even said that the finest specimens could be used to carry water: a nice way of cooling oneself down! The hat, in any case, became indispensable in Panama, and its success was such that other countries began to produce their own versions. Ecuador gave its authorisation to sell the precious straw. Peru and Colombia also began production – their output was smaller, but they participated in their own way in the history of the hat by introducing other types of weaving, and other designs.

At this time, Panama was not just the most important trading centre in South America, and the future leading light in a project that had the world holding its breath: it was also an international centre of revolutionary activity, one of whose principal actors went by the name of Eloy Alfaro.

Eloy, the son of Manuel Alfaro, arrived in Panama at the age of twenty to take over from his father. He was an excellent businessman who made his fortune largely from toquillas, which he attempted, though too late, to rename "jipijapas". He was intelligent, cultivated and strong-willed. He had a passionate nature, a noble heart and a yearning for justice. He became the first liberal leader of Ecuador, and brought his country through the most massive political, social and educational transformation in its history; he was also twice appointed President of the Republic. To attain his goal, he had to leave the country for many long years, during which he

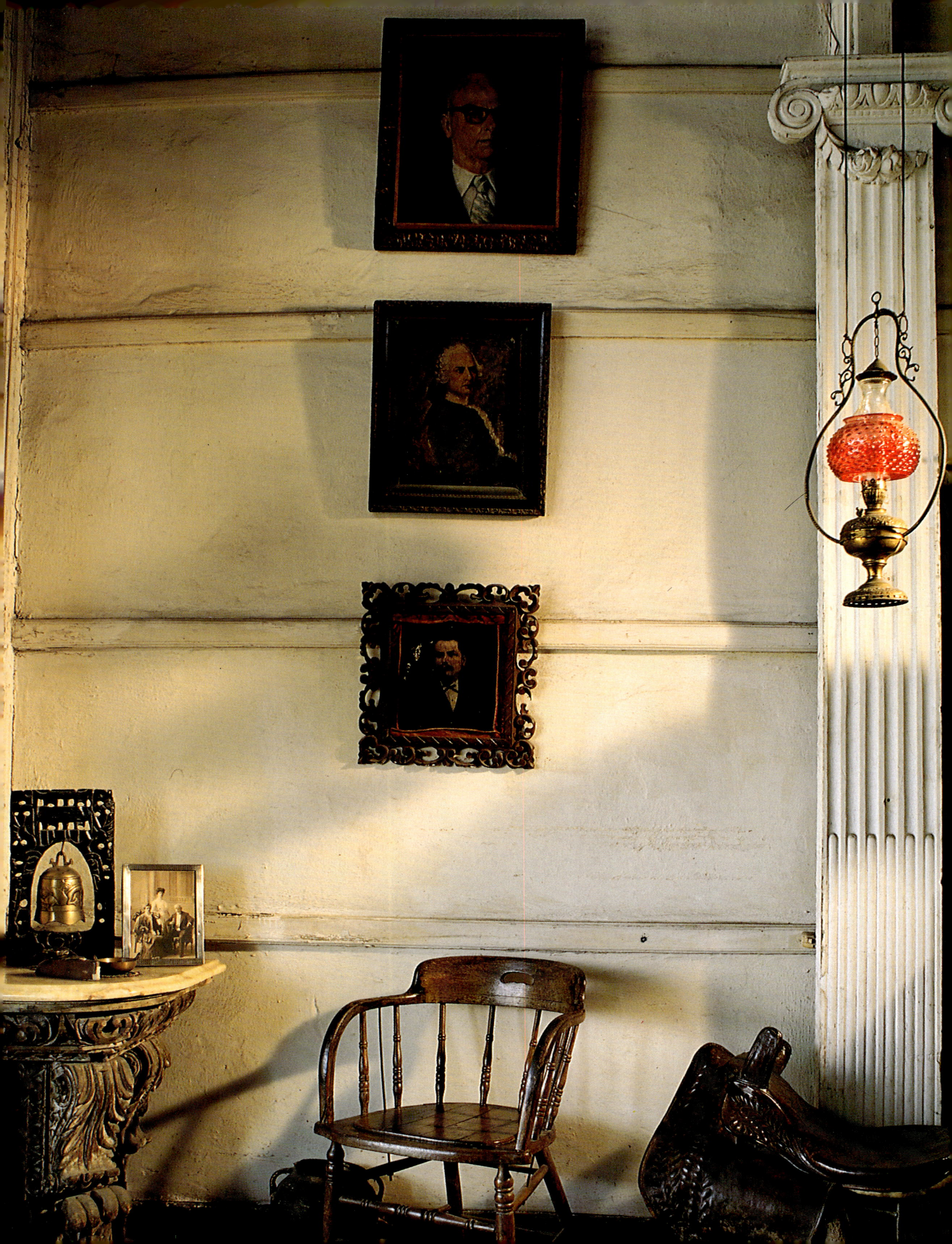

Ecuadorian national hero and emblematic figure, *Eloy Alfaro* helped finance his liberal revolution through the export of panamas.

Opposite page
*The home of Eloy Alviles Alfaro, the grandson of the celebrated Ecuadorian president.
On the wall are the portraits of several generations of Alfaros.*

became the patron of the revolutionaries. This led Tom Miller to comment, in his work *The Panama Line*, during a conversation with Eloy Alfaro's grandson, Eloy Alviles Alfaro, that "It seems obvious to me that the panama hat was responsible for the great liberal revolution in Ecuador". The generous soul of the future General Eloy Alfaro was not interested exclusively in his own nation: he followed to the letter the testamentary thinking of Simon Bolívar, according to which "America is the motherland", and helped other South American nations, particularly Cuba, to gain their independence.

Indolent, cheerful, always full of life, the island of Cuba also lives in the shadow of the panama. Of course there are planters of sugar cane and tobacco, for whom the straw hat is an inescapable necessity. But there is also the style. And Cuba is chic, Cuba likes to party, Cuban men are handsome. So, for over a century, these South Americans of the Caribbean were among Ecuador's best customers. When, in 1895, Eloy Alfaro became president of his country, the effect of his victory spilled over beyond the borders of Ecuador; the cheers resounded as far away as Cuba. The liberalism and extraordinary dynamism of the new president brought new life and intensity to Ecuador. There was construction, and reform, and hope.

A new railway line was begun. It was to cross the Andes, and so link up the coast and the Sierra, those warring sisters. It was to change everything, but the hats of Cuenca did well out of it. The Guayaquil traffic became heavier as a result, the port relived the great age of cacao, and immense haciendas spread out all around the town; these belonged to the rich latifundistas who comprised the country's oligarchy. Their names were Piedrahita, Manzano, Puga, Carbo, Reyre, Azpiazu, Seminario, Guzman, Rosales and Aguirre. In Los Rios province, less than twenty families provided a living for forty thousand people! But the most impressive property was undoubtedly that of the Ballen family, with its million cacao trees. Several decades later, this hacienda was to be bought up by one of the most successful of all Ecuadorian businessmen, Louis Noboa Naranjo, who converted it, under the name of "La Clementina", into one of the largest and finest banana plantations in the world.

The land in the provinces of Los Rios and Guayas was uncommonly fertile. There, the river which stretched out parallel to the ocean, and the immense estuary of the gulf of Guayaquil, created unique conditions of irrigation for the plantations. The largest port on the Pacific coast became a trading town and also an important shipyard. But the region was also hot and marshy; life there was difficult. Since 1860, the kings of cacao had tended to hand over the management of their lands to agents, and to spend their time in Europe. Almost all of them chose Paris, where they set themselves up in houses and mansions in the elegant *quartiers*. Some of them put down roots – which caused one of the descendants of the Manzano family to remark, much later: "It was cacao that made us French".

In Paris, this was the *belle époque*. The industrial epic dynamised the century and intoxicated its contemporaries. Ostentatious entertaining was the order of the day, with voyages in wagon-lits and steamships, which were at the height of their opulent luxuriousness. "Polite society" was all-powerful, and, although the nobility of Europe was quietly opening up to the new American "aristocracy", during the Second Empire, Paris continued to dictate fashion.

Despite the uncontested genius of Fabergé, and the splendours of Tiffany, the world bowed down before Cartier, who made Paris the capital of high-class jewellery, at a time when Lalique, Christofle, Boucheron and Mellerio were also embarking on their brilliant careers. The Empress Eugénie became the most faithful client of Worth, who was then inventing *haute couture*. European aristocrats and American heiresses, having become unconditional devotees of the couturier, were the crowning glory of fashionable society, and provided material for Proust, who described the salons of this extravagant period in *Le Côté de Guermantes* (*The Guermantes Way*). This golden age also marked the saga of the panama hat. The top hat had been *de rigueur* but, gradually, it was displaced by the bowler and the felt hat. The summer season brought straw hats into fashion, with the appearance of the boater, but Napoleon III, Edward VII and some other aficionados established the reputation of the panama, which took its place as the prince of straw hats. After its presentation in Paris at the World Fair, it was to be found in the great hat-makers' establishments. Starting from 1856, the nephew of Gibus began to import the finest panamas, after which it was the turn of Gelot and of Motsch. In London, it was Herbert Johnson who had the choicest specimens on offer.

The elegance of the "montecristi" conquered Europe, which gave itself up to the cult of the beautiful. Men followed fashion, and the arrogance of the dandies fascinated the bourgeoisie. People had a taste for luxury, and knew quality when they saw it. Boni de Castellane and Gabriele d'Annunzio, who were veritable Stendhalian heroes and arbiters of elegance, wore their panamas with style, and with a satisfaction worthy of connoisseurs. The success of the hat was such that it quickly became very popular — a little too popular for the liking of certain gazettes, which reckoned that it had "fallen into vulgarity", while acknowledging, a few lines further on, that "there are few experts" where this fine accessory was concerned.

For indeed the term "panama hat" covered an infinite variety of qualities, and, by the same token, a large range of prices. Thus, a panama of less fine straw, and with a less regular weave, remained an admirable hat, and more affordable, but also more banal. This type, which was very popular in the United States, had a more unstable life in Europe, where fashions came and went continually. In reality, the myth of the panama was built on the "finos" that came from Montecristi and Jipijapa. It was

Previous page
Buyers and sellers of panamas in 1910 in Santa Ana (Manabí province).

said that the rarest could pass through a wedding ring, or be hidden in a large matchbox. The price was of little importance: what people were looking for was fineness, suppleness and regularity; the ivory tone. This kind of panama cannot go out of fashion. It has its admirers, its unquestioning worshippers, its specialists. There was competition in quality, style, designs; there was a desire to amaze. It was the halcyon day of the hat! The *dolce vita*, in this declining century, opened up its road to all the capital cities.

After Paris and London, Berlin and Rome fell into line. It was a companion to the most ravishing journeys. The luxury of new means of transport had made other continents accessible: people thus went to Egypt, India and Morocco to be dazzled by unknown images. Summer resorts experienced a runaway period of growth. People would move to Biarritz, Nice or Monte Carlo for an entire season. They moved around a lot, and they did it in style. Vuitton trunks were an elegant way to transport imposing wardrobes to the most sumptuous hotels. There were wonderful climates to discover. In this quest for blue sky, the panama became indispensable. It triumphed on the Riviera, where any other form of hat became unthinkable. In his treatise on "masculine elegance", Abel Léger recommended "wearing the panama with a simple band of black cloth".

The first years of a new century changed nothing in the habits of this privileged society, sunk in its voluptuous existence. With Europe becoming more bourgeois, the United States pursuing its astonishing progress, and work on the Panama canal proceeding relentlessly, Ecuador was experiencing its great years of liberalism under President Eloy Alfaro, who ruled uncontested over the cacao, with its thirty-one million trees.

The history of the straw hat continued. It was now found regularly in the columns of the international press. By turns praised to the skies and trailed in the mud, in any case it seemed to interest the newspapers. In 1900, the

Opposite page
President Theodore Roosevelt during his visit to the construction of the Panama canal in 1906.

Sporting a panama on his visit to the canal, Theodore Roosevelt makes the front pages of newspapers the world over, and popularises the hat.

A panama in the sun in Marseille, during the famous "card game" scene in Marcel Pagnol's film Marius.

famous American cartoonist Thomas Nast sketched the banker J.P. Morgan, superbly hatted. In France, after Napoleon III, there were drawings of Edward VII, a great fan of the French hat-maker Robert Gelot, who, from a Parisian base, relaunched the panama in Europe. Then it was President Theodore Roosevelt who made world headlines in newspapers and magazines during his inspection of work on the future Panama canal. *L'Illustration* carried a major report on the event, with drawings and photographs. His "fino" was never out of sight; its photograph went round the world, and thus achieved undying popularity.

The hat made the front pages of the newspapers, but it also made regular appearances in the fashion magazines, which were henceforth better informed. More and more, it was a question of a hat made in Ecuador, and no longer just in Central America. Differences in style and quality became known about. And even the different kinds of straw were recognised: wheat, palm tree or wood; straw from Italy, or from the Far East, with its infinite varieties (Bangkok, Manilla, Baku, Bengal, Parabuntal, Shantung), or again English picot and Madagascar raffia. But the true panama was unrivalled. In England, it belonged to the panoply of elegance, with the cigar, the brogues and the tie. The press and the socialites had a practised eye for the sartorial subtleties of the gentry. No longer was there any question of incongruous rumours, such as the idea that panama hats were produced by plants, and that there was a season during which they were harvested! After the century which had made its name, the panama had still many more splendid years in front of it.

The first half of the 20th century took away nothing of its glory: a considerable increase in production took place in the North American and South American markets. In the United States, the celebrated hat-maker Stetson became an influential firm, manufacturing and distributing large quantities of different styles, like its main competitor, the Resistol firm, which now belongs to the ultra-famous Levi-Strauss group.

*Mr Witte and Mr de Rosen leaving the landing stage
of the Hamburg line in a cab.*

During this time, luxury shops opened up in New York, San Francisco and Los Angeles to sell the rarest "finos", whose prices attained hundreds of dollars, and in some cases a lot more. Mexico and Brazil had also become major markets. But one of the best, without doubt, was Cuba: for many years, indeed, it bought up the entire output of the small coastal town of Febres Cordero.

The 1940s were the great years of the panama hat. In 1944, it won the coveted glory of being Ecuador's number one export product. It is, however, true that a destructive fungus, named "the witches' broom", had put an end, once and for all, to the fabulous history of cacao. The decline of what had for a century been considered as the economic motor of the nation was categorical. And cacao had not yet been replaced by the products that were to revolutionise once more the country's economy, and to thus become its major exports: the banana and the oil.

In 1944, the hat was in the limelight. This was a place of honour and fulfilment. At last it was fully recognised by one and all. Its world tour had been dizzying, then it had got used to success and honours. But nothing can match the recognition of one's equals. The glamour of the 1940s contributed greatly to this success, given the fact that Europe now looked towards America, and that Hollywood was the maker and breaker of fashions. The good-looking Americans reinvented seduction. They had masculine souls and the serene look of conquerors. The hat suited them well. Silhouette and image, it became an object of infatuation. It was worn by the biggest names – Orson Welles, Humphrey Bogart and Gary Cooper, among others – and was immortalised in a number of cult films. Artists, gangsters and politicians made the name of the panama,

Following pages
*Right : Tobacco plantation (Cuba, 1920).
Left : Count Etienne de Beaumont, standing, with Mr Buster
and the Marquise de Polignac, seated, at the Monte-Carlo Beach.*

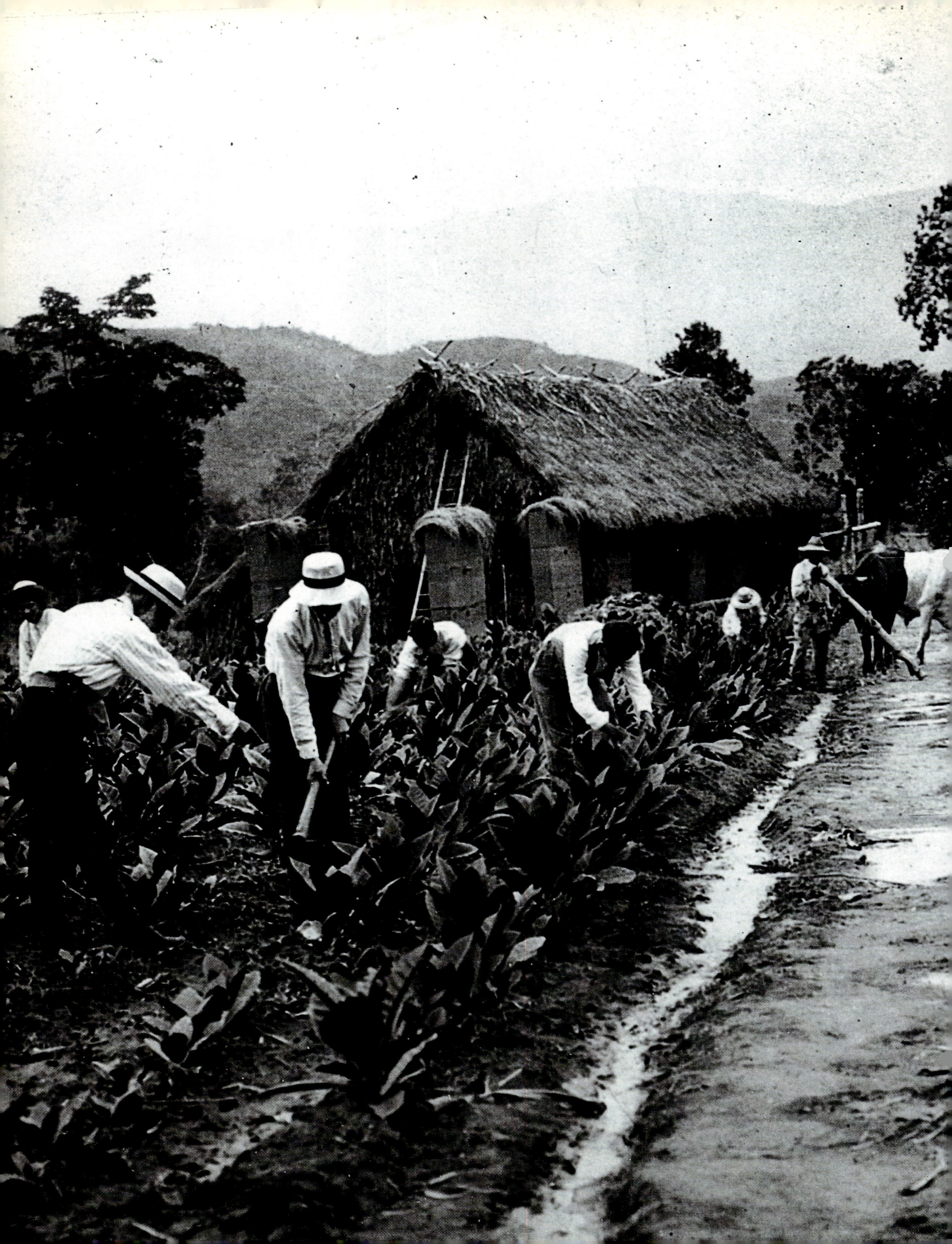

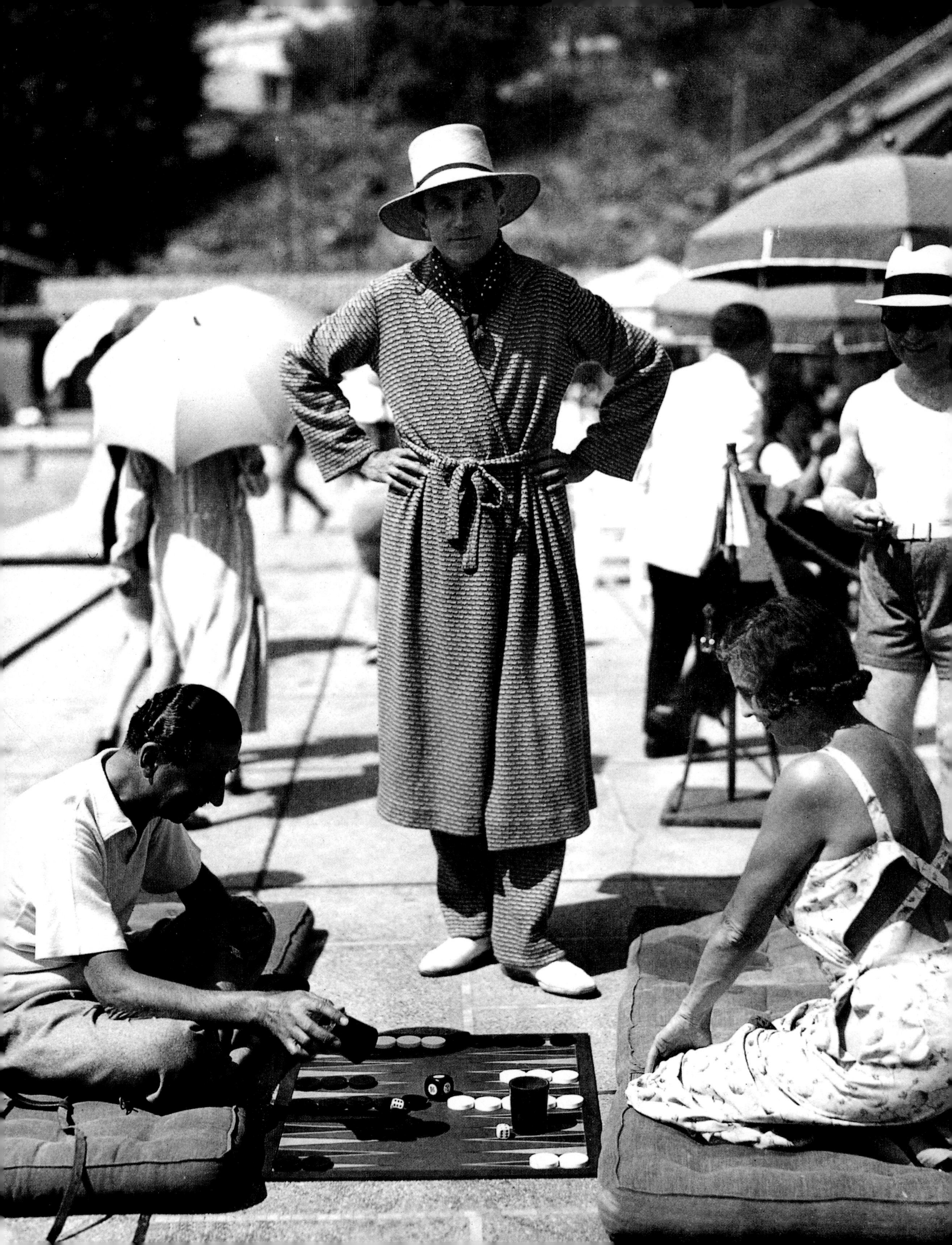

which took different forms according to its wearer. The best known was the "borsalino", from the name of the celebrated Italian hat-maker who had invented its shape. Then there was the "stetson", which the no-less-famous American hat-maker of that name created for the cowboys of the West. But the "planter" and "colonial" styles were also popular. The most chic remained the so-called "natural" panama, which one shaped oneself, and whose form was never fixed once and for all. This required straw of high quality, which in general was only to be found with the "montecristis". It was up to the connoisseur to locate it, and to recognise it!

With the right build, presidents and senators could adopt the Hollywood look, and the cinema stole a march on everyday life. The image started to acquire power in a world filled with promises.

Ecuador, in those years, possessed one genuine asset. His name was Galo Plaza, and he had a profile like Marlon Brando, as well as the same kind of charisma and stature. He was the grandson of the liberal president Leonidas Plaza, and had grown up between the best schools in Boston and his hacienda, "Zuleta", on the high plateaus of the Ecuadorian cordillera. From this background he retained a taste for contrasts. He loved the land and the open spaces, but also encounters, business, and public life. He was appointed ambassador to Washington, and became President of Ecuador in 1948, between two periods during which the presidency was held by another illustrious figure of those years, José Maria Velasco Ibarra. Galo Plaza had a sense of the image, and loved his country. Who could do a better job to promote the famous artisanate of the hat? And he did it with elegance and brio, letting no occasion pass by to wear one, or to present one to the heads of state he met. He knew well the value of these "toquilla" hats, having himself gone to Montecristi to buy his panamas. Don Rosendo, the old merchant, recalled this unusual amateur – a warm, imposing figure, who arrived in his storehouse to choose a panama without even mentioning the question of price, being fully aware of the work that it represented for the weavers of his country.

The post-war period in a bruised and battered Europe began, however, to change things for the flourishing panama market, given that Ecuador was no longer the only country that produced straw hats. An industry had sprung up in Italy, and China had also set out on the royal road traced by the panama. Of course the raw material was different, but there were takers for products of every quality, in these markets of the sun. In the States, the ultra-liberals occupied the centre of the stage, rejecting everything that could be taken as a sign of conservatism. Thus began the era of the "Sin Sombrerismo" ("hatlessness"), and the new bare-headed generation found an idol in the person of the young and brilliant J.F. Kennedy. There was no one better to symbolise the ardour of the Sixties.

Unlike this seductive hero, Russian conformism, with its status of openly-declared enmity, kept its hat on its head. It was a mark of the difference between two generations which co-existed in time, but which in reality were different in every way. Kruschev, at the head of his political structure, haunted the Western newspapers with his jovial countenance, the paradoxical symbol of a redoubtable power. He wore a hat as he wore his coat – out of necessity, and as a social signal. Good weather was the reason why he too went for the panama; and it appears that he had a collection of them. Perhaps they were presents from his friend Castro?

The year 1962 forced Cuba to close its doors. Confrontation with the USA had turned to crisis. Ecuador also broke off diplomatic relations with the dissident cousin, which had dramatic consequences for the people of Febres Cordero, who were forced to reduce by three quarters their output of panamas. They were not, alas, the only ones. The peacetime world had found new weapons to fight with, and the era of economic wars was launched. Liberal dress codes, and their new markets, were dark clouds for the artisanate of the panama.

The straw hat gradually took a back seat, and the weavers learned other trades; Ecuador turned towards new conquests. There were other challenges, oil prospecting, banana plantations, shrimp farming. The wheel went round, and these activities took leading roles in the internationally-orientated economy.

The limelight has faded, and the panama hat has adapted itself to the latter part of the century. In the face of the imitations whose assaults it has suffered, it possesses strengths that are not negligible: its composition is unique, it needs the best weavers in the world, and its reputation goes back over a century. Maturity, as a gift bestowed by the passage of time, has taught it to beware of fads and fashions. And if it makes concessions to a passing fancy of the crowd, due to one of its fellows passing across the screen in a successful film, this is always with inner serenity. Its real client is the sun.

The panamas of today journey towards lands and seasons that are warm throughout the year, bringing with them a softness and a brilliance that is peculiar to Latin America. The finest of them still reach a few high-class hat-makers, but unfortunately these are getting rarer all the time; almost as rare as the connoisseurs whom they continue to protect with a shadow of elegance.

Opposite page
The beach at Etretat in the Twenties.
Following pages
*Left : Panama from
Cuenca, belonging to the Plaza family.
Right : President Galo Plaza on a journey to the Sierra.*

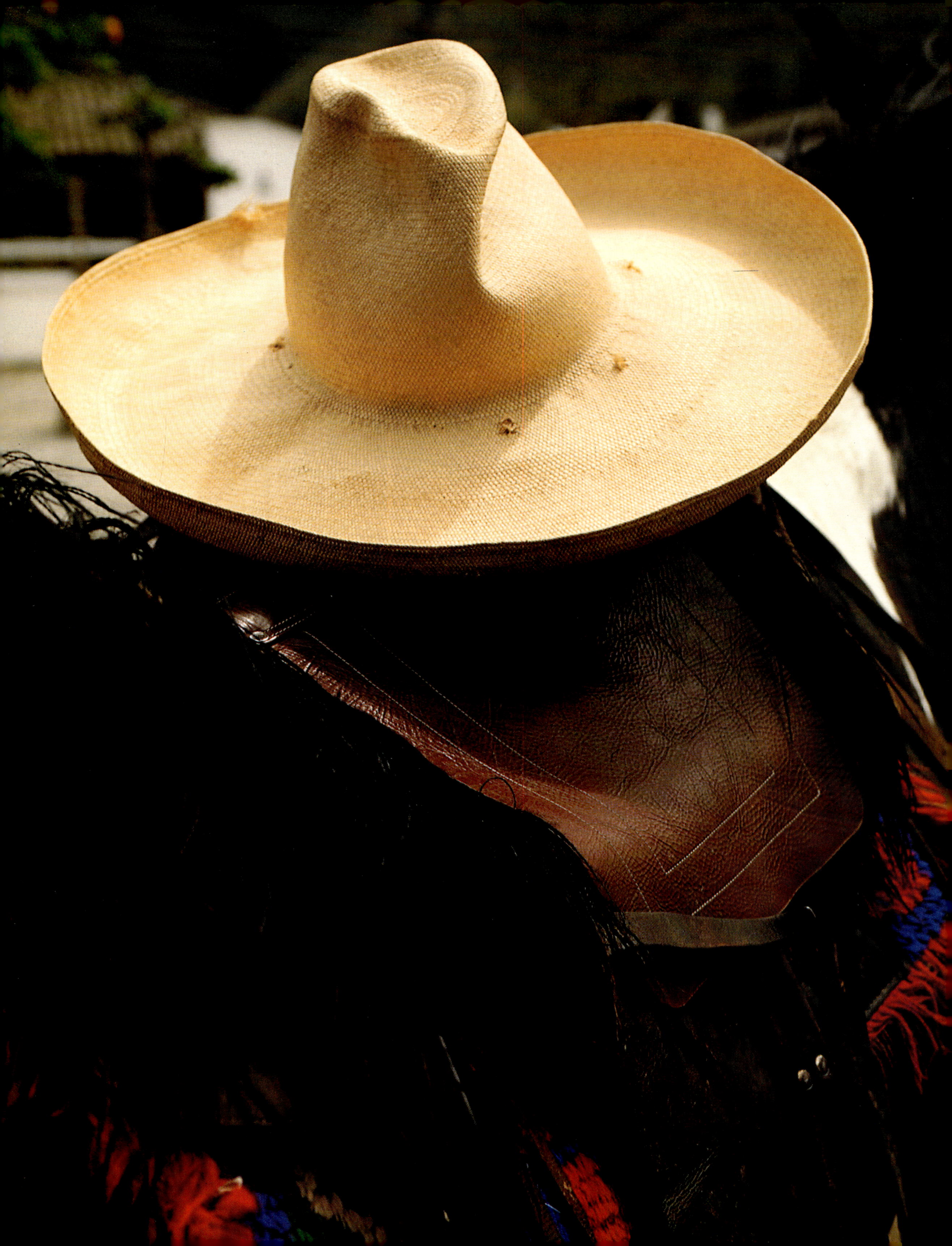

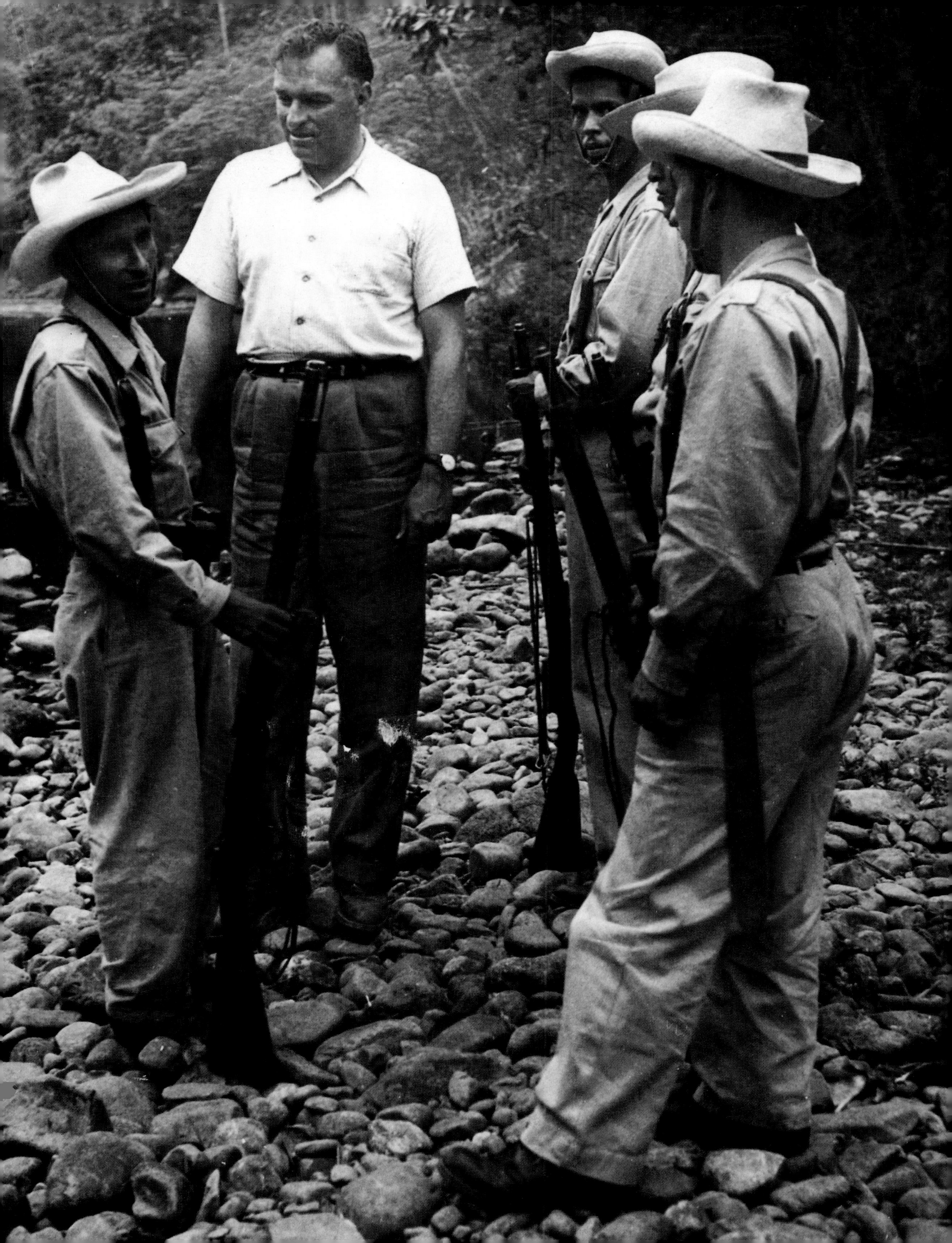

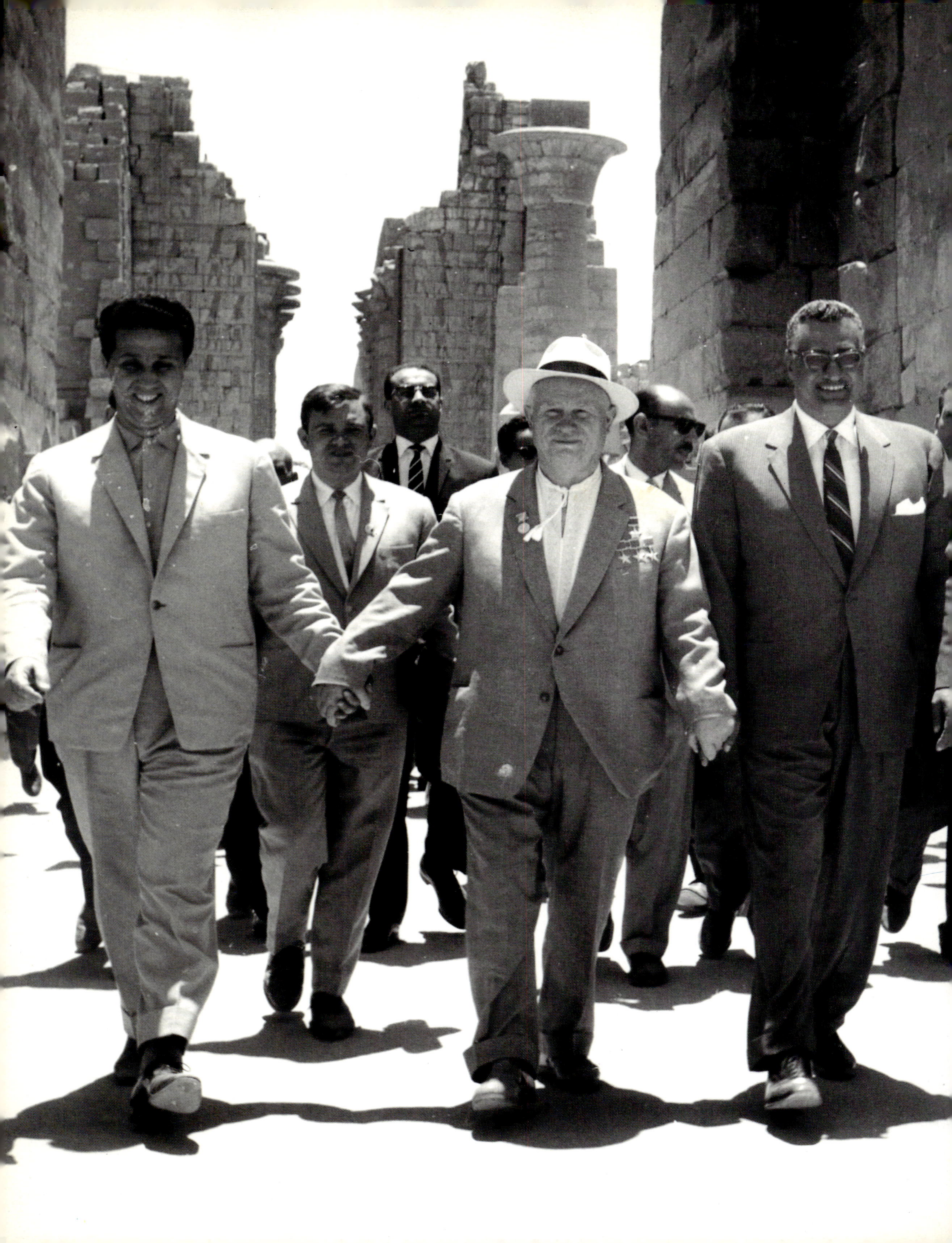

A summer hat by tradition, the panama lends prestige to statesmen all over the world.

Following page
President Galo Plaza during a meeting with President Harry Truman (Washington, 1950).
Opposite page
Kruschev, Ben Bella and Nasser during the inauguration of the Aswan dam in 1964.

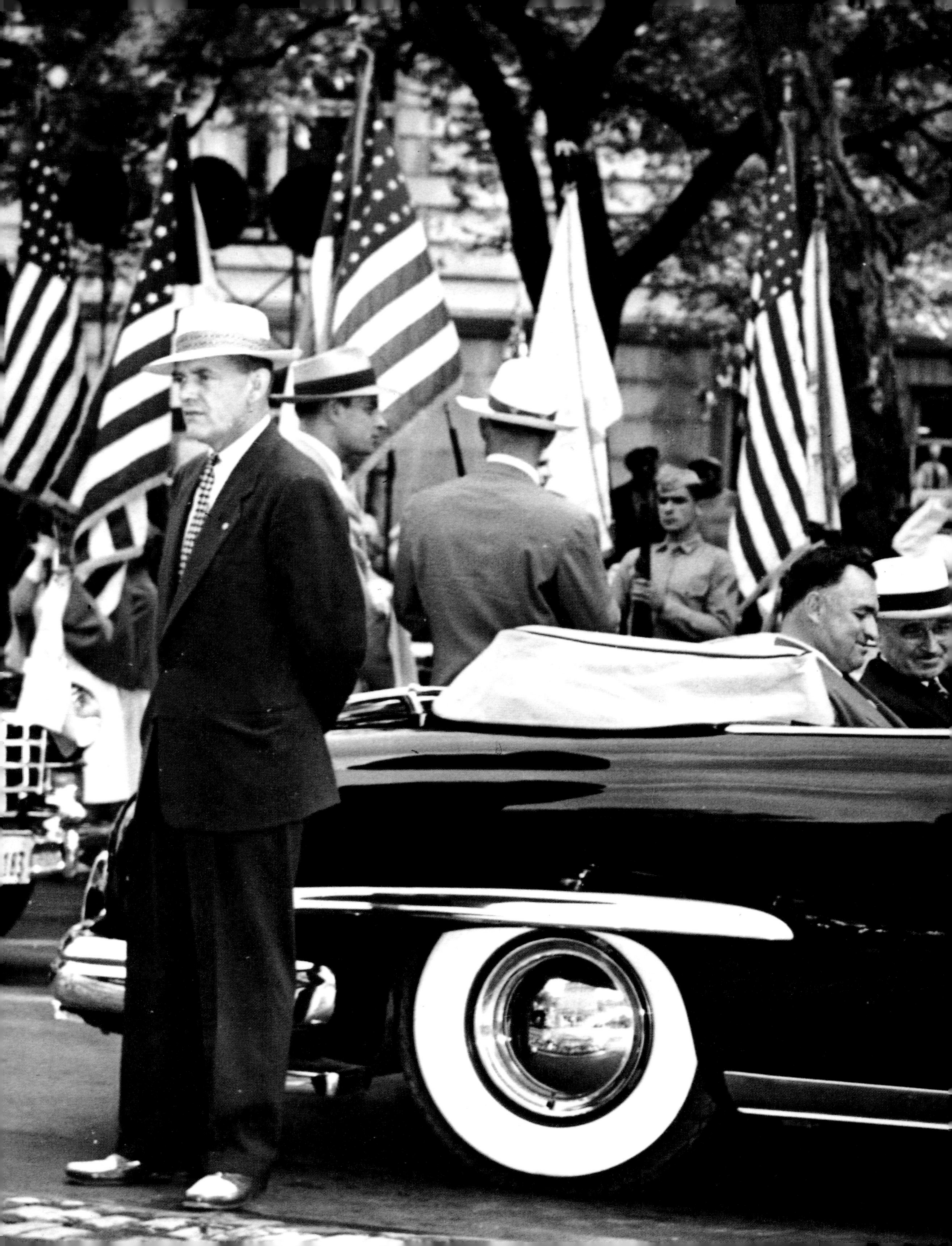

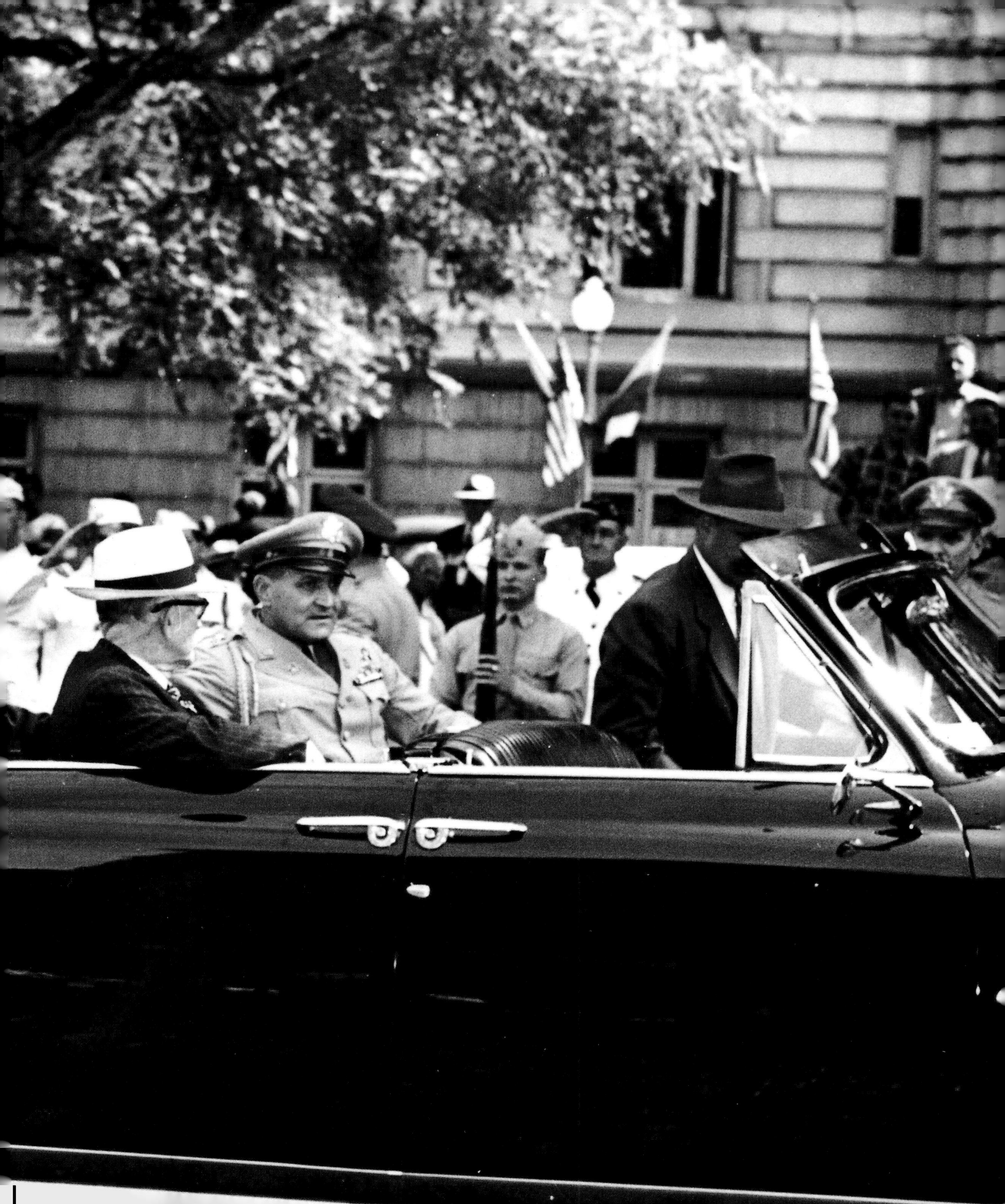

2

The Myth of the "montecristi"

Like his village, Manuel Lopez Espinal seems to have stepped straight out of a novel by Gabriel García Márquez. Solitude and fatality have conspired with time to mark his face, as they have marked the deserted streets of the little town of Pilé, with its thousand inhabitants.

The town, which is hidden away at the end of an interminable dust road, is home to the best straw weavers in the world: those who make the "montecristis". These artisans with their golden hands have always woven knowledgeably, artistically, with the obstinacy of insistence on perfect work and an object that is unique. In his house built on stilts, made of wood and bamboo, Manuel, who is one of the village's maestros, has been weaving since the break of dawn. He knows his straw, which likes the softness of the early morning air, and takes a shape perfectly as long as one avoids the hours of intense sunshine.

Behind a wooden stand made of a shaft with three legs, which serves as a support for the form and for his hat, he weaves. His torso is supported by other forms which he has added so as to make his position more comfortable and maintain the piece he is working on. His head is lowered, and he is gazing into the straw as he works on it. His hands are sure, agile and infinitely gentle, moving quickly. He weaves with three fingers of each hand, whose nails are fine, hard and extremely long; these are the tools of his trade. To achieve the best shape, he dips the ends of his fingers from time to time in a little bowl of water placed beside him. This is how he keeps the straw damp. Like the other weavers of the village, Manuel awaits the sun. He will have worked for almost three hours this morning. It will then be time, after a coffee, to go out and help in the fields. Weaving will not begin again until the evening, at the hour of prayer, when night falls and coolness returns to the air. By the light of a bulb or a candle, the ancestral work will then recommence for several hours. For generations, this is what weaving has been all about.

The old weaver remembers having learnt his trade at the age of twelve, more than sixty years ago. He has never stopped since then, and has himself taught his children the secrets he learnt from his father. And so it goes, life in this little town in a remote corner of the world. The night is full and the stars have invaded the sky of Pilé. It is fatigue that forces the artisan to call a halt. He covers the hat with a cotton cloth, which will protect it from dust and insects. He is proud of the colour of his work: a soft, uniform, luminous ivory colour, which he hopes

Opposite page
The legendary suppleness of the "montecristi" panama.
Following pages
Left : "Toquilla" straw, when fresh, looks like coloured ribbons.
Right : The same straw ribbons, after being washed and bleached, have taken on their definitive appearance.

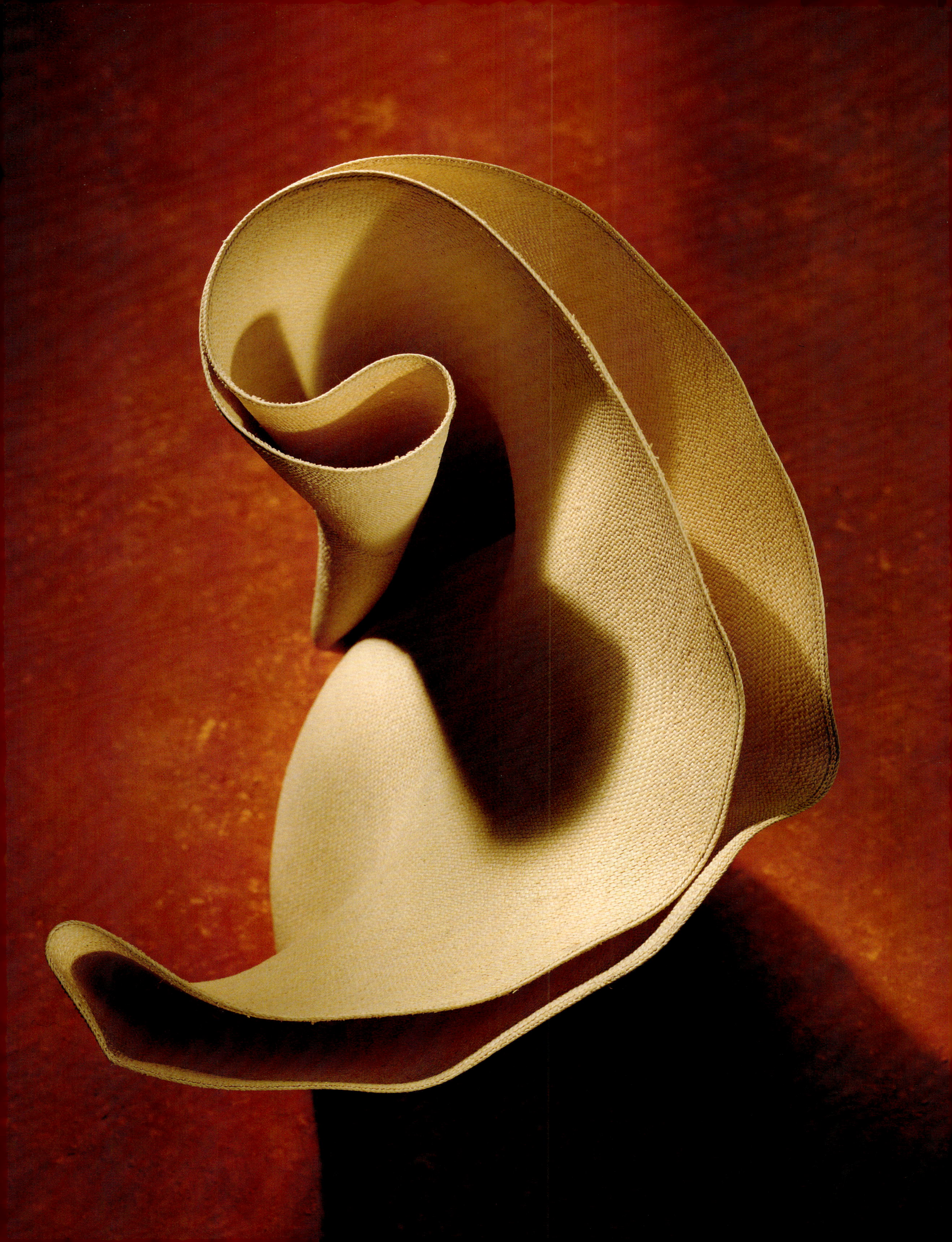

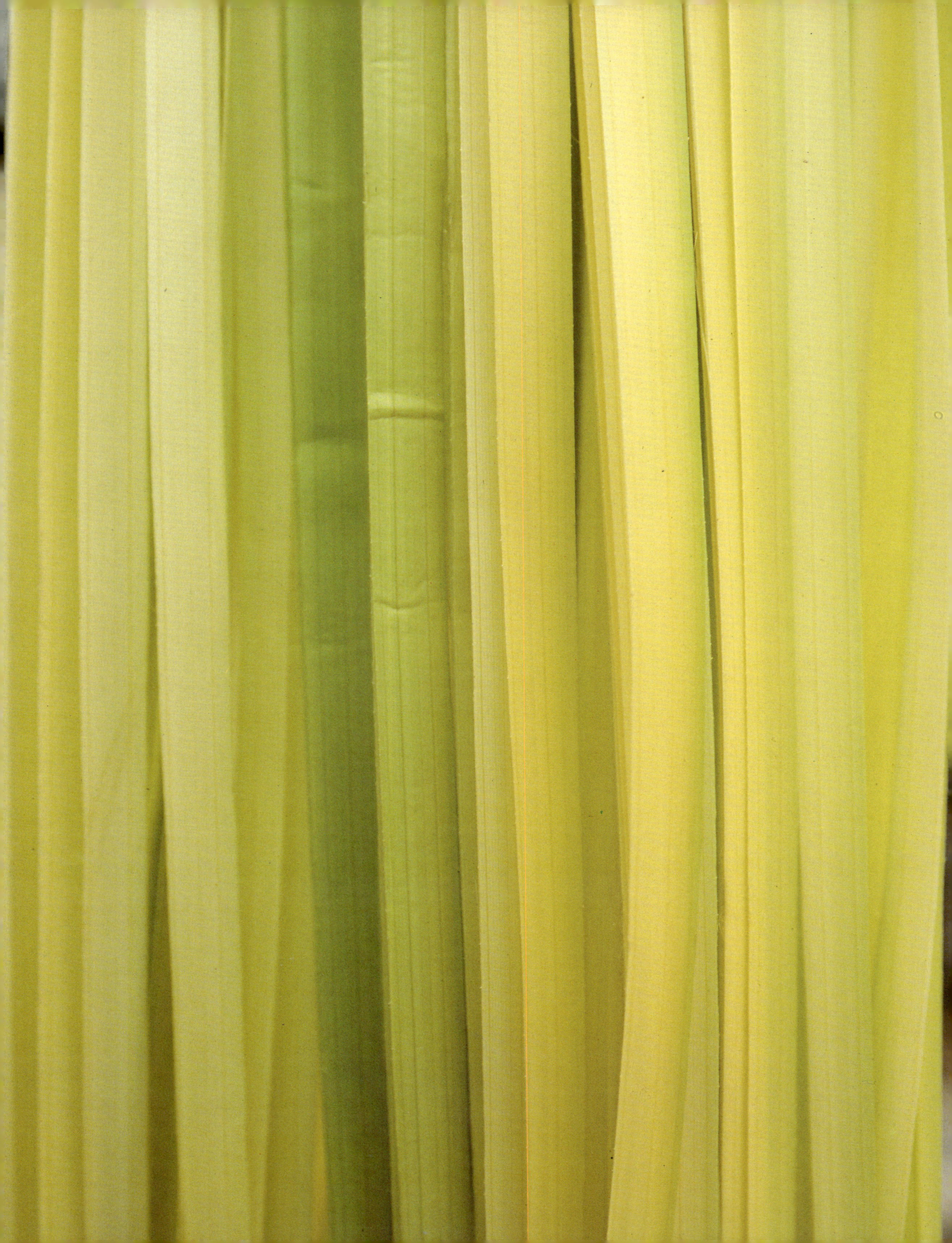

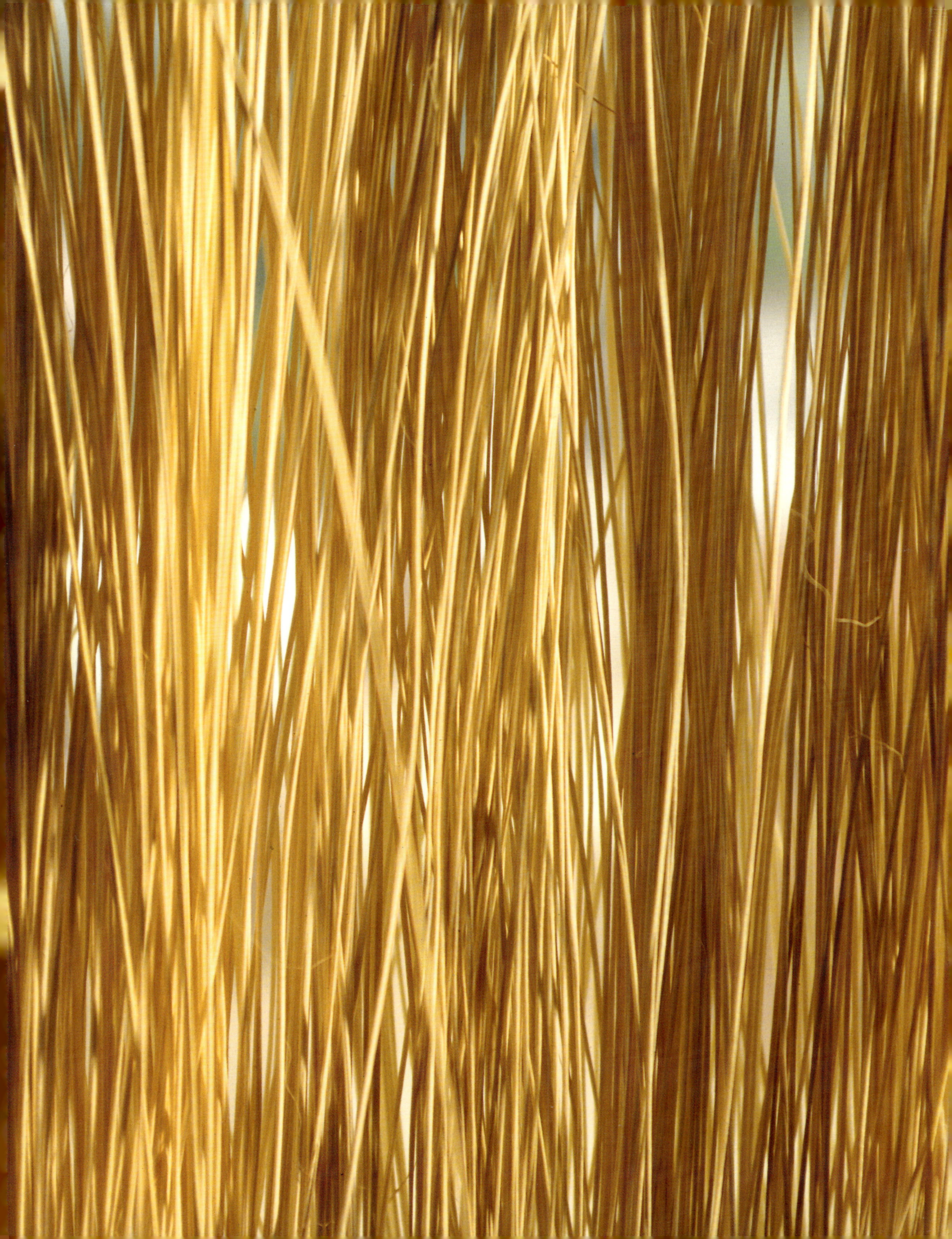

will be spotless and without the least imperfection. He has chosen the straw himself; generally he buys it from Maria Lopez de Delgado, who lives just a few houses from his own. Maria does not do any weaving herself; her role is to treat the straw. She too learned her trade from her mother, and will pass it on to her children. This straw, the vegetable fibre called "toquilla" in this part of the country, grows at a few hours' walk from here in this same province of Manabí, though also in the provinces of Guayas and Esmeralda. Its qualities, which are unique, are the result of a hot, damp climate and a coastal soil which is particularly fertile, rich in salt and lime.

The largest plantations of "toquilla" are fifteen kilometres from the coast, on the lower slopes of the western cordillera, swept by cool winds between the rainy season and the tropical moistness. The plants, which belong to the palm family, are long, high and light, of a fine bright green. The end of their stalks are adorned with leaves which spread out like a fan. It is these leaves which, as shoots that have not yet fully developed, are cut for turning into straw. They are harvested throughout the year, but the time when cutting takes place is important because the shoot, still sheathed in green, must be young and yet at the same time already firm. Whether it is a reality or just a belief, the phases of the moon have as much importance for the cutters as the age of the plant or the temperature of the day. Poetry remains an influence, amidst all this.

The "toquilla" plantations of Pilé, Manglar Alto, Olon, Valdivia and elsewhere are veritable tropical forests. They are worked by the villagers, who often get the actual cutting of the plants done by "pajeros".

The shoots, or sheaths of immature leaves, look like stalks of about a metre in length and a centimetre in diameter. In Ecuador they are called "cogollos". Gathered together in bundles, the green straw is then transported by lorry or by mule, according to its destination. As she does every week, Maria Lopez de Delgado has chosen her toquilla. The firm green stalks pass through her expert hands one after the other. With a knife, she makes a notch in the middle of the stalk and frees the stretched-out, soft, pale leaves; these she separates from the veins, filaments and other thick parts, already mature, which have to be thrown away.

There remains no more than a sheaf of silky "ribbons" held together by a small piece of stalk. These are boiled in large earthenware pots for about twenty minutes, then dried in the wind, away from the rays of the sun, for one or two days. At this point, Maria's house disappears for a time behind a huge curtain of vegetable matter. The "cogollos", which are hung on ropes, dance in the wind, and the ribbons begin their process of retraction. They roll up upon themselves, to the point where they form perfectly cylindrical shafts, blond and fine, which Maria watches over tirelessly. She shakes them so as to separate them properly, because if they happened to dry too close to each other they could stick together, and would then be unusable.

Maria's task is long and thankless. It needs a great deal of patience. But she also knows that her role is determinant for the quality of the future hat. The colour and strength of the hat will depend on the way she treats the straw. And she works at it with all the pride she takes in a job well done. The last stage is to bleach the "toquilla". After being washed once more, the straw is laid on a clay slab over a brazier in which sulphur is burnt for an hour or two. This produces the subtle ivory-like colour. The curtain of vegetable matter forms again, for a last drying. Then the dry straw is selected according to the whiteness, suppleness, dimension and fineness of the fibre. The quality of a panama, and thus its price, depends, to begin with, on this selection process.

Opposite page
Don Rosendo at Pilé, a town of weavers near Montecristi.
Following pages
Traditional bamboo house on stilts in the town of Pilé.
Family of weavers in Pilé.

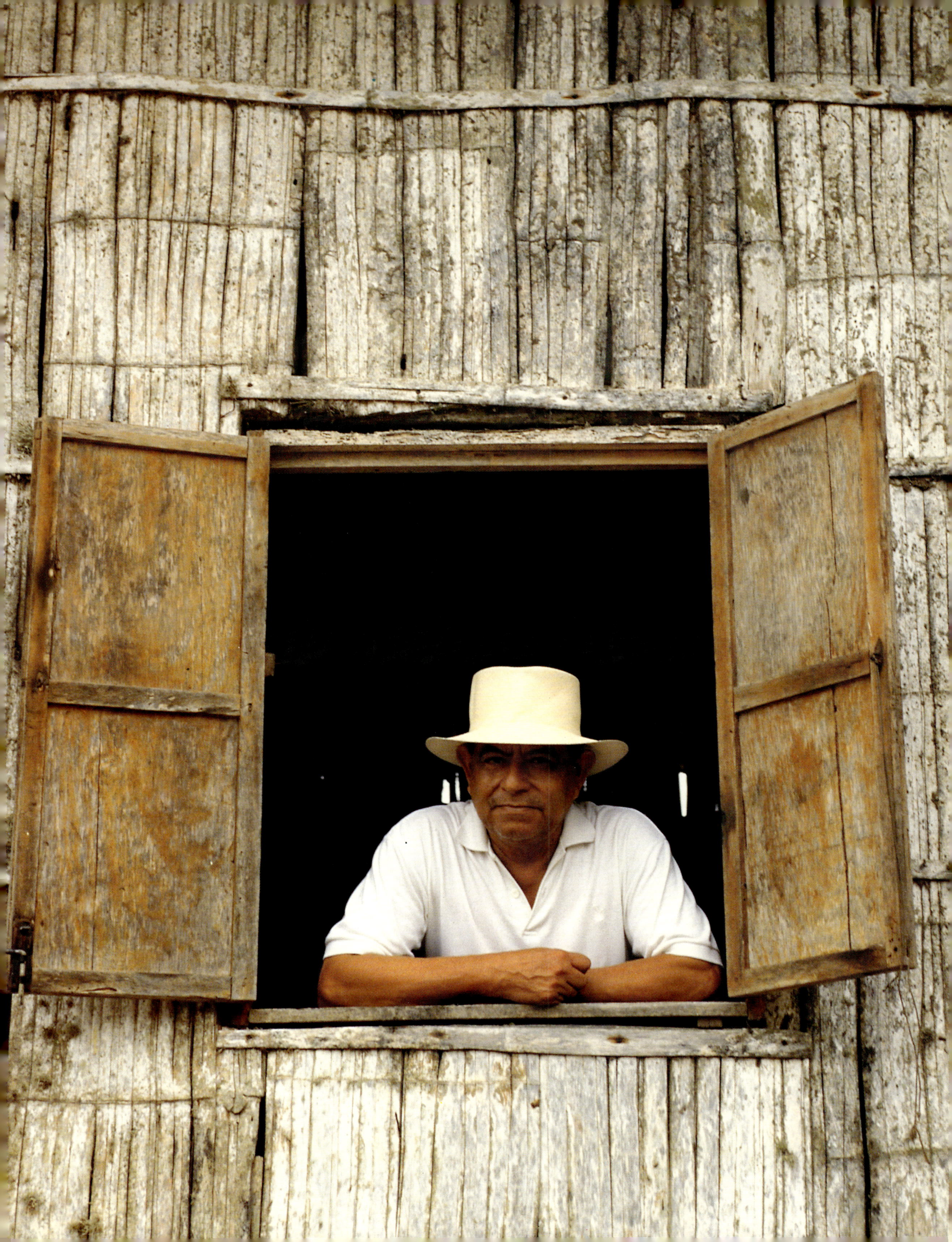

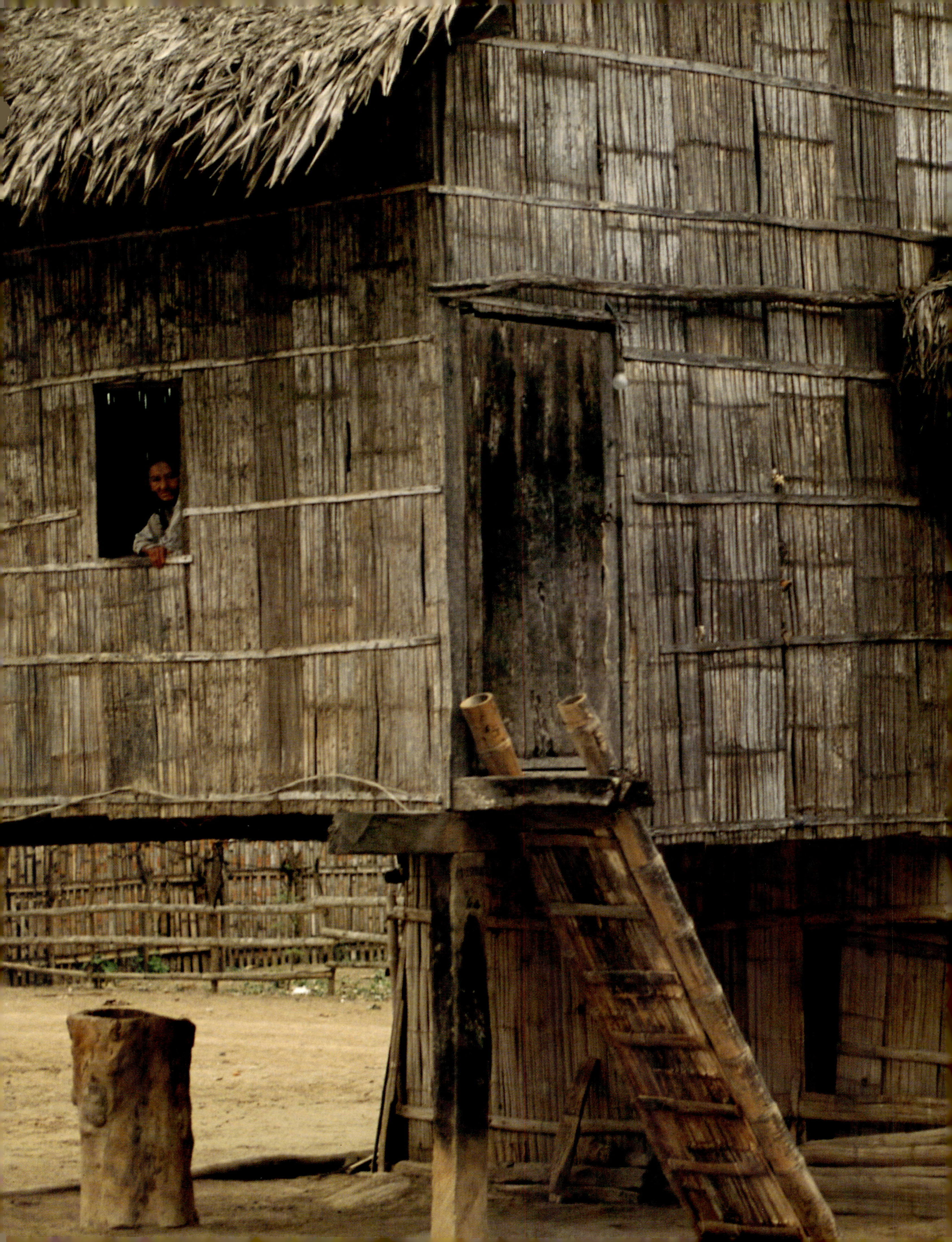

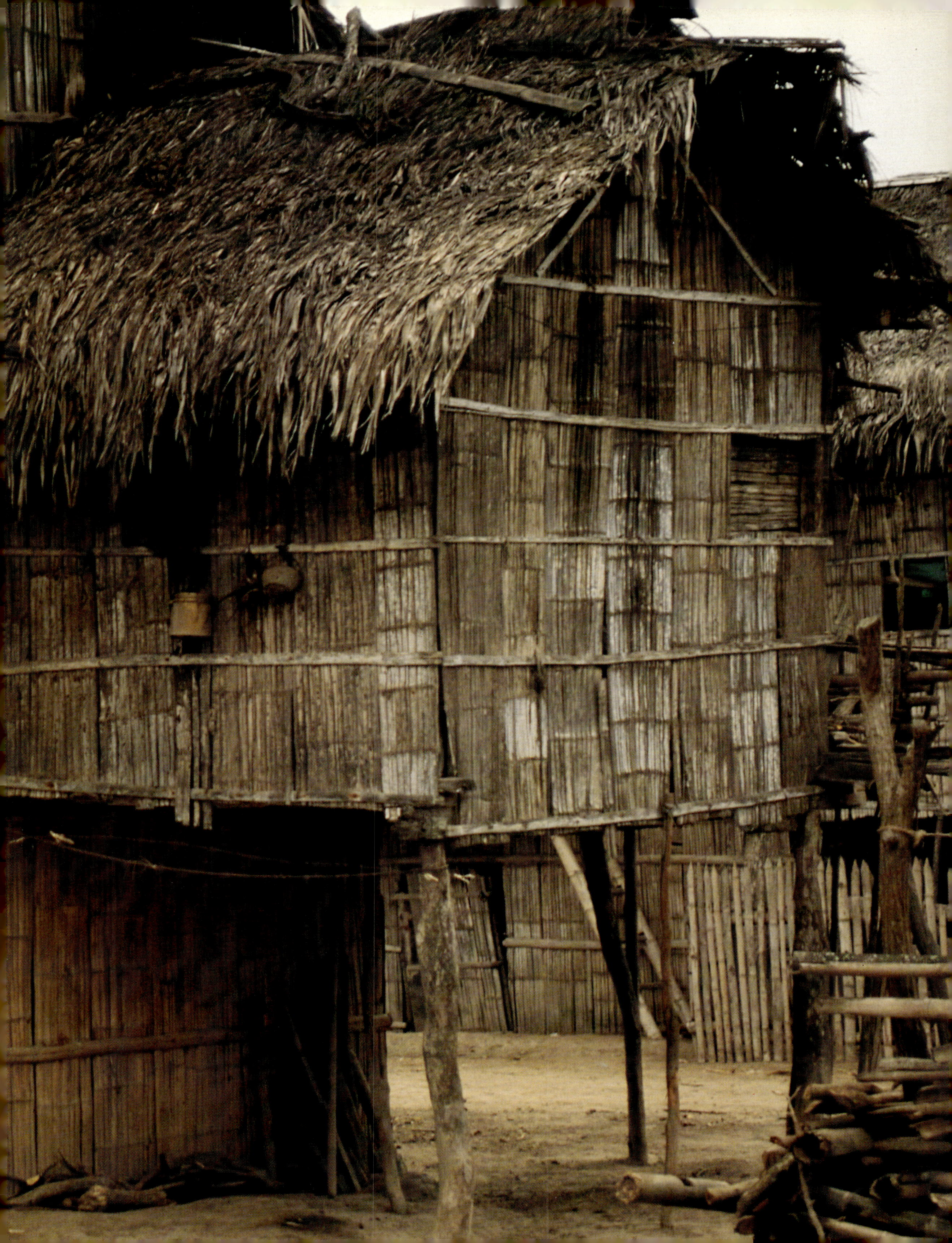

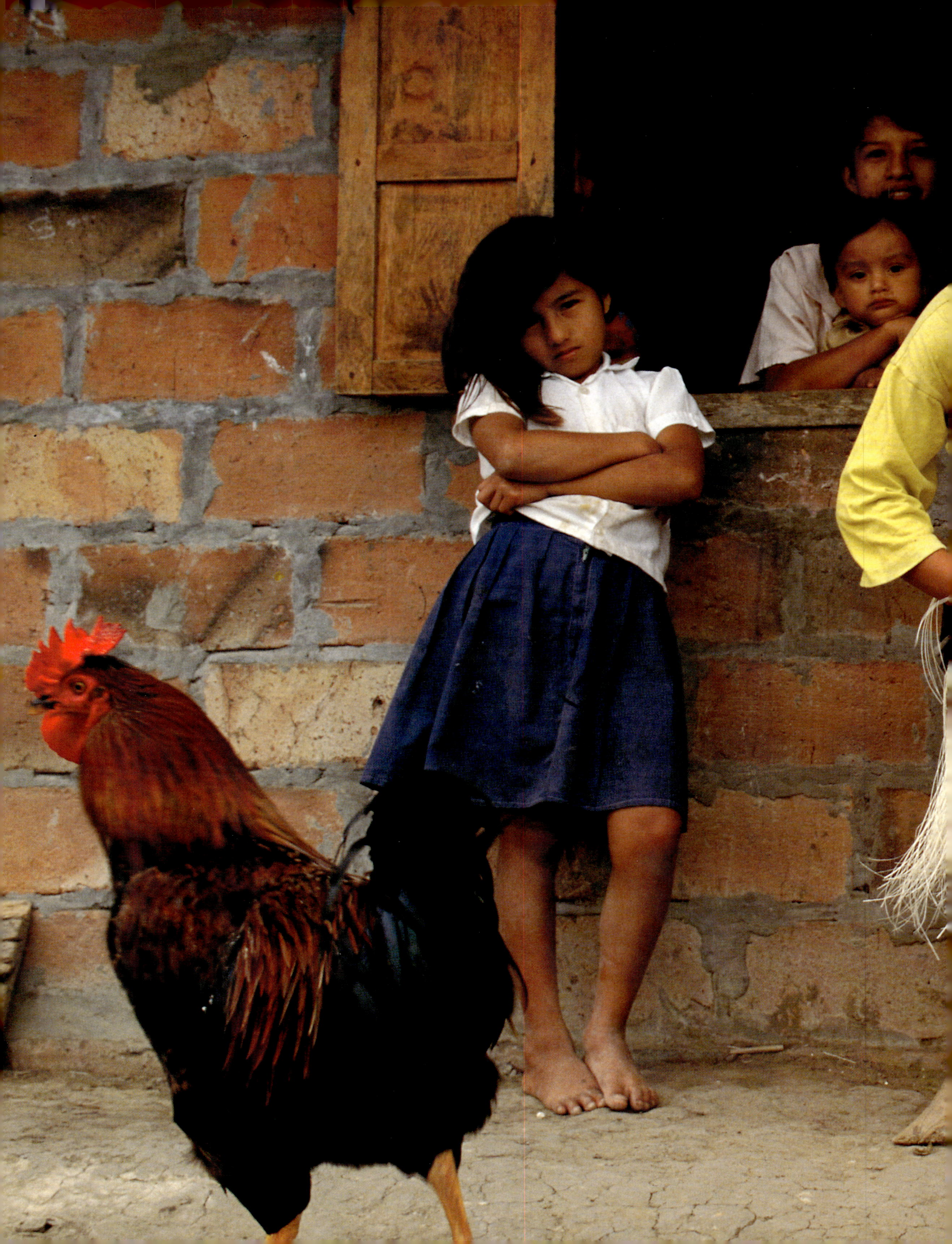

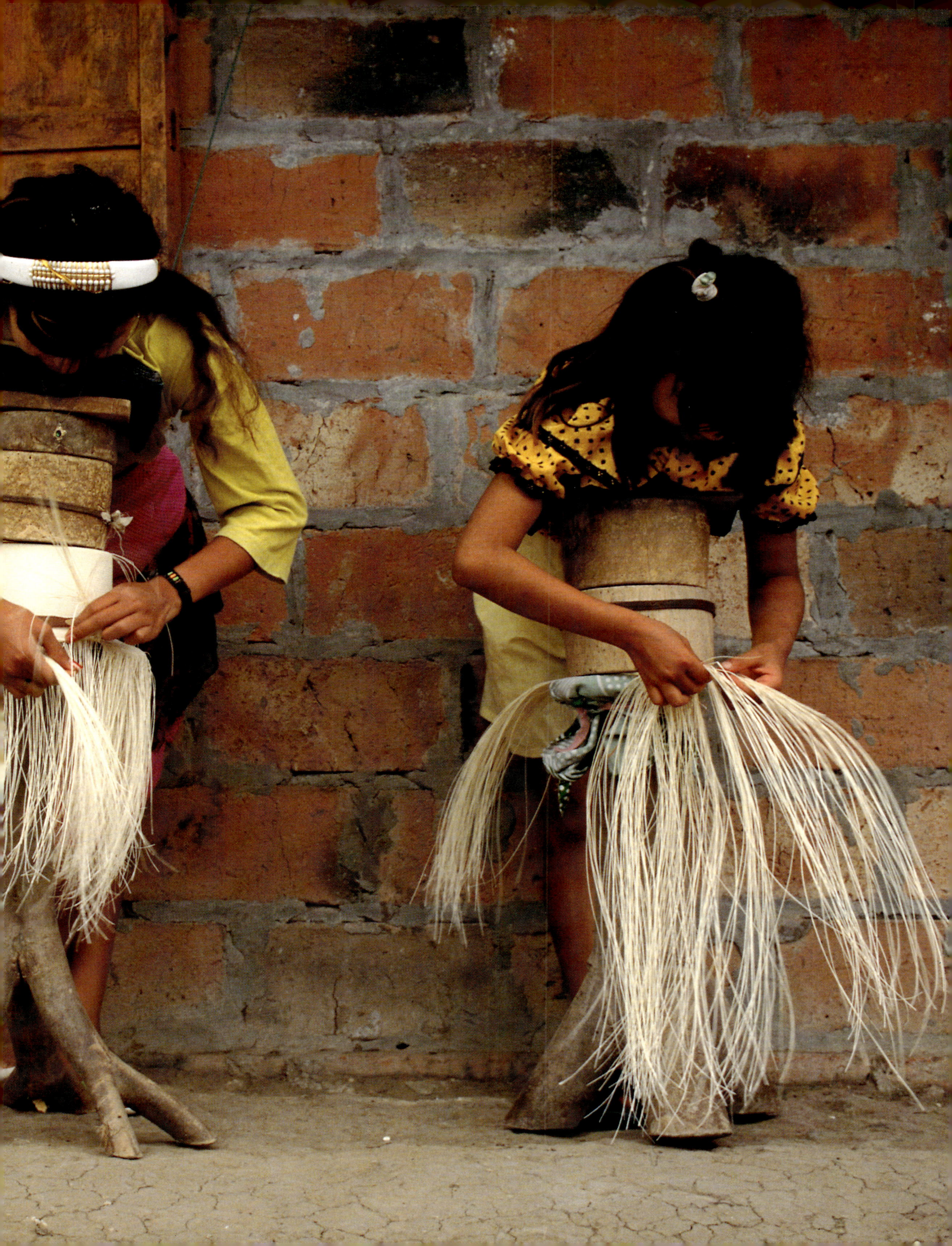

For certain special orders, Maria even has to work on each fibre individually, dividing it in two, three or four, then washing it one last time to obtain a still finer, suppler straw, almost like thread. The straw is now ready to be woven, and the weavers of Pilé will come to choose their "toquilla" according to the hats that they intend to make – the finer the fibre, and the longer the weaving process, the rarer will be the panama.

Maria's reputation is such that it allows her to sell her straw to weavers in other small distant villages, and even as far as Montecristi, the historic birthplace of the world's finest panamas. Sometimes, she even works for a "toquilla" grower. In just a few days his straw will have been treated and packed in large sacks, ready to be sold in the surrounding markets.

Manuel Lopez Espinal has already ordered his straw. His talent and experience make him one of the most gifted weavers in the village. His weaving is of extreme fineness. His next "montecristi" will take at least four months to make; it will be a marvel of lightness and purity. Already, he can see it. He recalls a time when he took on even more ambitious projects, for in fact it can take more than six months to make a "montecristi"! Long ago, his mother, who was a highly-esteemed weaver, took eight months to turn out the most incredible of panamas. It was a true ivory-toned jewel, a "fino-fino" of twenty-eight rows that had taken more than sixty cogollos to make. The one he is currently making will have taken him almost three months. It will be a "fino" of fifteen rows, and will have consumed thirty-five cogollos – it will be a panama that he can be proud of. But the next will be even finer. It will be an "extrafino". His agent has already ordered it, and a client is perhaps even now awaiting it, somewhere at the other end of the world.

Opposite page
The weaving of a "montecristi" begins with the egg in the centre of the rosette, as shown here.
Following pages
*Left : Bundle of treated straw, ready for sale.
Right : Bottom of the crown
of a "montecristi",
in the course of being woven.*

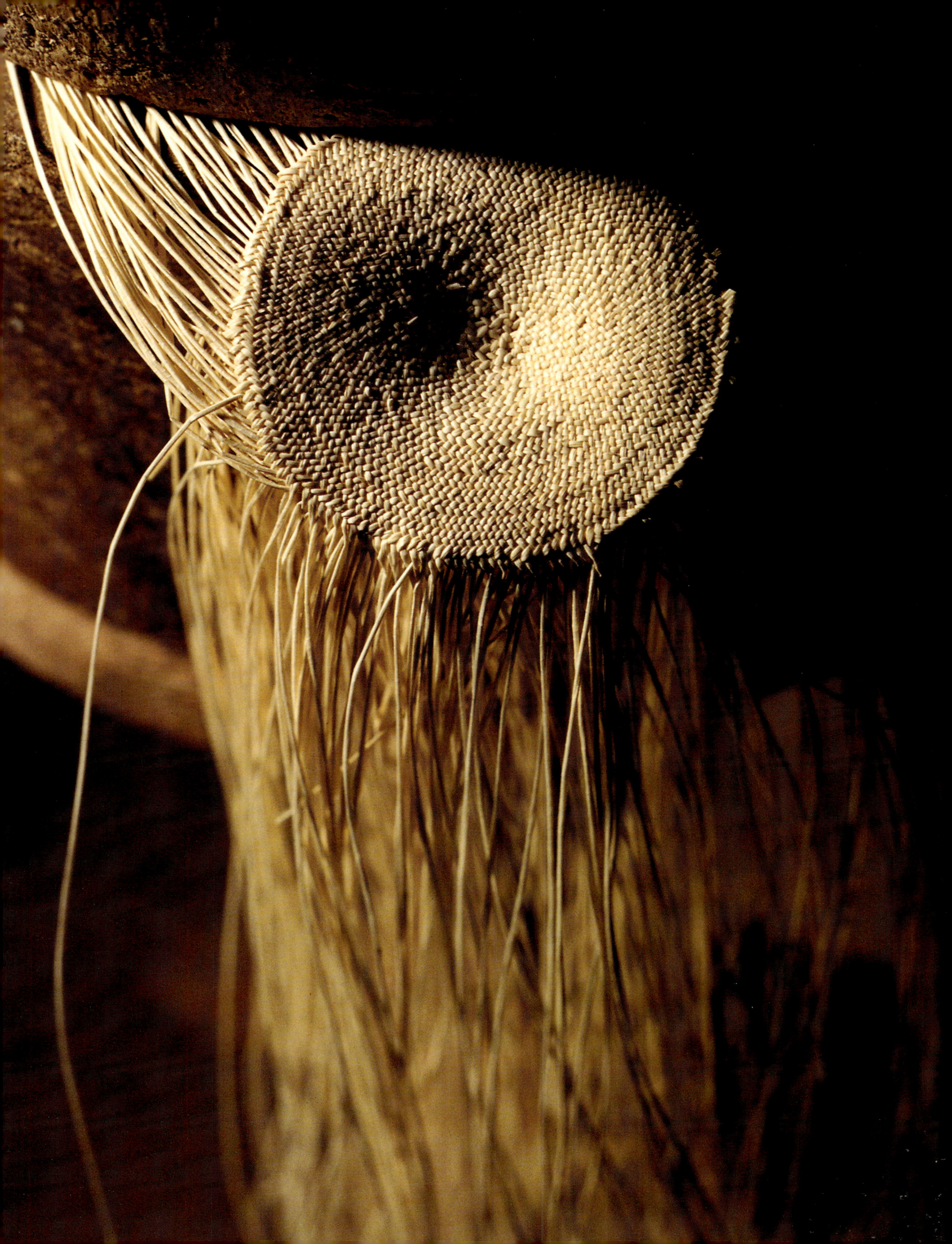

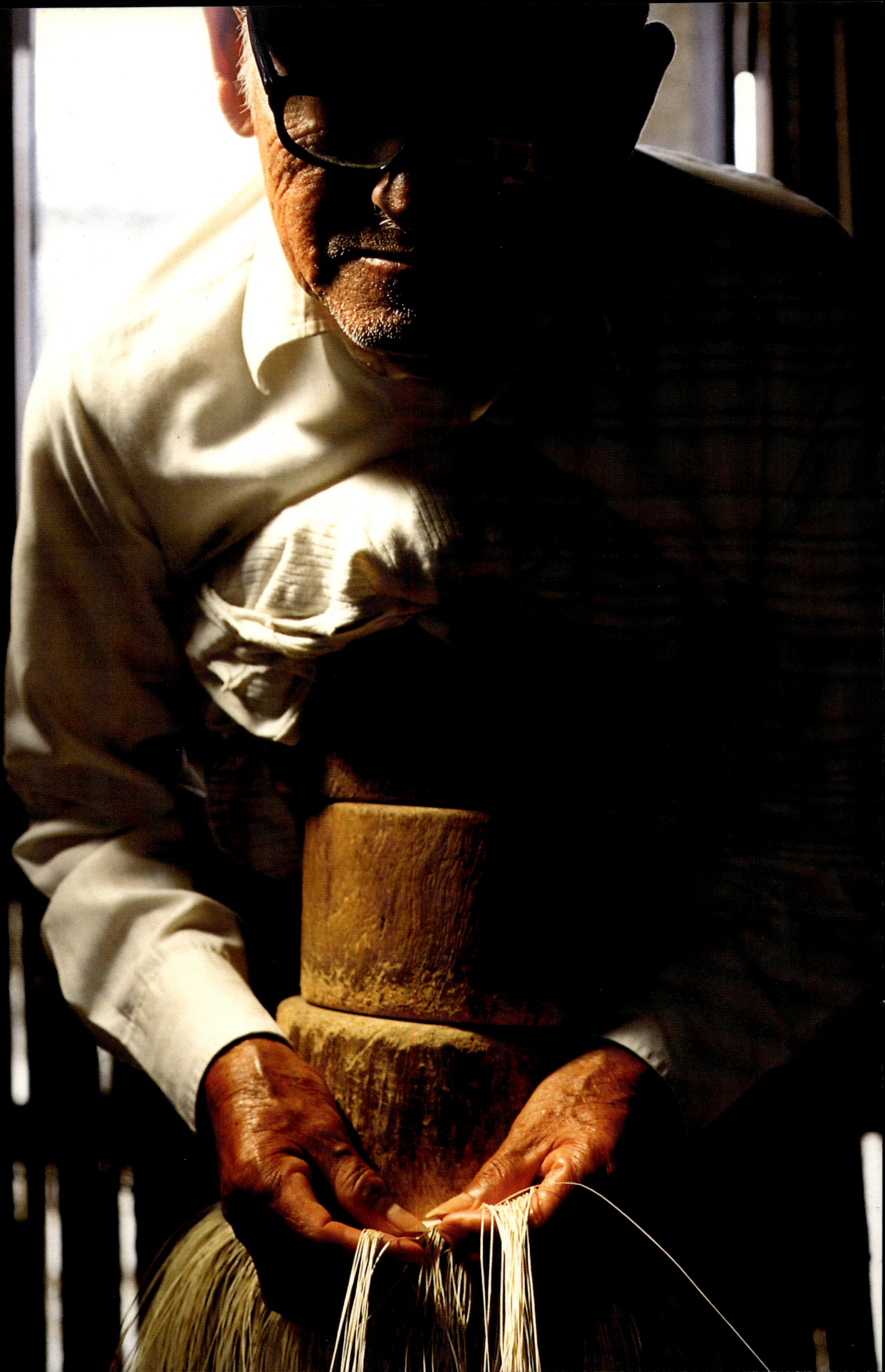

There remain today only a dozen weavers capable of making the finest straw hats in the world *montecristi superfinos.*

Opposite page
Manuel Lopez Espinal, a weaver since the age of 12 and an expert in "montecristi finos".

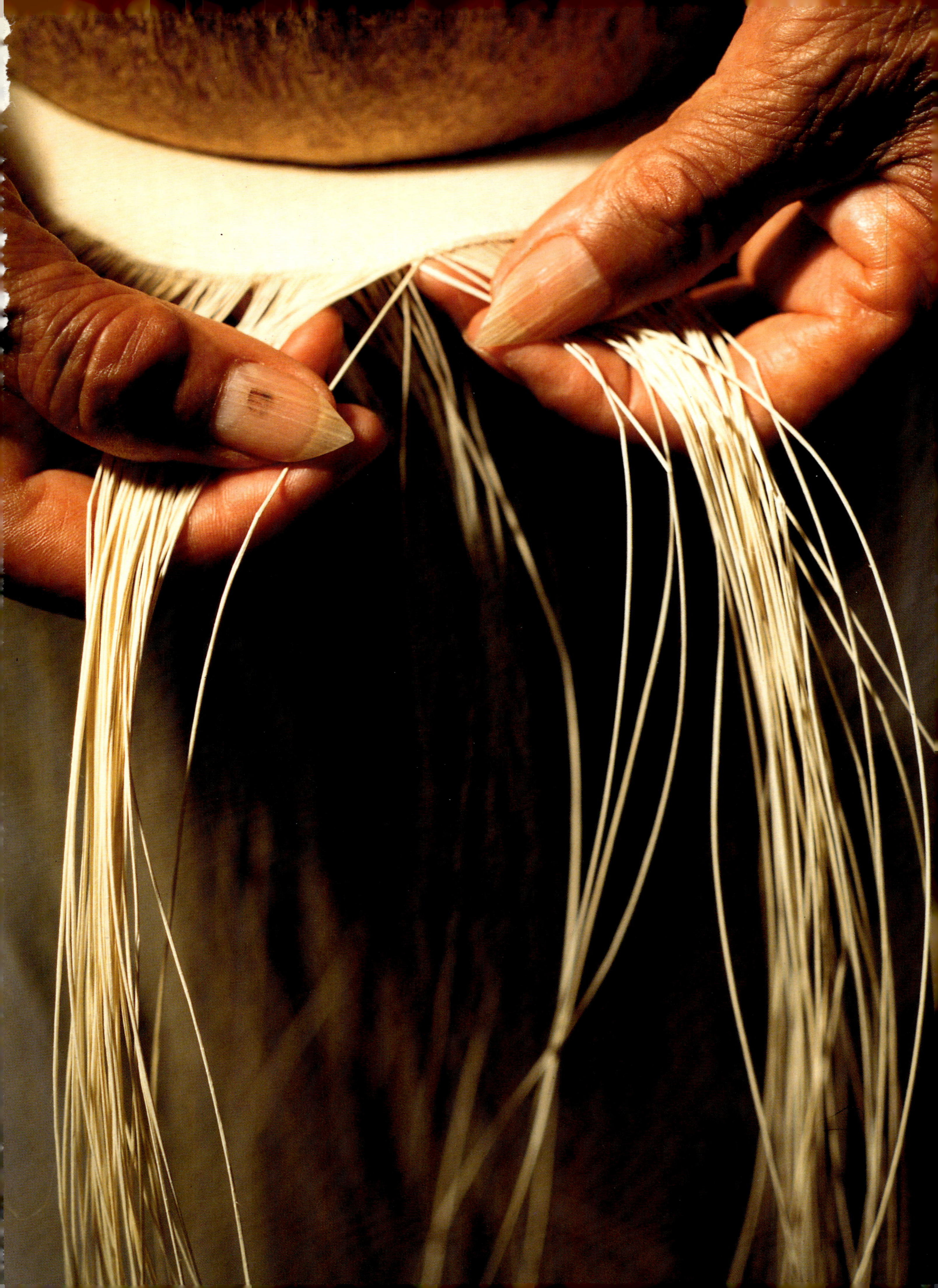

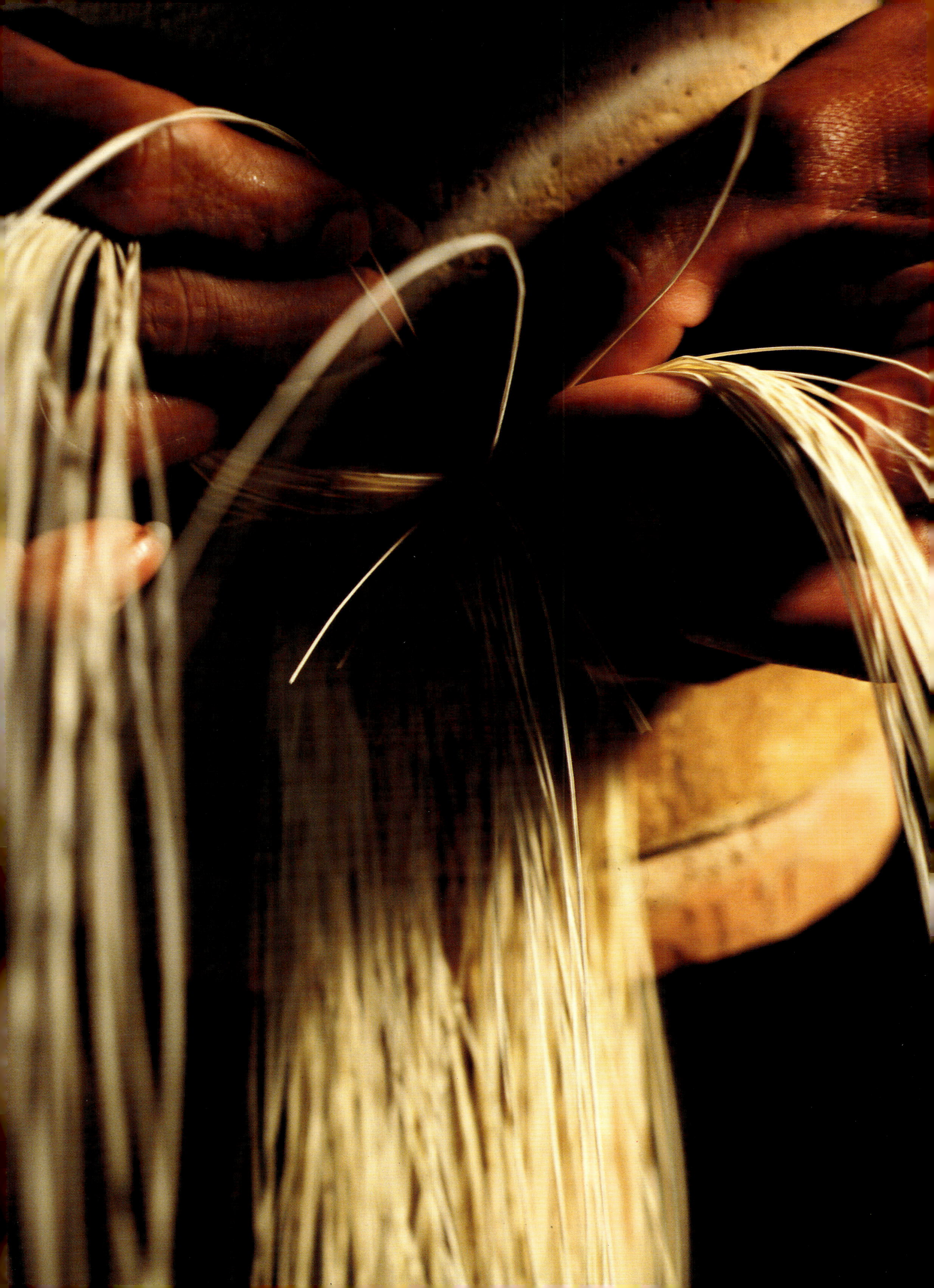

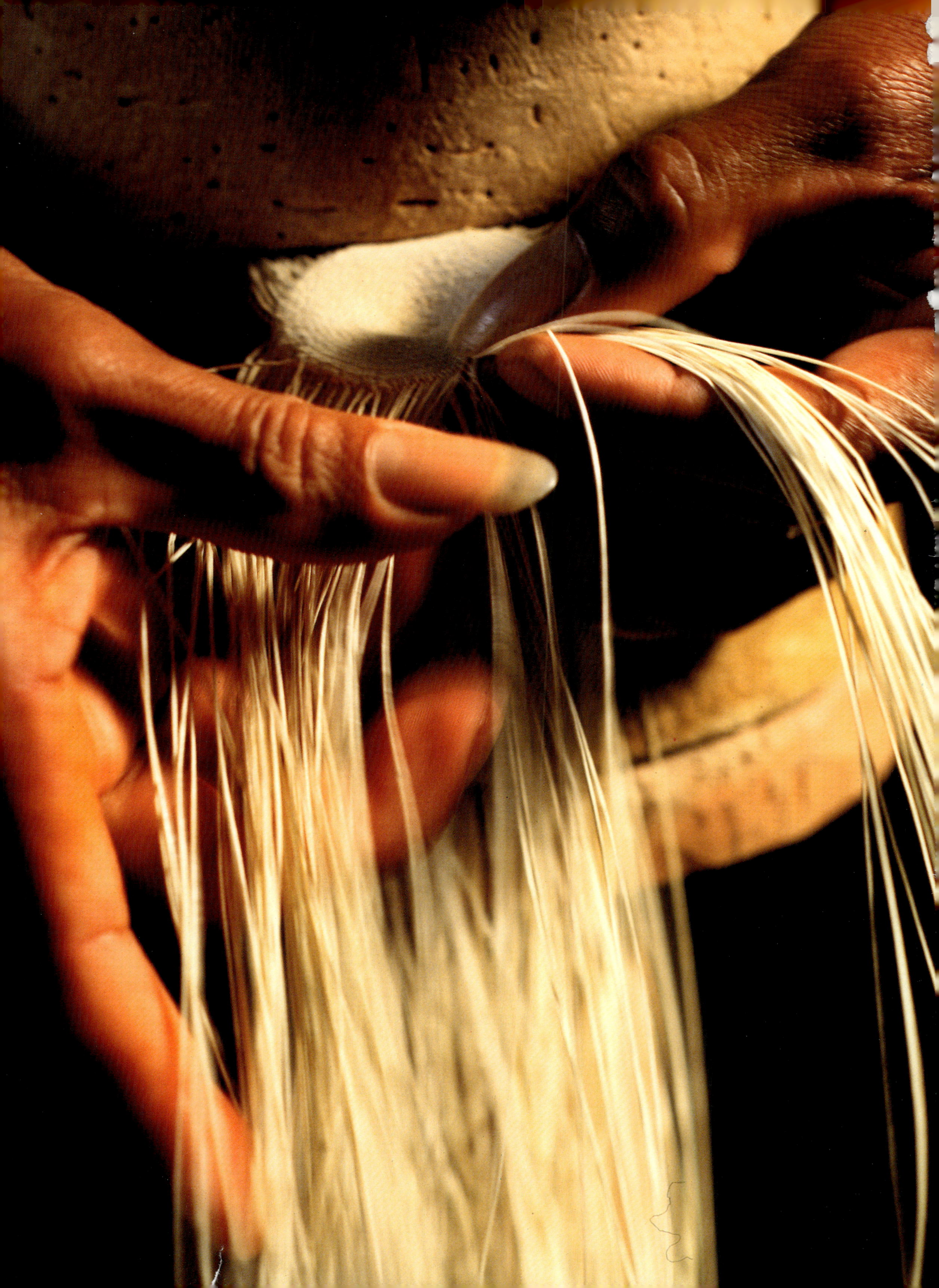

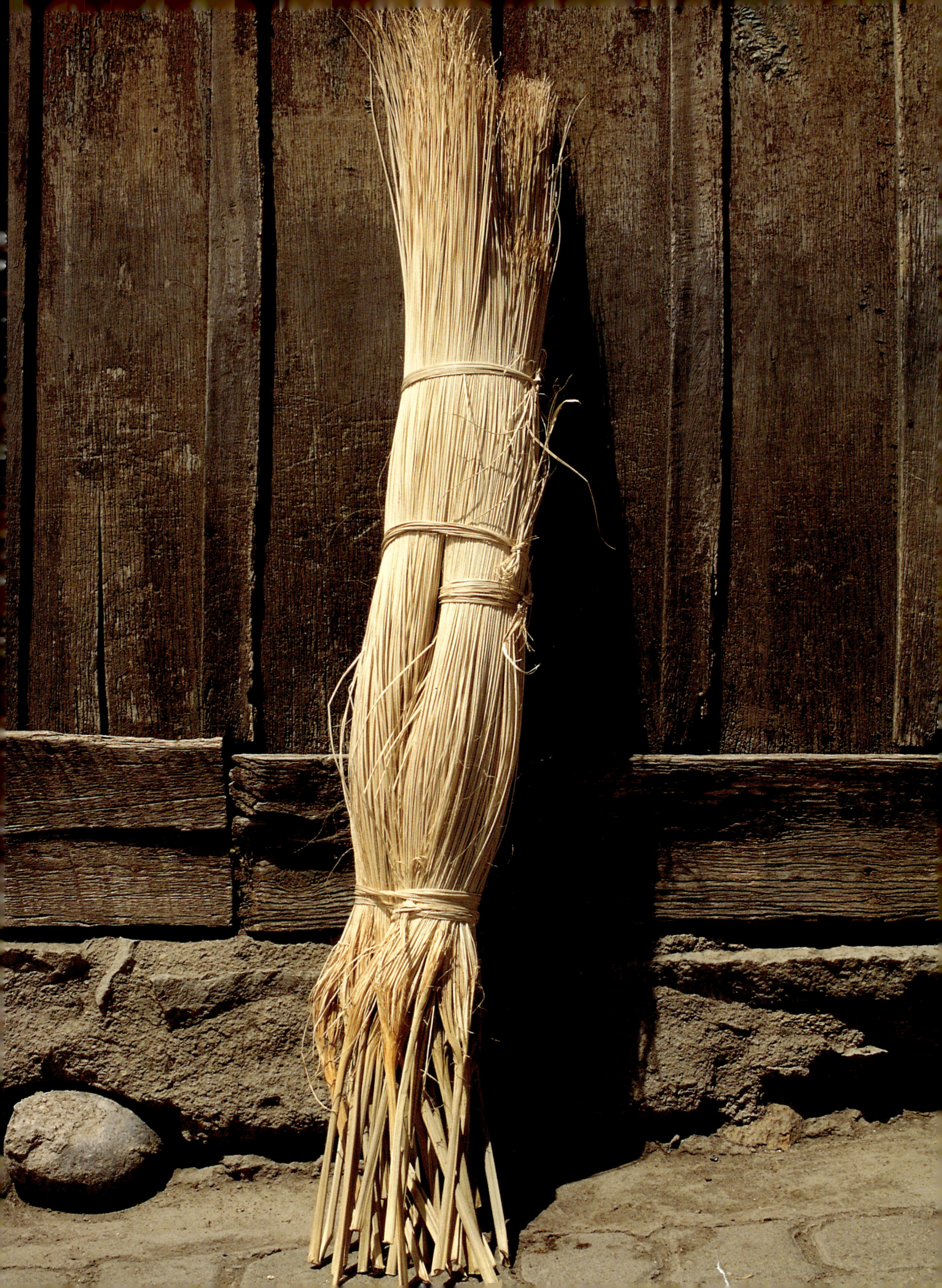

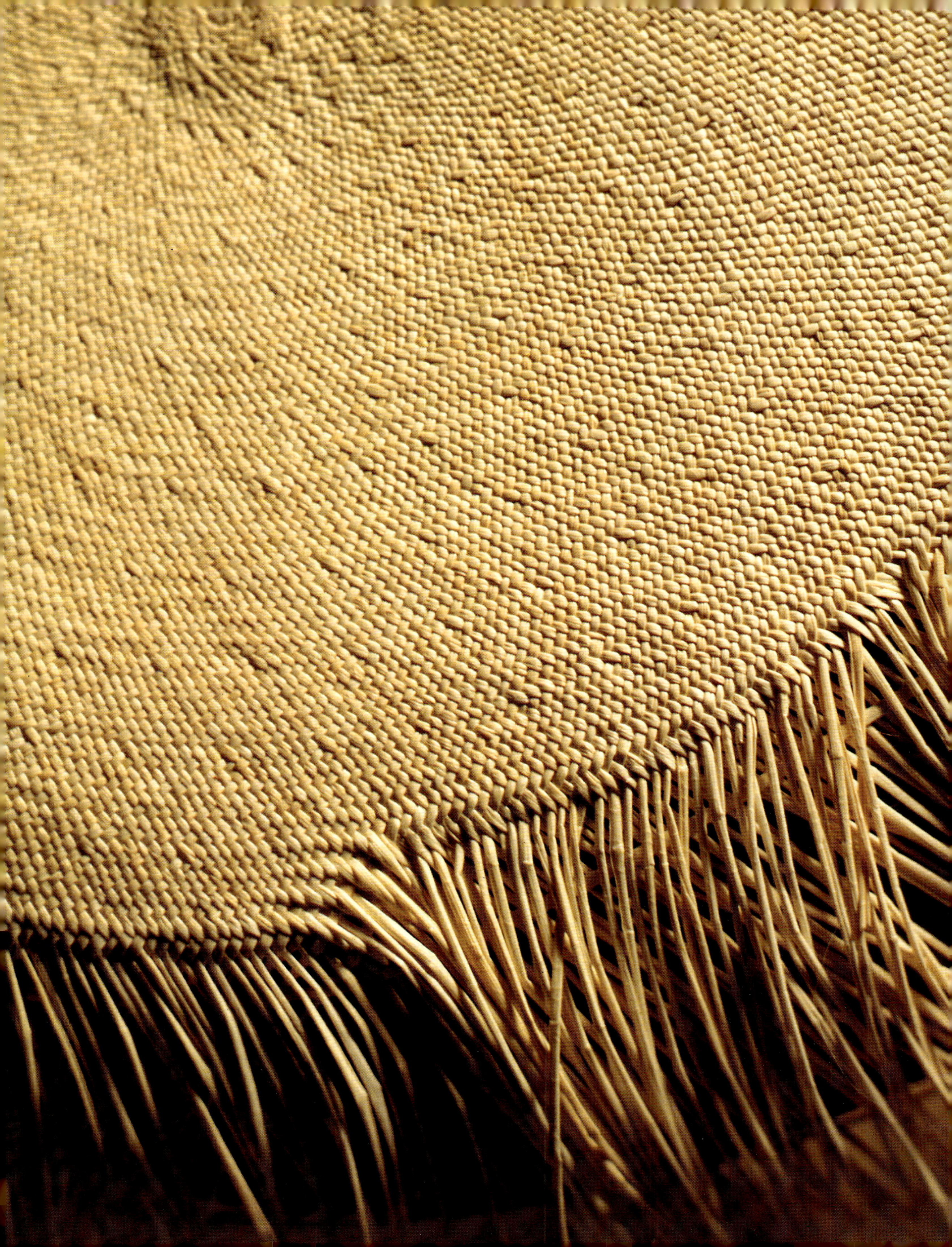

The "montecristi" has always been considered the prince of panamas. The quality of a "fino" depends on the selection of the straw, the fineness of the weave and the regularity of the brim. It is judged by the quantity of rows that make up the crown of the hat, and, finally, by the appearance of the finished product. The rows, which are arranged in concentric circles, starting from the centre of the hat (called the "rosette"), can be made out when the hat is placed in front of a light. Their number, which is synonymous with a more or less serried weave, is an important indication of quality, when all other criteria have been satisfied.

Upon his return from Maria's house, Manuel lays down his straw in a courtyard near the main room. Another day ends in the village, where the silence is scarcely disturbed by the voices of the children playing in the bare earth of the streets. A little further on, lights come on in the small church, and the vultures, which have long been a feature of life here, break off from their wheeling to await the night. A light breeze springs up. It is time for the old man to return to his work. The day has been a full one, what with the weaving, the fields and his visit to Maria. And yet he is anxious to get back to his task; he wants to get this hat finished.

He began work on it almost twelve weeks ago, and although each "montecristi" is unique, the successive stages remain the same. At the start, he created the rosette, the centre of the crown. This was made with eight fibres in a tight lattice. As the weaving proceeded, he added new straws so as to enlarge the circle, and thus brought the crown up to the desired size. This part of the hat can be made in a seated position. It takes a lot of order and skill, and straw of great suppleness. When the end of the crown has been completed, the piece must be placed on a form which is itself set on a tripod stand,

Opposite page, left
Toquilla straw being dried.
Opposite page, right
The start of work on a "montecristi superfino",
seen here on its work stand.
The wooden forms press down on the crown to flatten it.

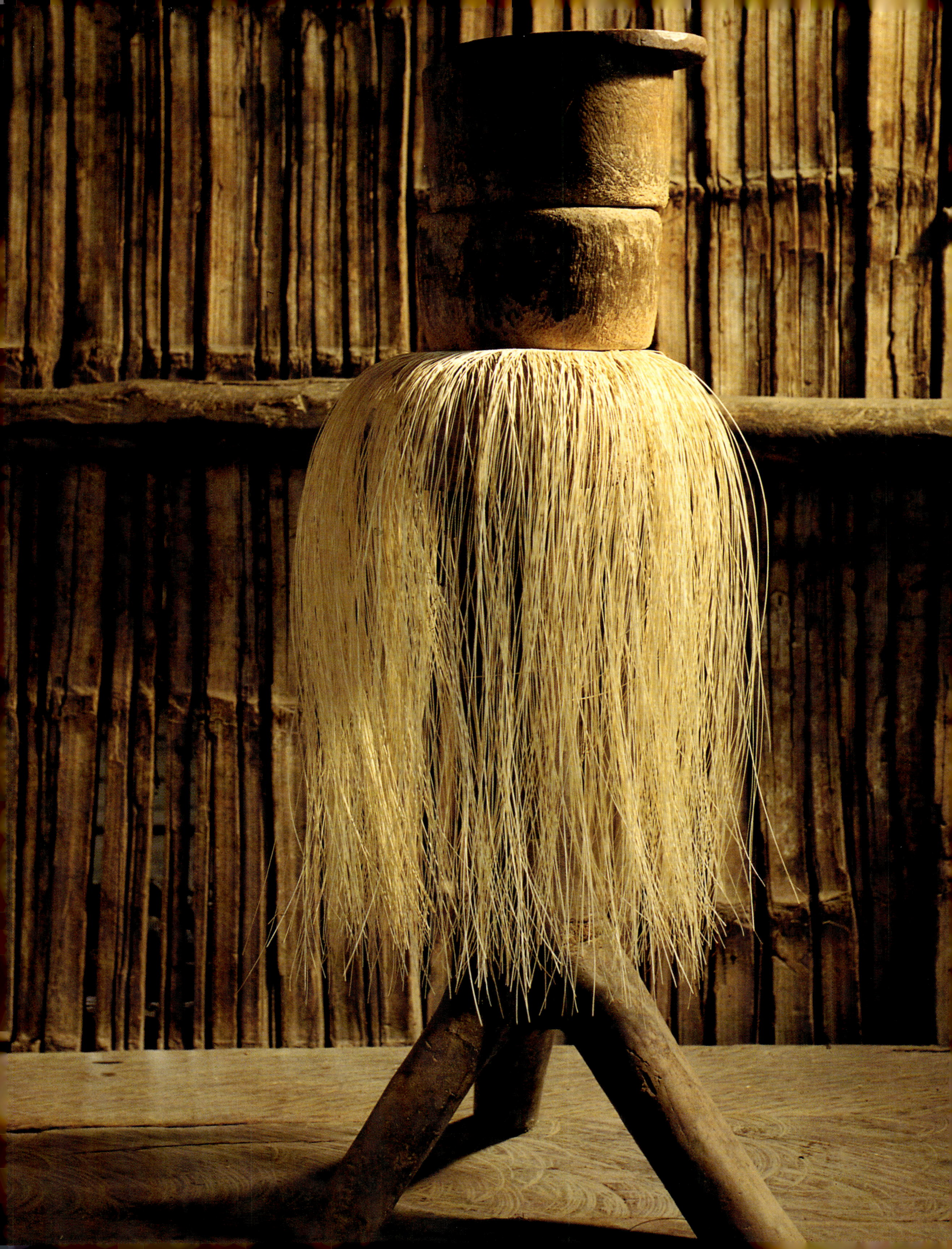

after which the work is carried out in the upright weaving position, such that the angle of the hat can be properly controlled. The flexibility of the straw makes it possible to bring this operation to an extreme point of refinement, sticking as closely as possible to the form. The continuation of the weaving is long, painstaking and periodic, the product of ancestral skills. Then comes the final part: the brim, which the Ecuadorians call the wings of the hat; its size is determined by the details of the order, and it is the eye, as ever, that is the judge of the ideal proportions. It is at this final stage of his work that the old man finds himself as night falls. He still has to weave the last rows, and knot the straw all around the brim to mark the end-point. And this will be the culmination of his task.

The hat is now finished. The light-bulb, swinging feebly, casts little shadows over the ivory whiteness which gives life to the large room. The old weaver steps back one more time to look at his work. The weft is fine and regular, the style is good, the colour uniform, and he does not see any imperfections. He is satisfied. Tomorrow, he will hand over his "fino" to Don Rosendo, who will give him the rest of what he is owed. This is the arrangement that has operated for some years between him and his agent, who pays him in three or four instalments, advancing him the money he needs to live on. In the middle of the room, the panama is spending its last hours in Pilé. Perfectly at ease on its stand, still encircled by a mane of golden hairs, the hat seems to attract to itself all the light in the place. The night becomes a showcase for this rare pearl. The old man is happy; now he can go and sleep. The road from Pilé to Montecristi is long and monotonous. Don Rosendo's old car, a victim of the jolts and the dust, is beginning its return journey, loaded with "toquilla" hats. The agent is happy with his trip to Pilé this morning; he is bringing back treasures, of which Manuel's hat is one. But there are also the two sisters, Juana Isabel and Maria Clothilde Lopez, who never let him down, and Senovio Italo Espinal, who has produced a miracle.

At Pilé, everyone knows how to weave, but those who are capable of making a "superfino" can be counted on the fingers of one hand. It seems, in effect, that in the entire region, there are now no more than ten real weavers. If they have no successors, their disappearance will constitute the definitive cessation of the production of "superfino" panamas, that is to say the finest, the most beautiful, the rarest!

Of course, there are still many Ecuadorians who make their living from straw. Senovio Italo Espinal has seven children, and all of them are good weavers. At the town hall in Pilé there are courses, financed by the Banco Central del Ecuador, which award young weavers a certificate of aptitude after sixteen hours of training. And then there are other small villages of weavers in the region, for example Las Pampas, a few kilometres from there, where Don Rosendo can find some excellent "finos".

But in reality the situation is worrying. The master weavers are getting fewer all the time, and the old man knows that it will be difficult to change the course of events. Working with straw is hard, and does not pay well. A weaver earns, on average, a tenth of the selling price of a panama – it does not amount to a lot, for so much work. Alphonse Cuesta expresses this well in his novel, *Los Hijos*, when one of his characters says: "Mas gana el hombre silvando que la mujer hilando" (A man earns more whistling than a woman spinning).

> In Pilé, everyone knows the art of weaving but those capable of creating a *superfino* can be counted on the fingers of one hand.

Opposite page
White cotton cloth, used to protect a "montecristi" in the process of being woven.

Such is the attitude of numerous artisans today, as they abandon, one after another, this noble calling for activities that are easier and more profitable.

The road continues across the immense, undulating desert of clay, which is dotted with dry shrubs and strange fibrous trees. Soon, the presence of a few houses indicates the asphalt road that leads to Don Rosendo's residence.

The small town of Montecristi, a few kilometres from the industrial port of Manta, looks like a setting that John Steinbeck would have chosen as a location for his favourite characters. It is said that it got its name from a certain Mr Criste, who made his home on the top of the hill there: the name Montecristi probably evolved over time, with the arrival of new inhabitants. Meanwhile, the winds have been blowing ceaselessly through the sloping streets of the town. And dust is the lot of this solitary outpost, where time seems to have stood still for the last century. Of its past glory there remains only the house of Eloy Alfaro, the national hero who was born there in 1842, and the church bell, which was a gift from the queen of Spain during the colonial period. Pride and poverty.

Don Rosendo Delgado Garay lives on the heights above the town. His warehouse and workshop are marked by a wall painted with the name of the Finos-Montecristi. The main room is cool, open onto the outside, and cluttered with straw objects and hats. It is here that the final touches are given to the hats that come from Pilé, or Las Pampas, or from one of the weavers of Montecristi itself. Don Rosendo has no sooner arrived than he heads for the back room, which is his storehouse. It is small, poorly-lit, and full of his latest acquisitions, arranged according to size and weave. He then goes back to his place in the larger room, to his armchair in a sunny corner, and sets to work on a hat. Like his wife and the other finishers working around him, his gestures are rapid, almost reflexive, as his eyes range over the hat. He looks to see if there is perhaps a small cut or a different-coloured straw: he corrects any errors he finds.

Following pages
Weaving of a "montecristi superfino".

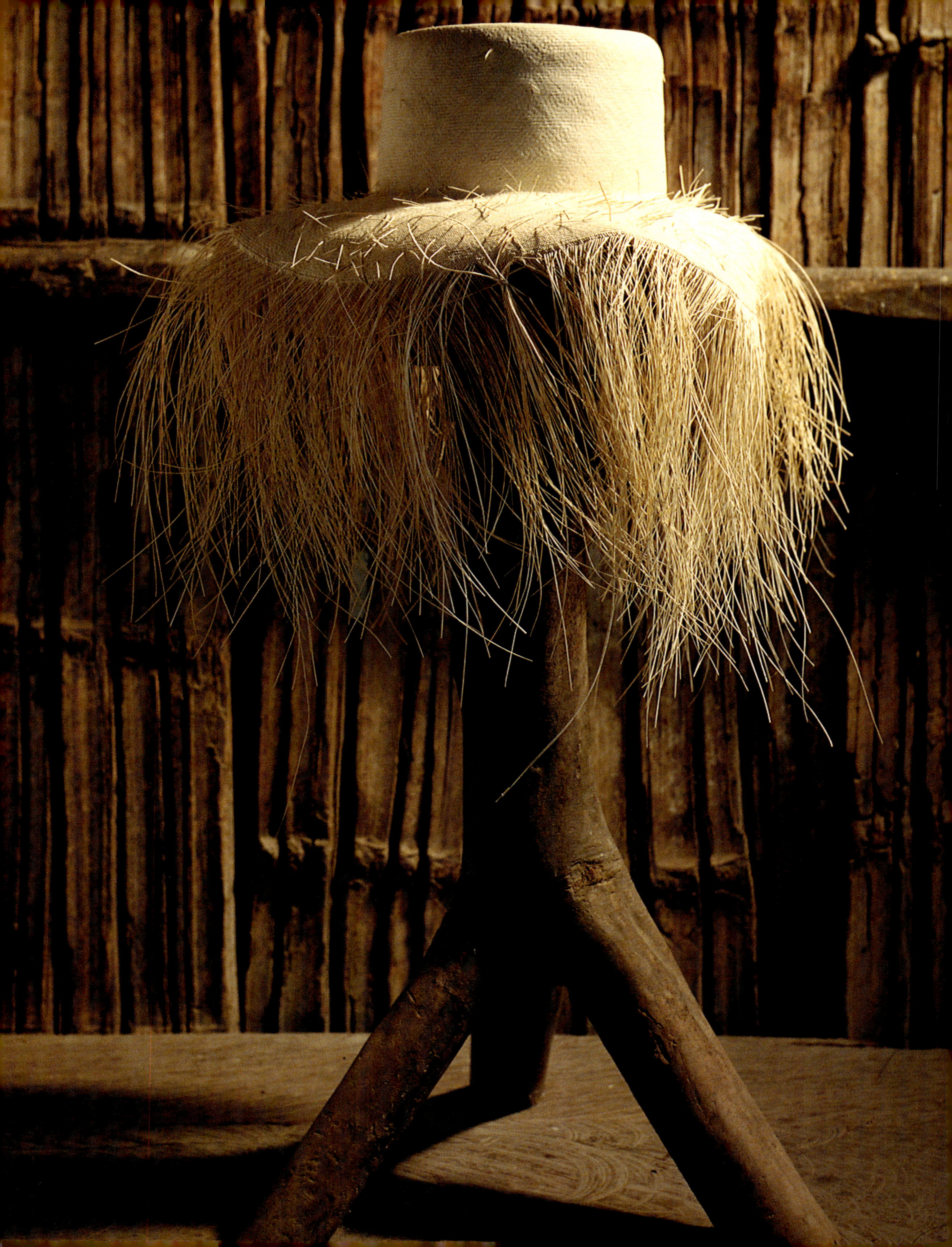

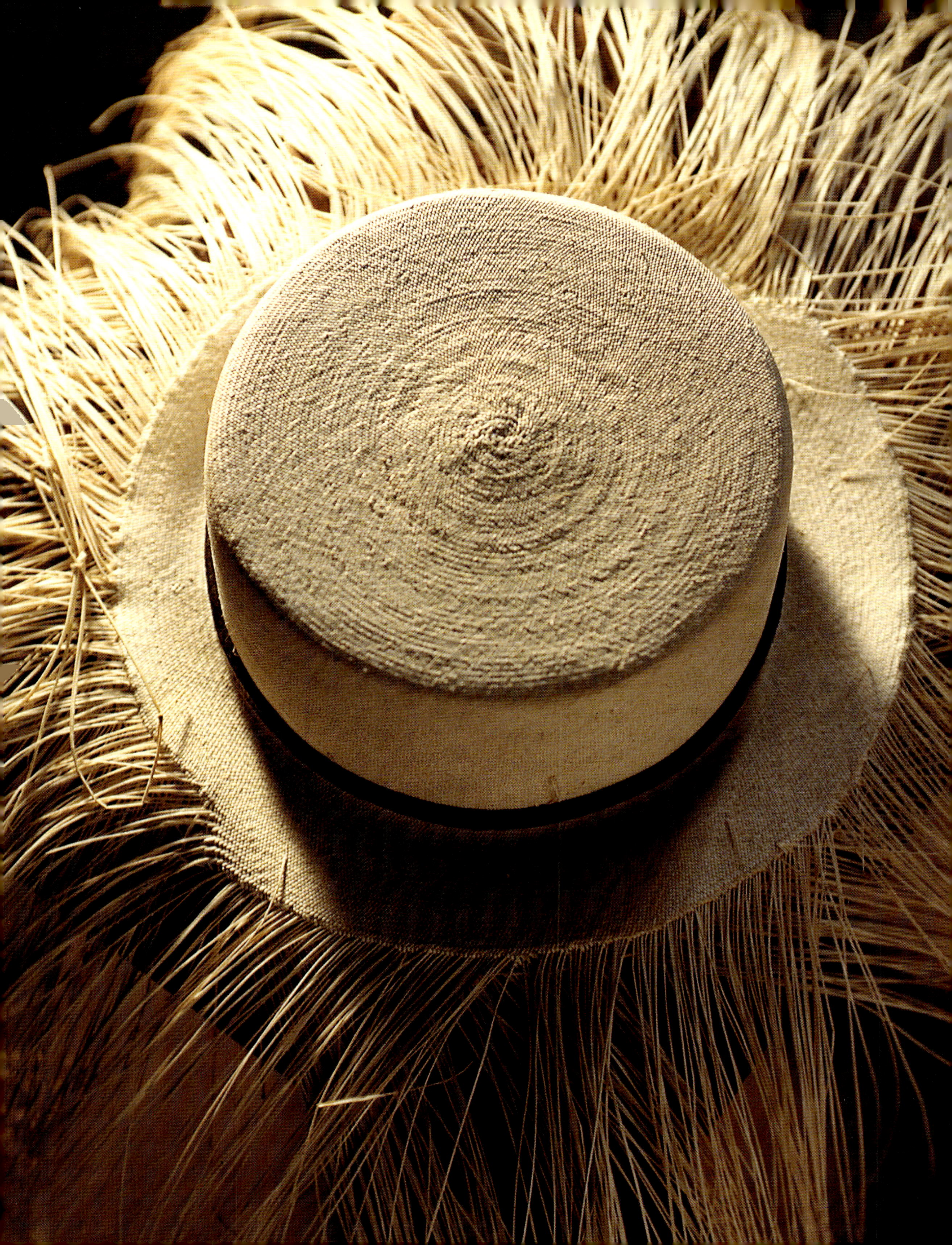

Then he cuts the remaining straw. Whether it be the isolated wisps in the hat itself or the shaggy fringe around the outside, he eliminates all excess. Finally, gripping each strand, he applies himself to constructing the brim, tying up the ends towards the interior. When the brim, thus disciplined, becomes a perfect edge, the old man knows that the hat is ready. He can then sign it, as a guarantee of the quality that he is so attached to.

The work goes on like this all day in Don Rosendo's house. Often, the "re-collectors", as they are called, will interrupt the rhythm of the activity, selling panamas acquired from the weavers of the surrounding areas. Knowing the old man's standards perfectly, they take his precise orders and scour the region in search of hats for sale. The finished "finos" are now ready for their great voyage. They will take their place in the restricted circle of "montecristi" amateurs that extends to the four corners of the globe. Welcomed into luxurious boutiques, they will be placed in the expert hands of those who are responsible for forming them. This is a rare talent, but those who possess it are able to create new, admirable forms. In New York, Paris and London, they all have the same respect for their material. This straw hat remains unique for them: it is a Garden of Eden, almost inaccessible. When silk was rare, it was measured against the "montecristi", whereas today it is compared to Shatoosh, which is a synonym of fineness, rarity and luxury. The expert hat-makers love this straw, which is like none other. Soft and flexible, it bends, rolls up and unrolls with immense docility, as long as it is moistened from time to time.

The good hat-makers know that a "montecristi" must not be too highly worked. They are content to concentrate on the oval and the brim of the hat, using a wooden form, with the help of a little steam. The brim can be ironed, or even trimmed according to taste, but the height of elegance is to hold to the natural form, which is already so fine and so perfect. All the work is done by hand, in the sole search for harmony and subtle equilibrium. It is the specialist who will find the style of his "fino", subduing the material without doing it violence, pursuing the ideal form for his client. Form can also be created by using the pressure of shaping machines. The result is achieved more rapidly, and is more sharply defined. It is the choice of some people, who favour fashion over inherent character. But it will never be that of the true amateur of the panama. Whatever the form and the means made use of, the last operation carried out on the hat is always the same: an interior trim is added, to stabilise the oval form of the panama, and a personalised hatband is chosen.

Since the 19th century, a simple band of black cloth has been considered as the most classic example of elegance. Today, the mythical image of the panama is still associated with this detail. Those with the most unbridled imagination choose a ribbon in navy blue grosgrain, or in camaïeu, but, as panamas go, this is generally the limit! And here the voyage of the "wrongly-named panama", as Don Rosendo always calls it, comes to an end. From the straw-cutter to its final owner, it has passed through the hands of a long line of artisans, weavers, merchants and hatters, who have in common their expertise and their love of their profession. It is now ready for other voyages. Of all its qualities, the greatest is often forgotten: its longevity. This prince of panamas has the gift of eternal youth, and takes delight in defying time. The years which pass can only add to its beauty, giving its colour a light honeyed patina. Thus it traverses the years with grace, pushing arrogance to the point of continuing to turn heads…

> The quality of a *montecristi* is measured by the fineness of its weave and the rows in its crown.

Opposite page
"Montecristi superfino" before finishing.

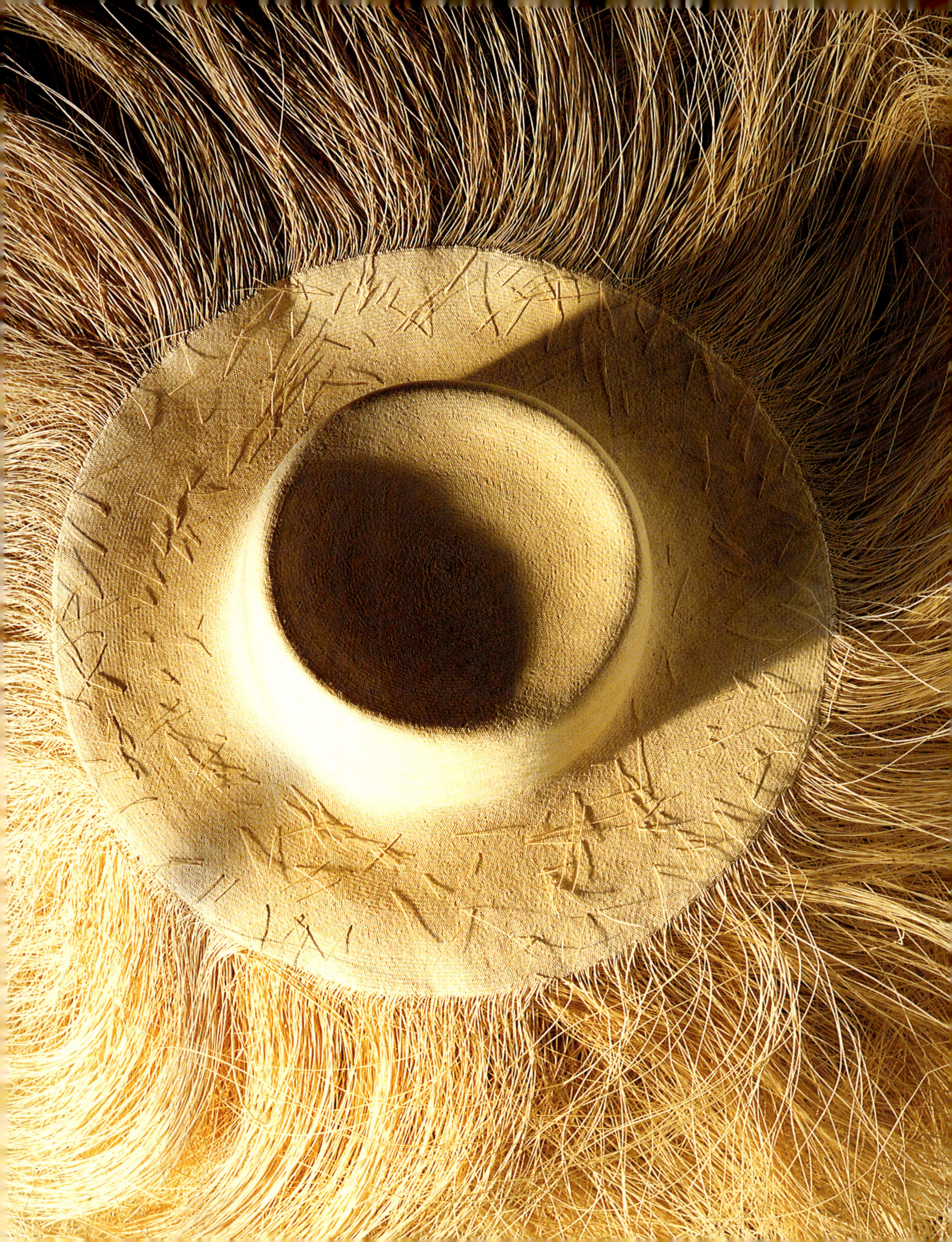

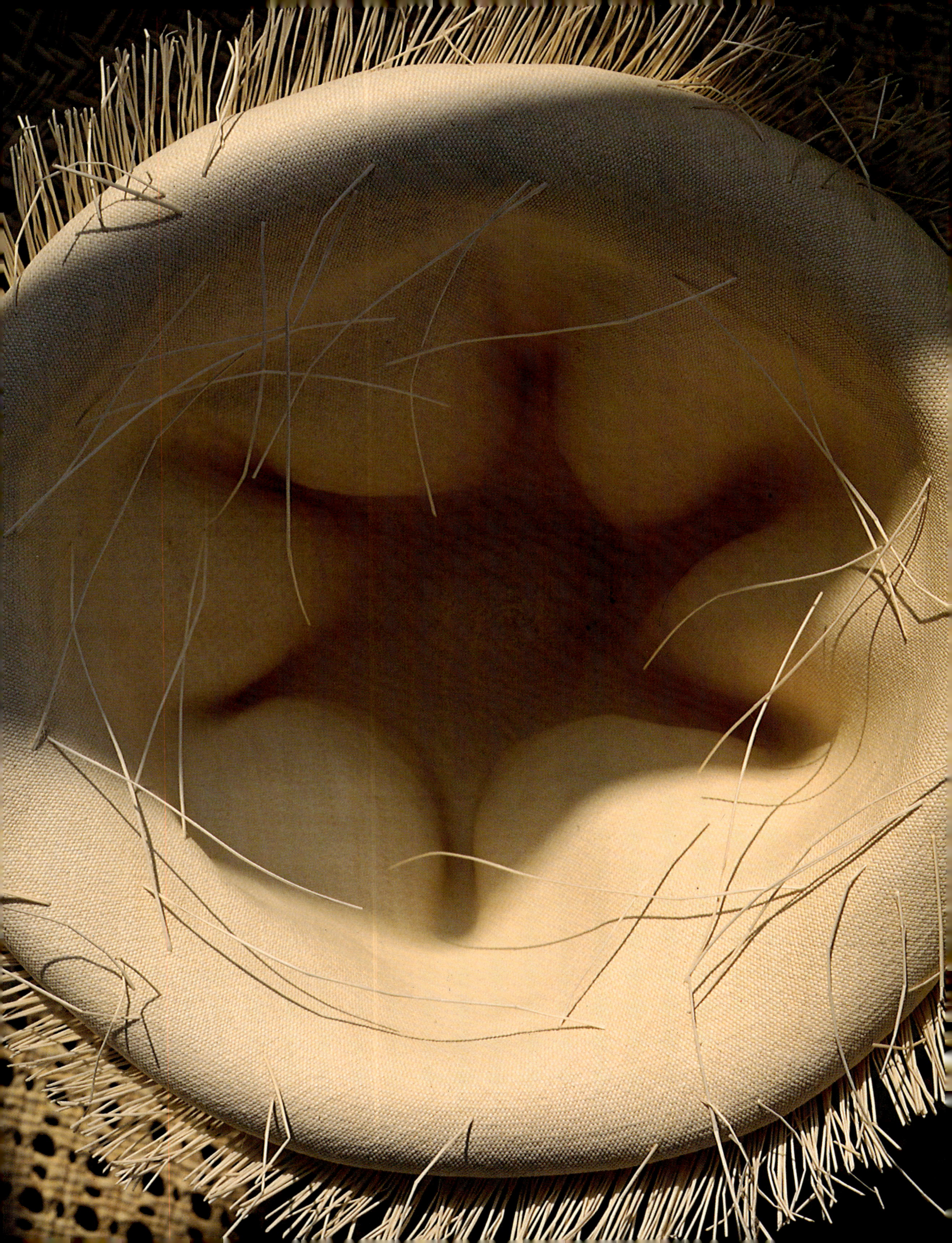

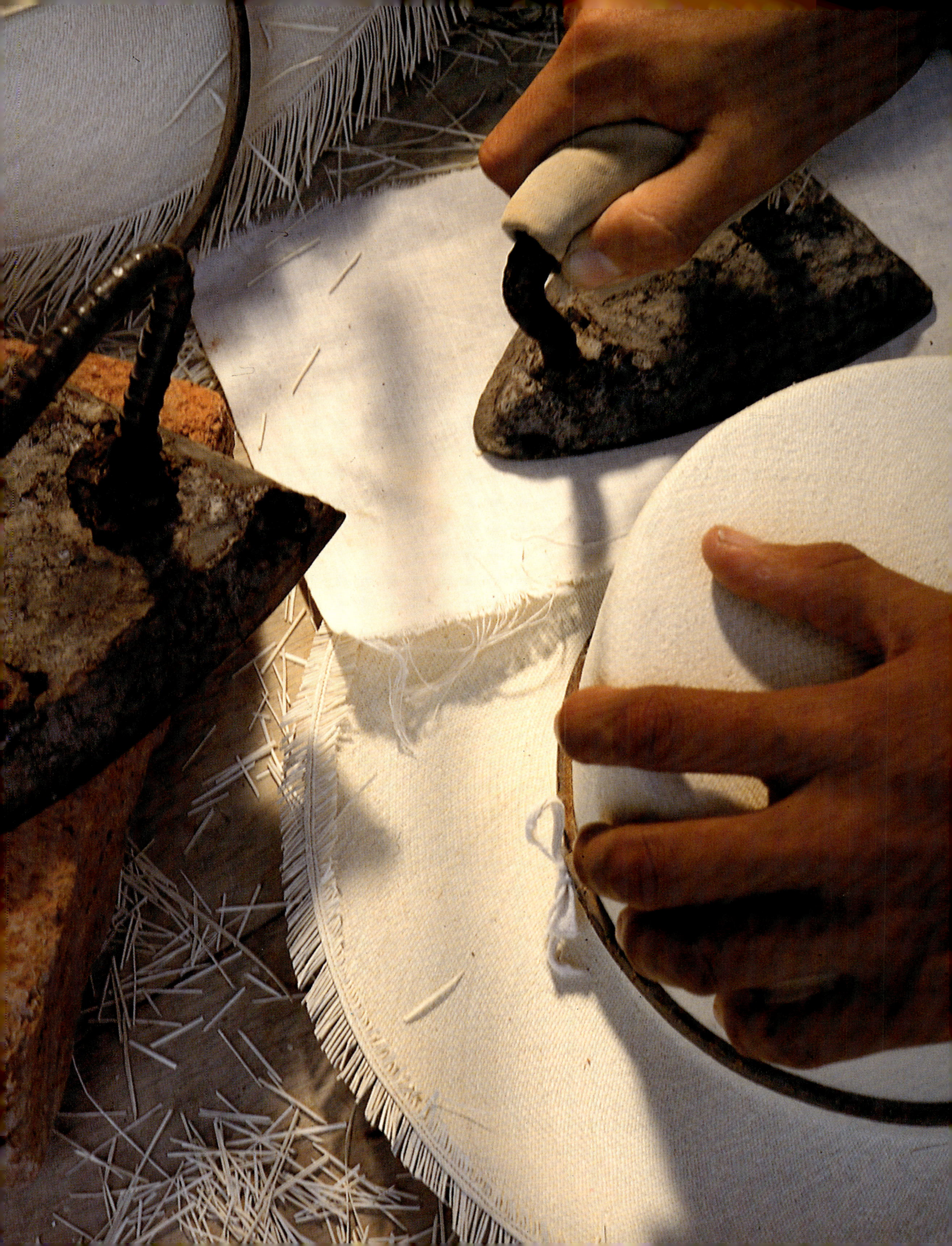

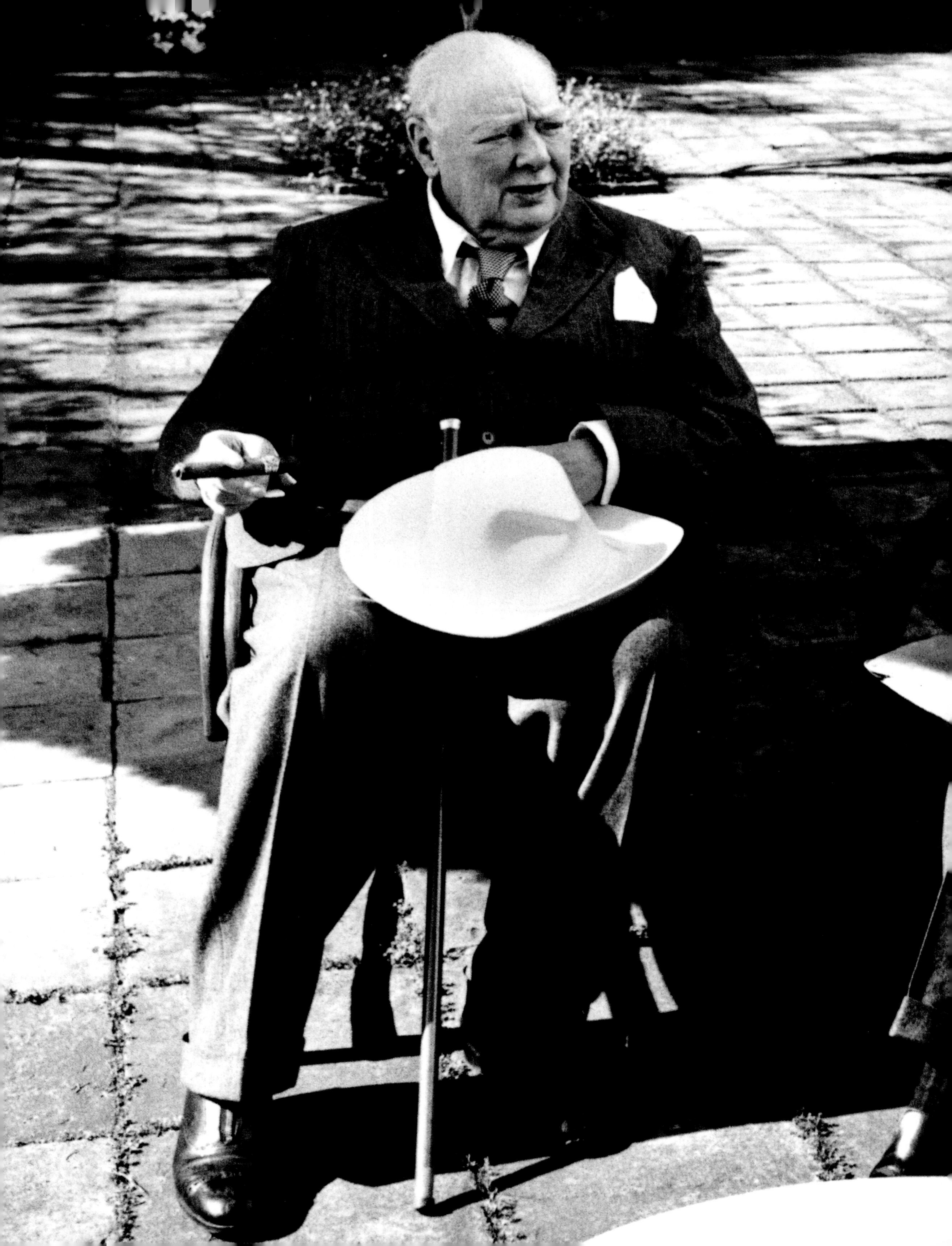

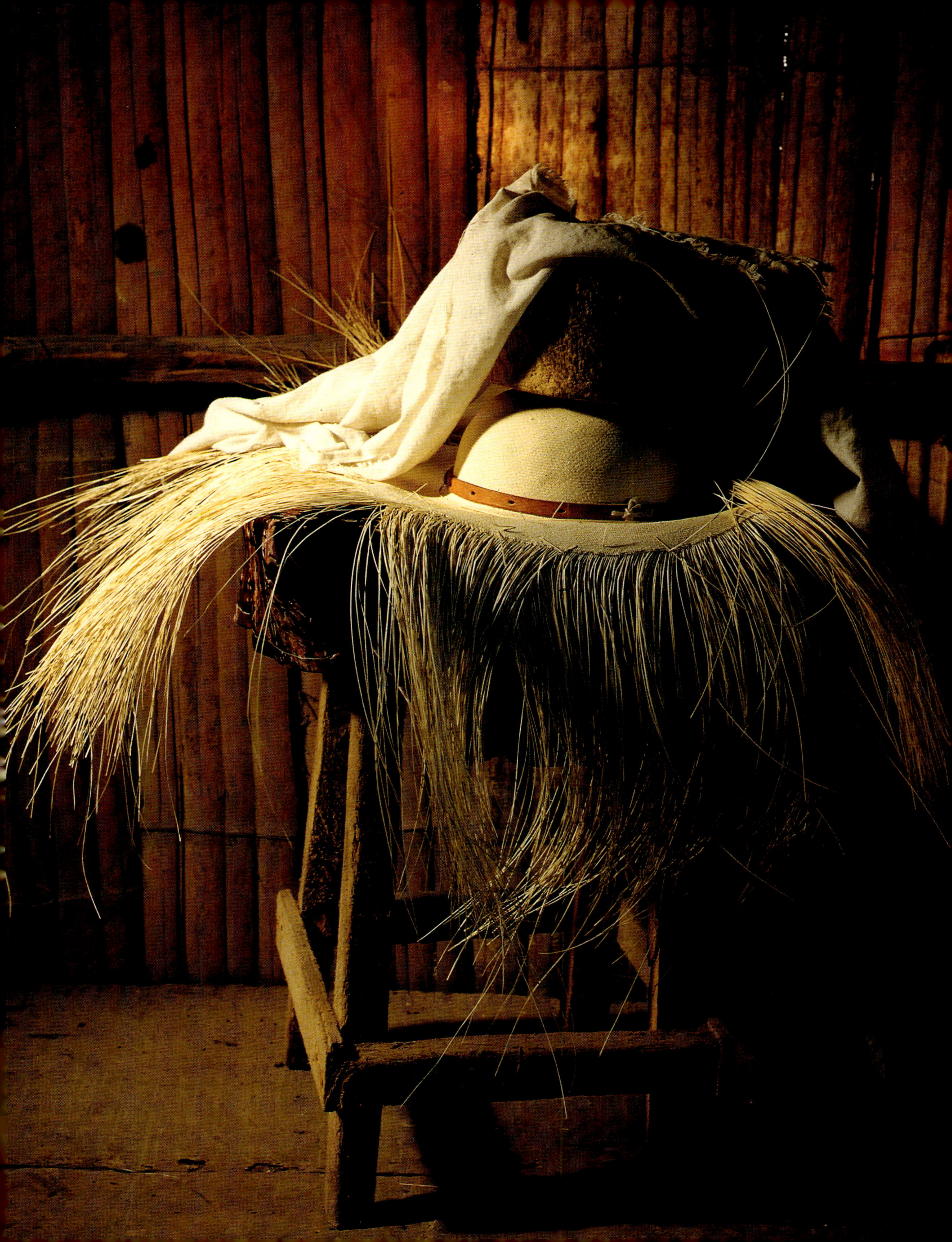

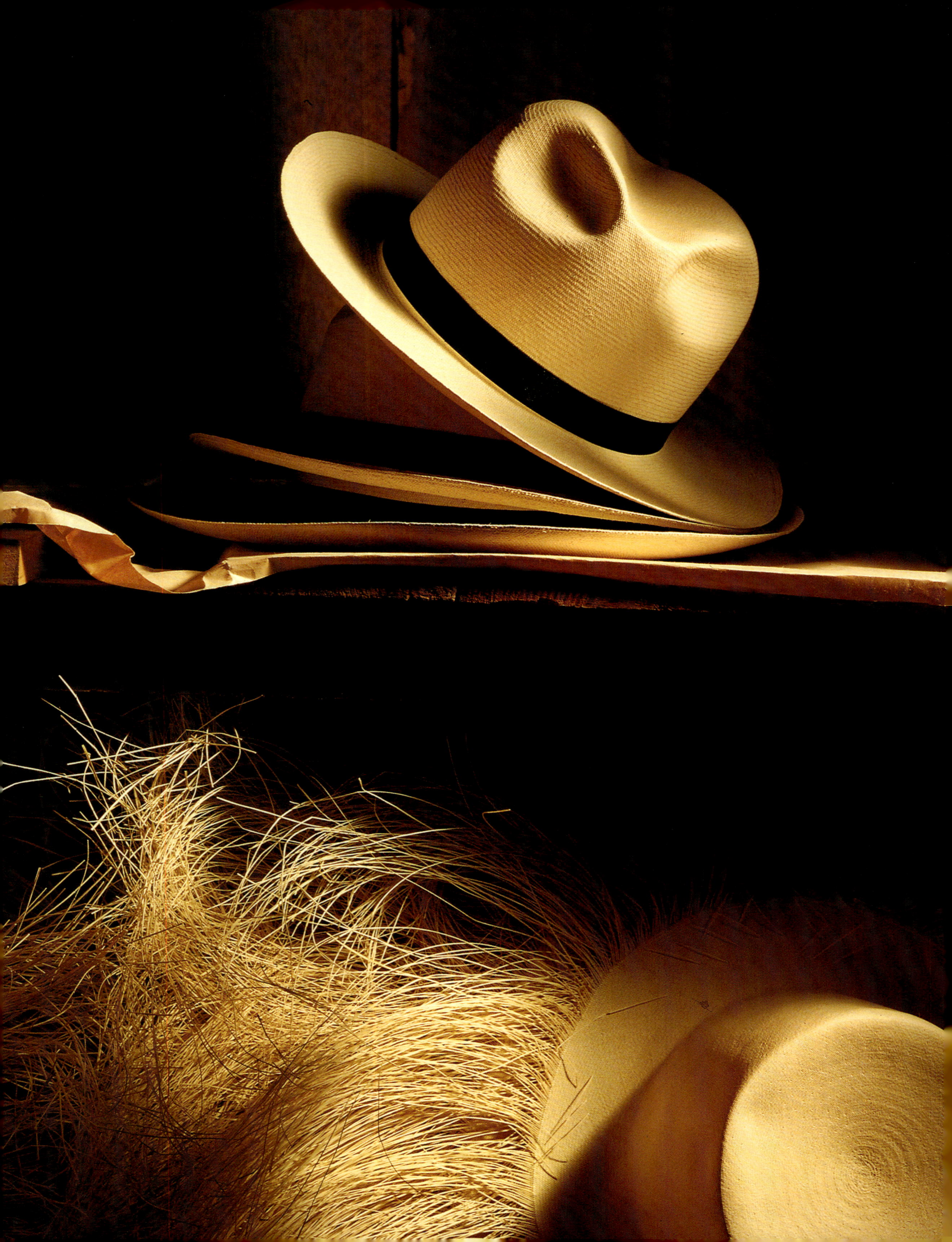

BANCO CENTRAL DEL ECUADOR
FODERUMA - MANTA
CONFIEREN ESTE
CERTIFICADO

A SR. Néstor Angel Espinoza

Por su participación en el CURSO DE TEJIDO DE PAJA TOQUILLA, realizado en Pile con 16 horas de duración

Since its first appearance, the Montecristi panama has symbolised masculine elegance.

Previous pages
1. "Montecristi superfino" being finished.
2. Ironing with an iron heated in the embers of the fire. The hat is treated with sulphur to give it greater whiteness.
3. Winston Churchill at Cap Ferrat in 1959. On his knee is a "montecristi fino".
4. While a hat is being woven it is always set on a form, and a leather band is placed around the crown.
5. Don Rosendo's house, with "montecristi finos" being formed in the "borsalino" style (at top), and "superfinos" before finishing (at bottom).
6. The Banco Central del Ecuador certificate which is awarded to apprentice weavers.

Opposite, left
Signor Baizinni, 1905.

Opposite, right
Crown of a "montecristi superfino".

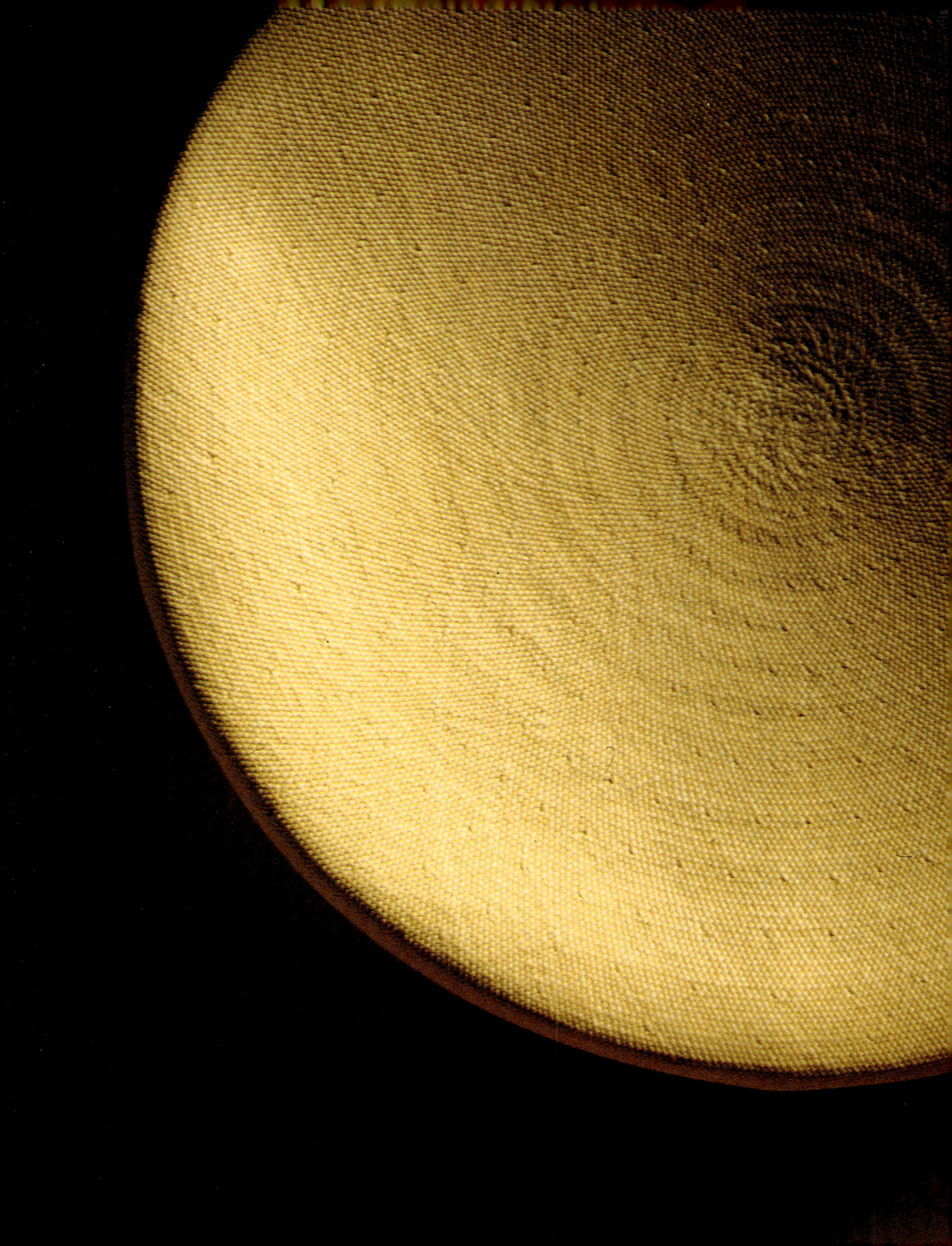

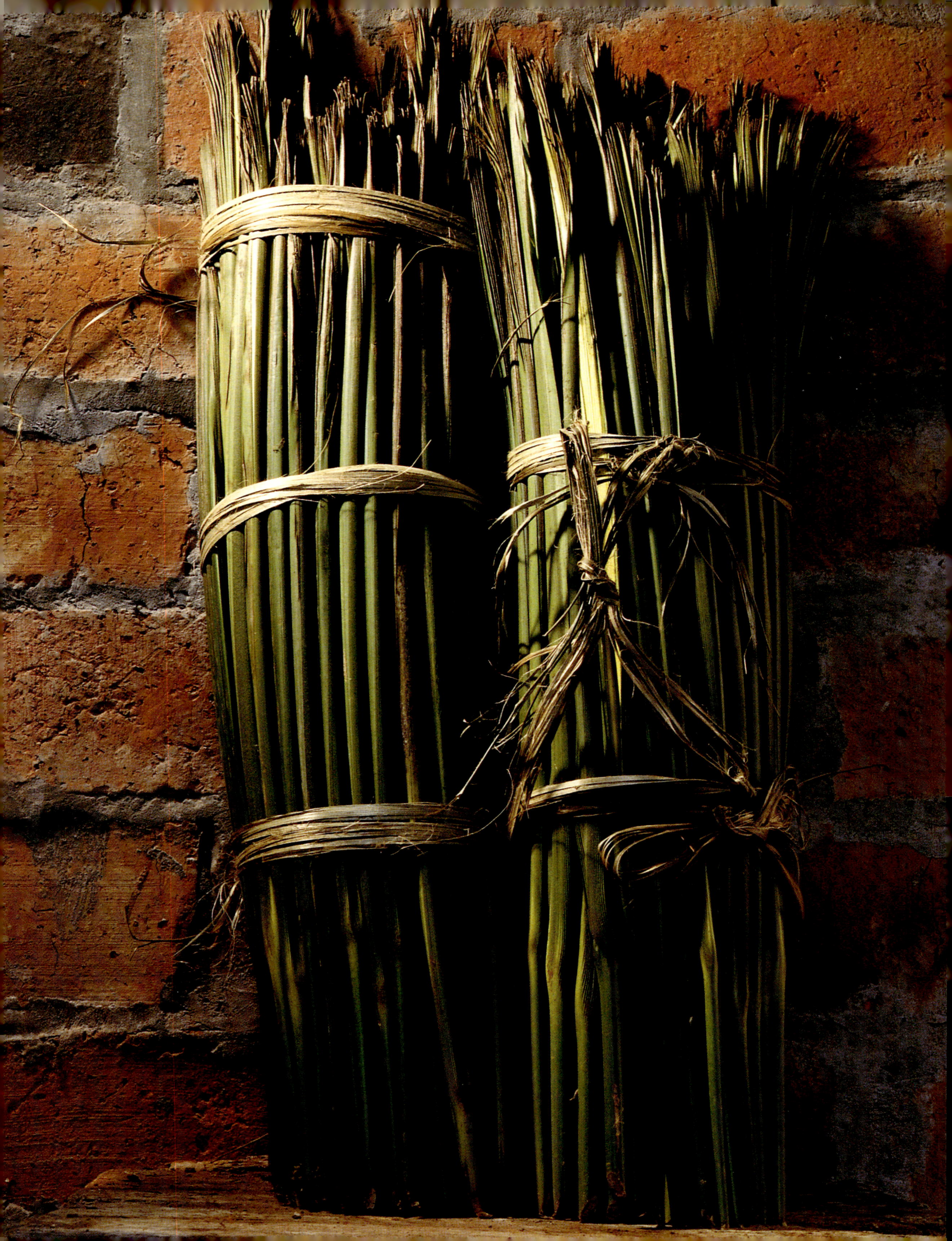

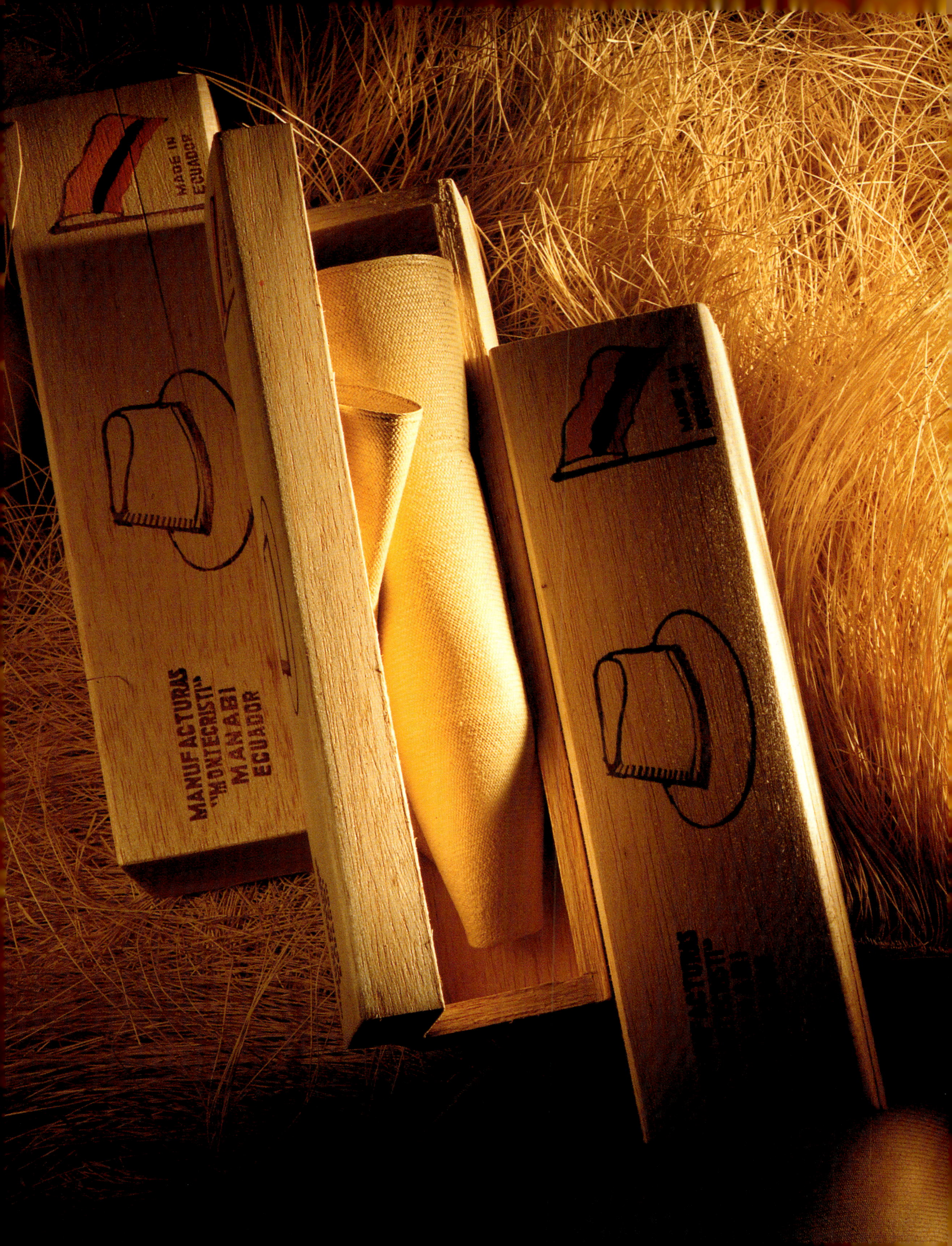
MADE IN
ECUADOR
MANUFACTURAS
"MONTECRISTI"
MANABI
ECUADOR

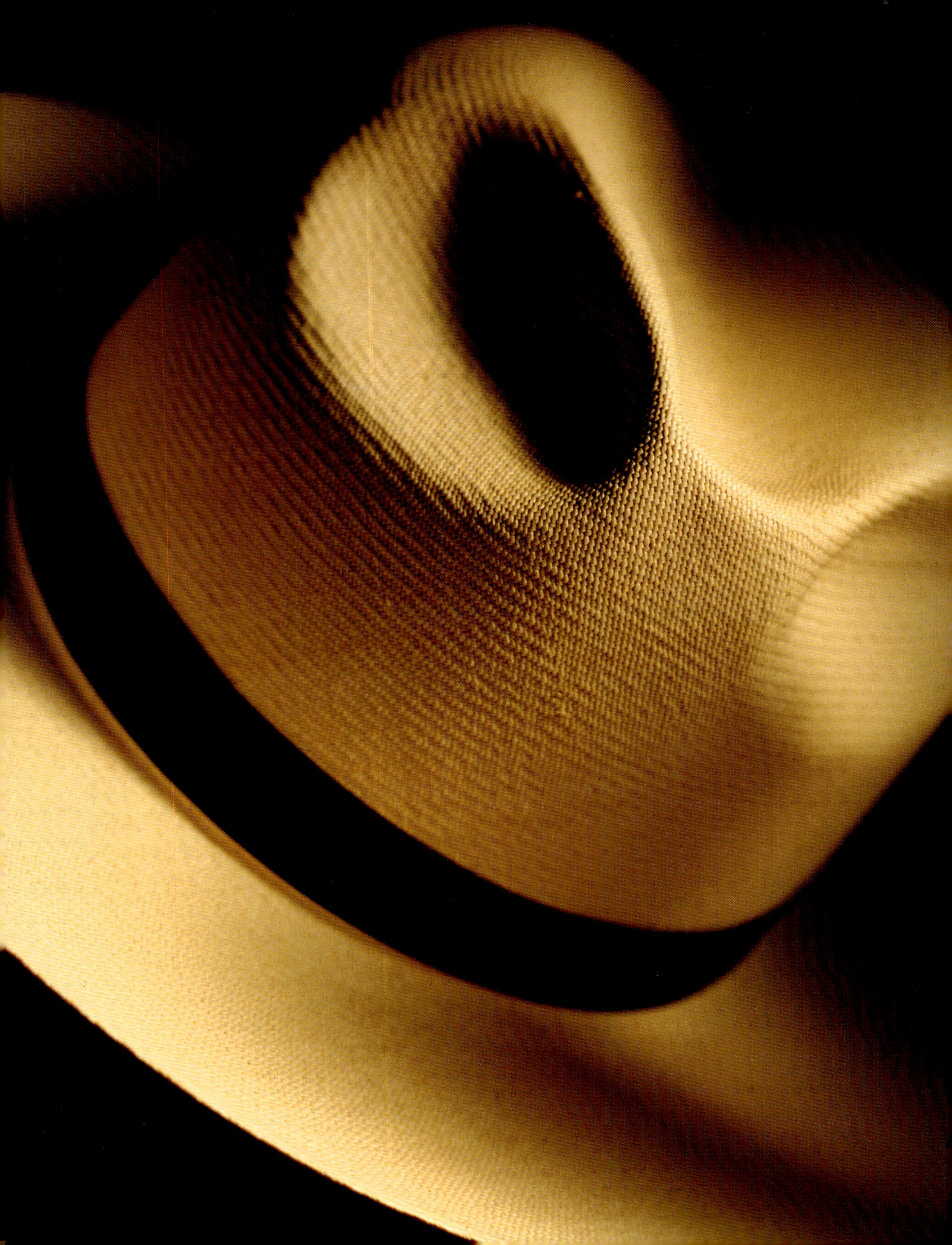

The simple band of black cloth has become a classic symbol of elegance.

Previous pages
*Left : Bundles of toquilla straw, freshly cut.
The green stalks are called
"cogollos" – they are palm leaves which are still
at the young shoot stage.
Right : According to the myth of the "montecristi",
the hat should be rolled up
and presented in a balsa-wood box.*
Opposite, left
A "montecristi" of the "borsalino" style.
Opposite, right
*H.M. Gustavus V, king of Sweden, at the
Monte Carlo Sporting Club.*

Glorified during the 19th century, the panama has since been considered the prince of straw hats.

Opposite page
Alberto Santos Dumont, pioneer aviator in 1906.
Following page
Death in Venice: *a scene from Visconti's film, which contributed to relaunching the myth of the panama.*

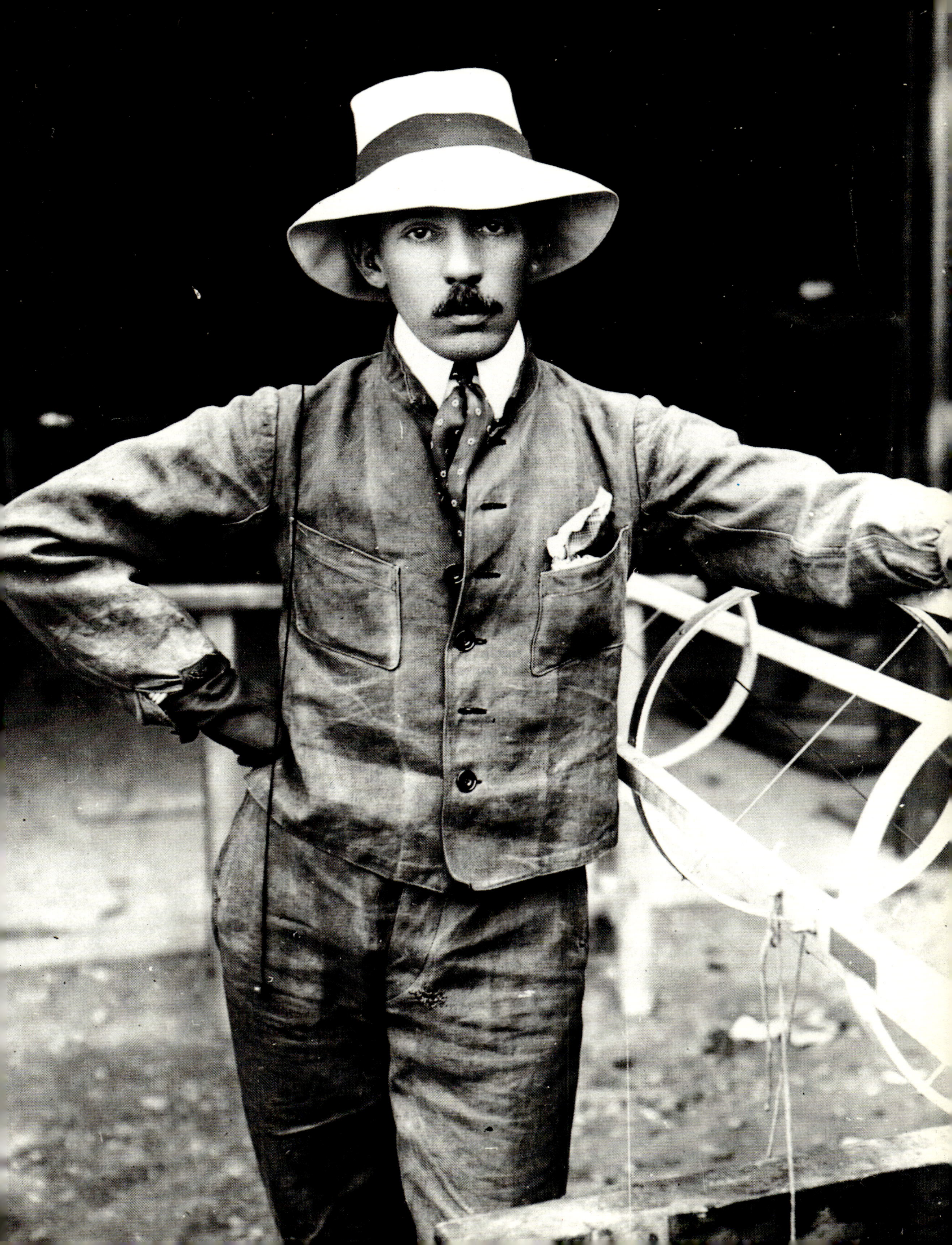

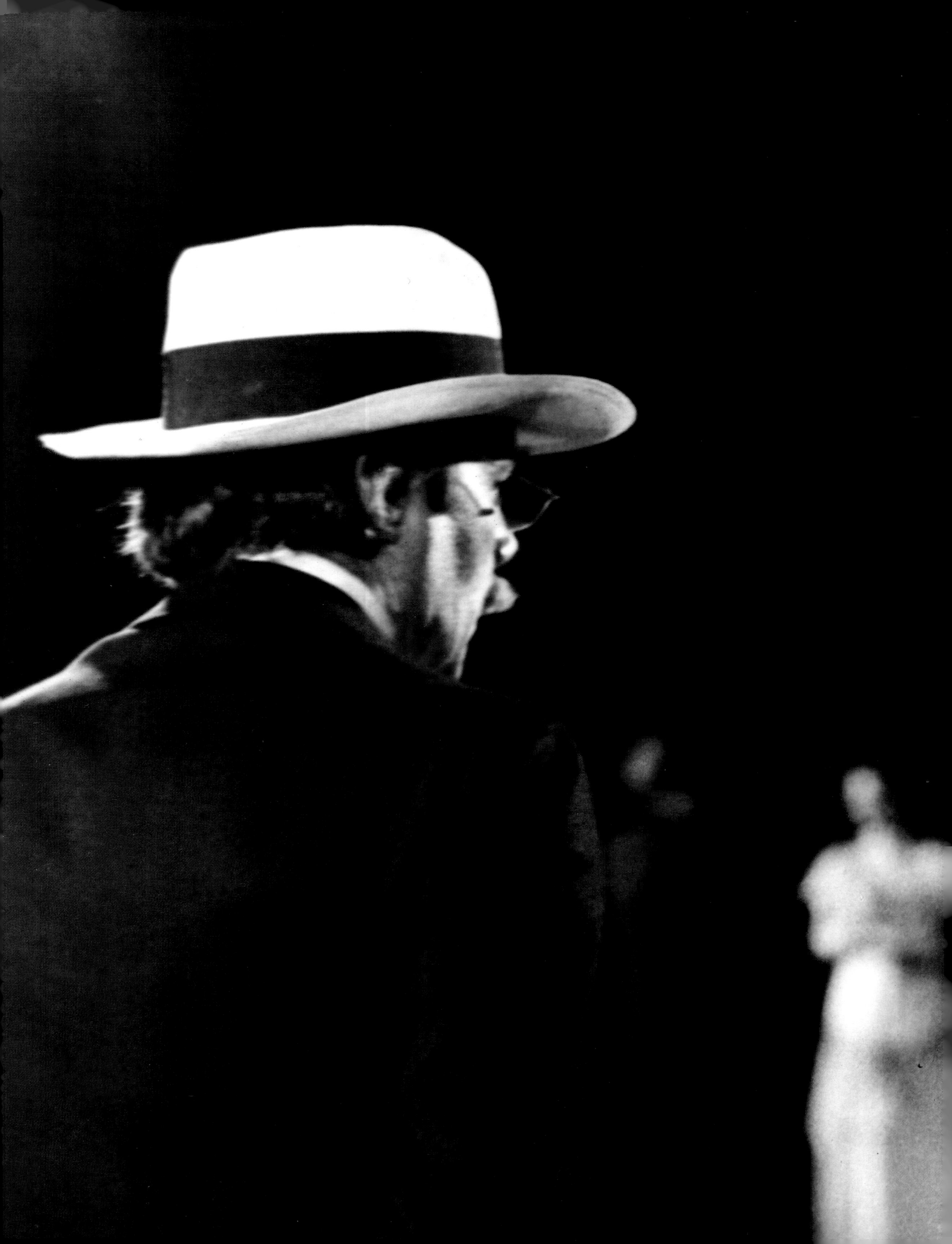

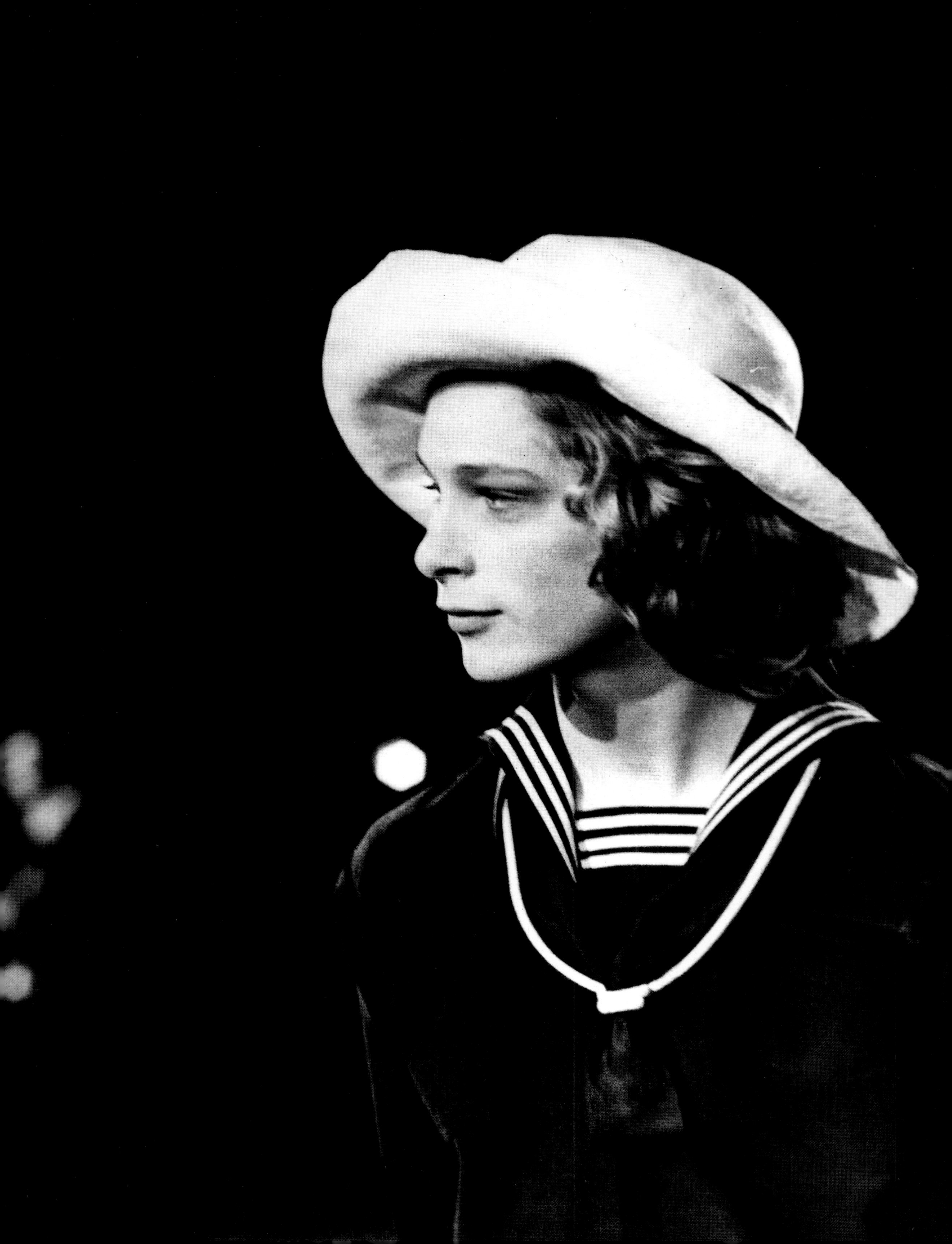

3

Cuenca : the Andes, around a hat

When Rodolfo Dorfzaun was asked the reason why he took up trading in panama hats immediately upon his arrival in Ecuador, he talked about his beloved motor bike and panama, which he had to leave behind when he left his native Germany in 1939. The sentimental aspect of this anecdote, to which no one had ever paid any attention, was discovered to be authentic when, years later, after his death, a photograph of the two objects in question came to light.

The arrival of Rodolfo Dorfzaun in the country of the panama hat coincided with the great export years. His nephew, Kurt Dorfzaun, who joined him shortly afterwards to assist in this flourishing business, is now at the head of one of the country's largest panama-exporting firms, with a turnover of around forty thousand dozen hats per year, which is twenty percent of Ecuador's total production. His son Roberto has set up a distribution firm in New York, which covers the whole of the United States. And yet, even with his five hundred thousand hats per year, there is nothing extraordinary about Kurt Dorfzaun. His direct competitors deal in similar or even larger numbers, and are also present in numerous markets.

Gerardo Serrano is without doubt the largest supplier in the history of the Azuay region. His workshop goes back a long way indeed, and the aroma of authenticity that lingers about the place gives it an atmosphere of warm reassuring legitimacy.

Homero Ortega, for his part, is proud to belong to a family that has been in the business for five generations. He himself is carrying on the line in the company of his five sons, who work with him. Four of them have opened "almacenes" in Spain, Italy, Japan and the United States. Like Serrano, Homero Ortega has a passion for the business, and dreams of being Ecuador's biggest exporter. He has a taste for the memorable catch-phrase, as much as for tradition. As he likes to say: "My heritage is my stock in trade".

Like a number of others, these three great exporters of toquillas live and prosper in Cuenca, in Azuay province. Set at an altitude of two thousand five hundred and eighty metres, the little town of Cuenca has kept intact the charm of its colonial past: a multitude of small streets with low houses and wrought iron balconies highlighted by flowers recall Seville. In reality, its Andean pride and innumerable churches are more similar to its big sister, Quito. As cities of the Catholic Andes, cities of greenery that touch the sky, they have a common history, a common distinctiveness. Quito has been influenced by modern times, as a capital city must be. Its colonial tradition has fallen away, and the different periods have begun to inter-

Opposite page
Piles of unfinished panamas in Homero Ortega's workshop.
Following page
School in the centre of Cuenca.

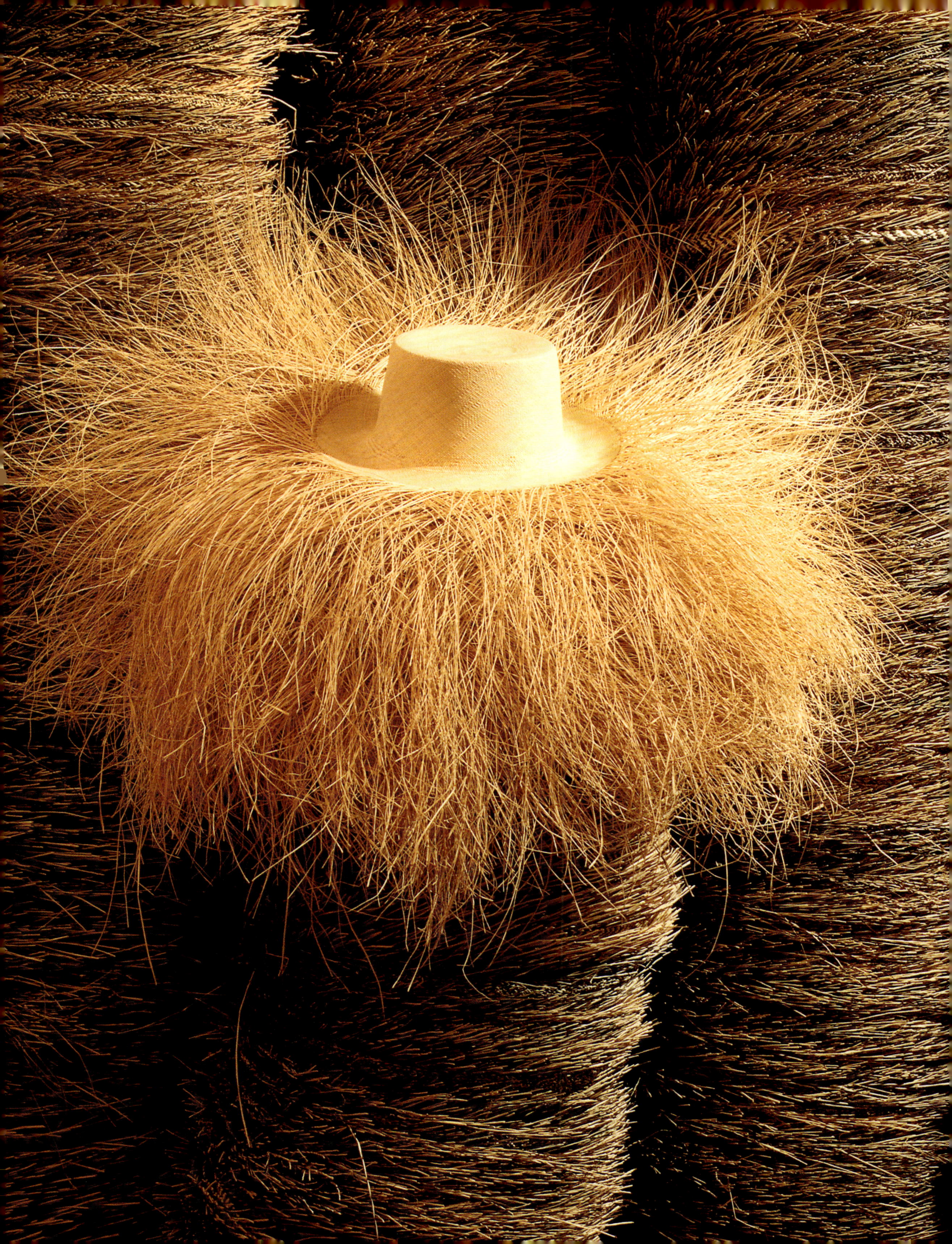

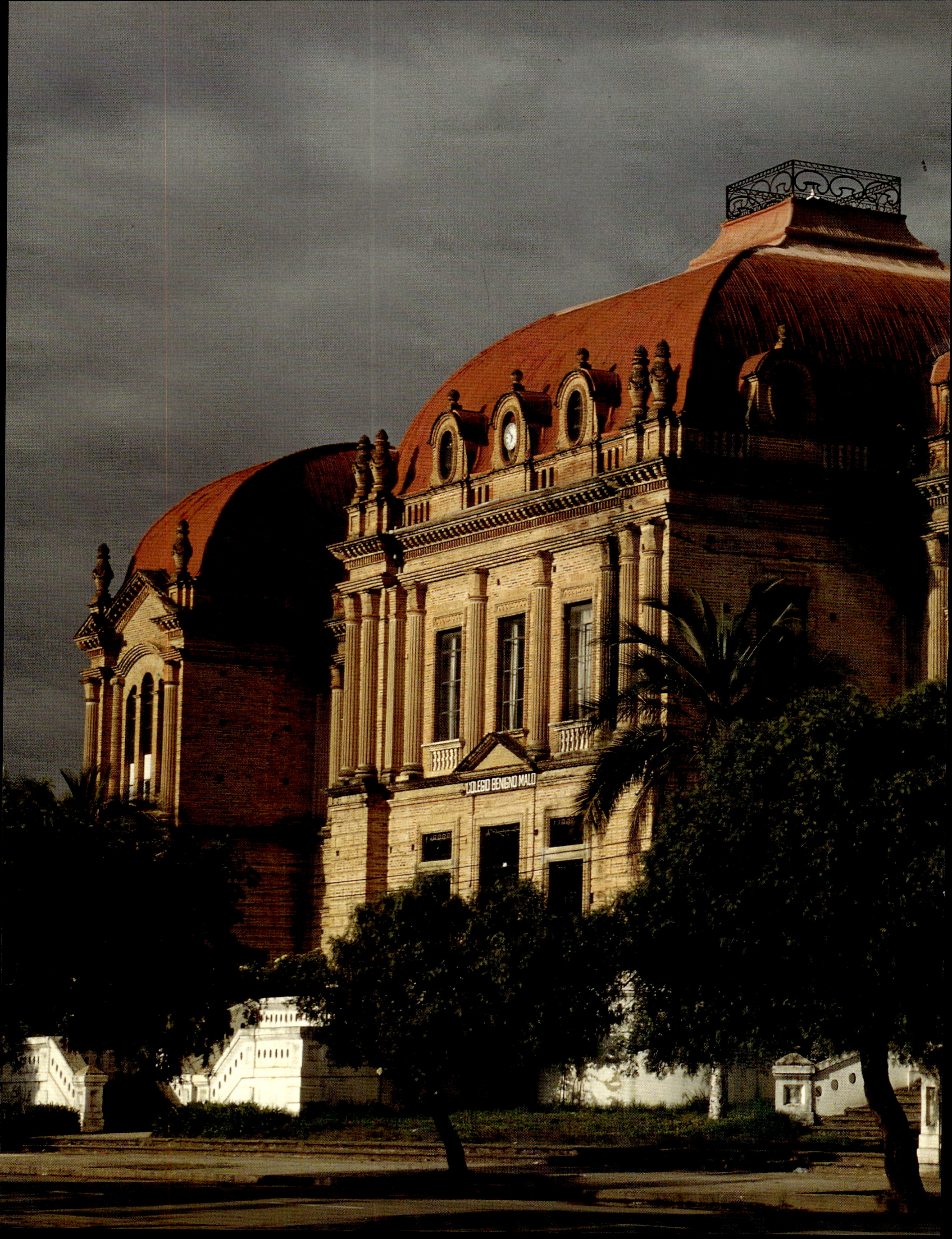
COLEGIO BENIGNO MALO

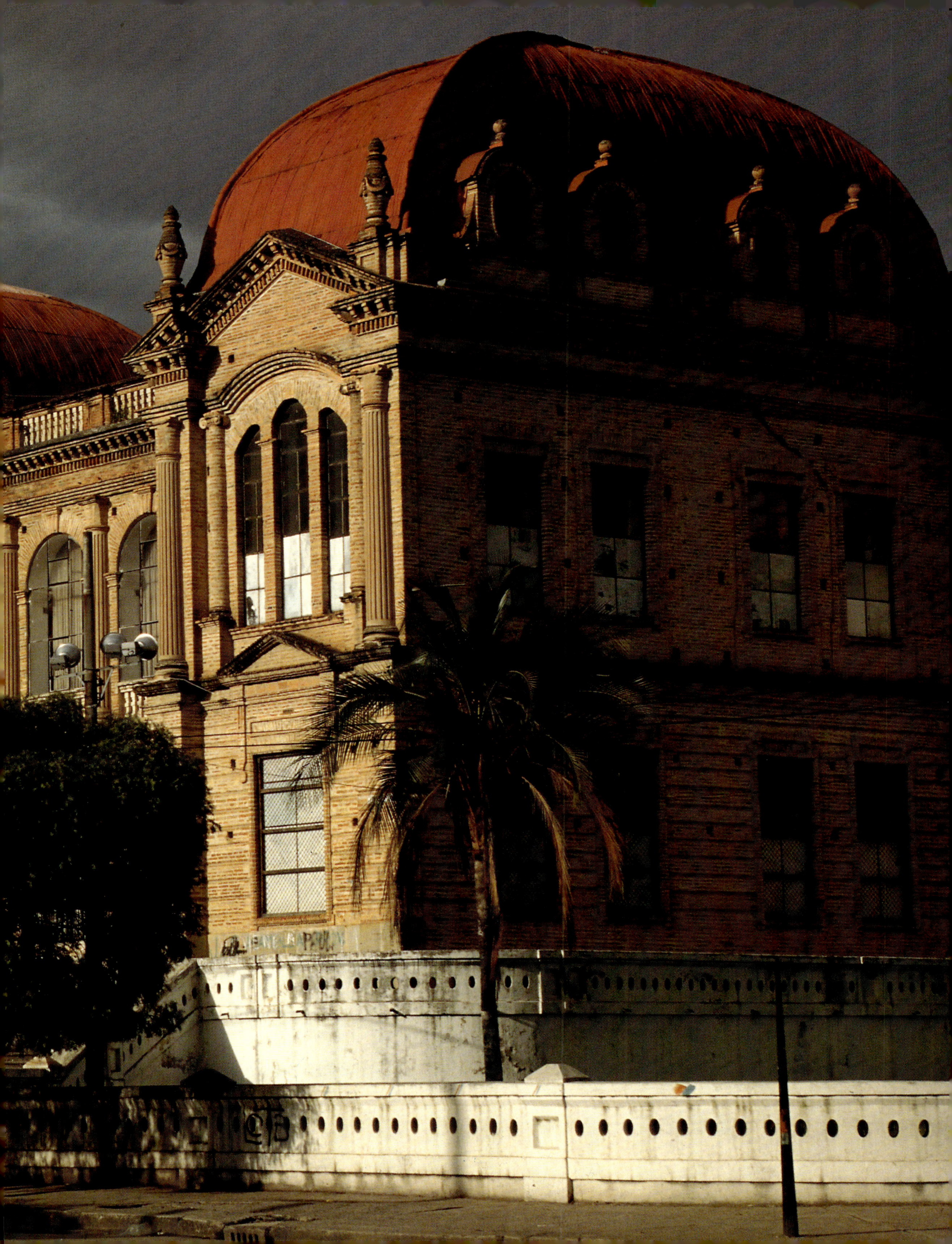

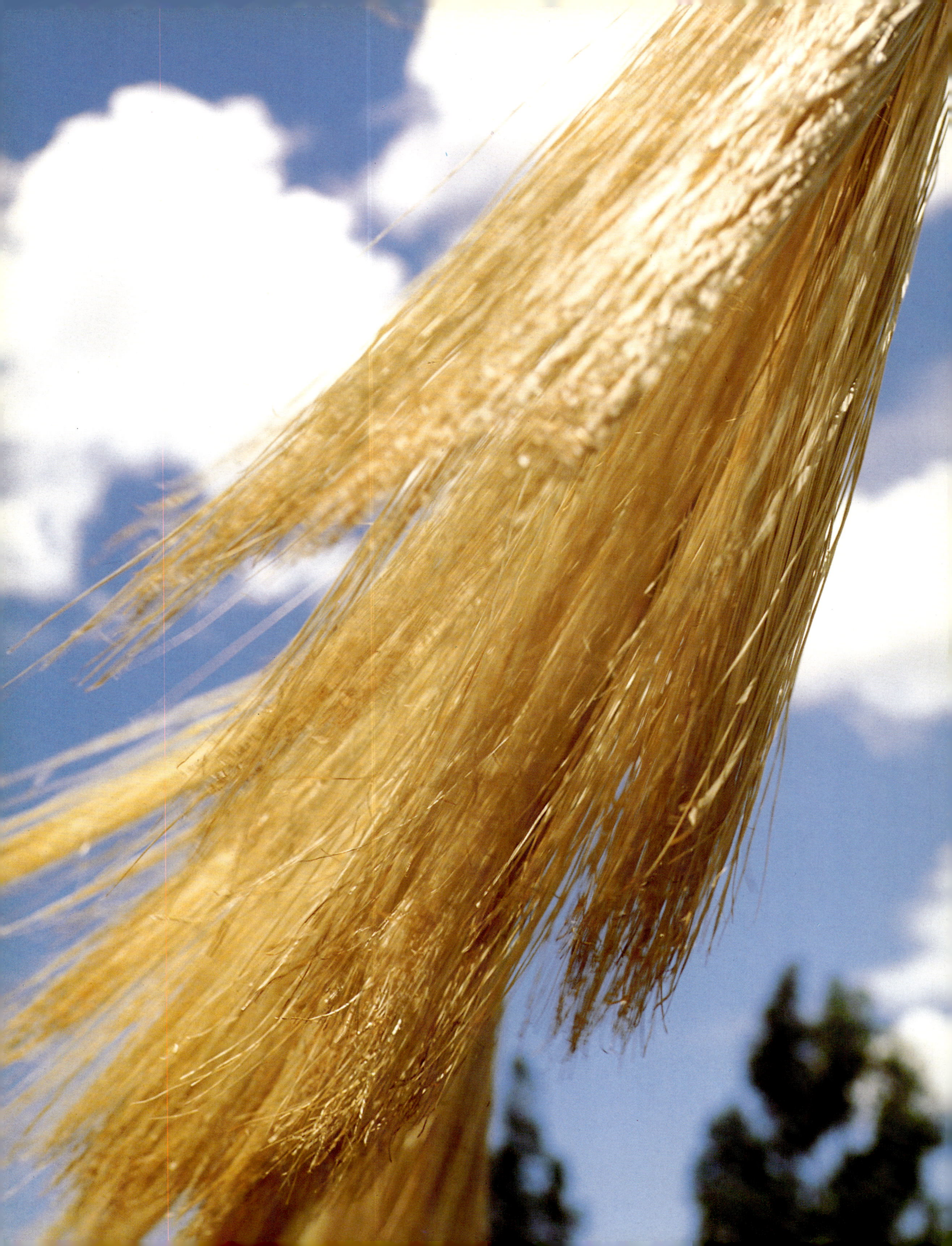

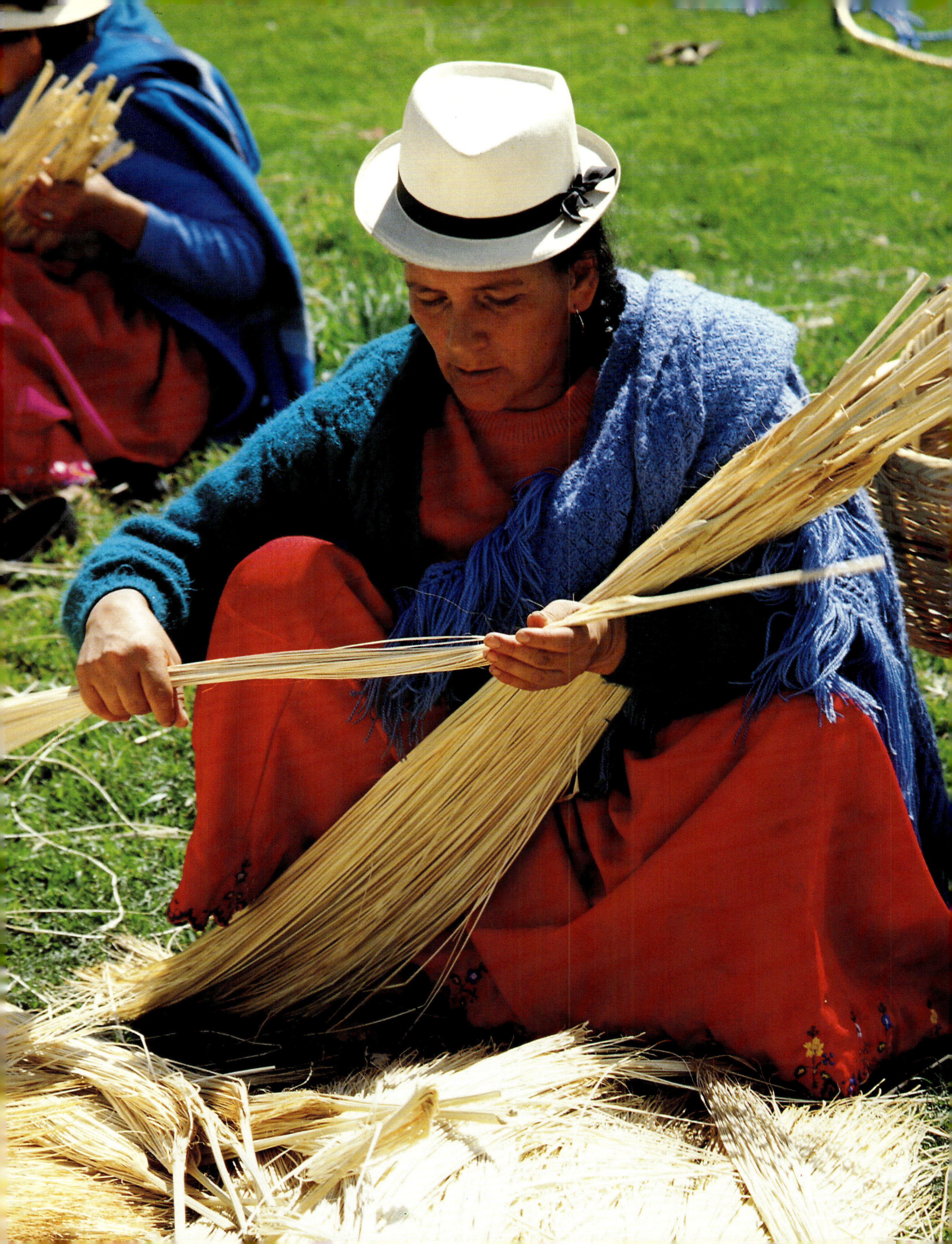

mingle. This is reflected in the practice of its artists, for example Guayasamin or Viteri, who project the culture and history of their people into their new forms.

But at the same time Quito has remained faithful to its history. Its centre, which it has kept intact, is of such beauty that Unesco has listed it as a part of the humanity's cultural heritage. The façades have been repainted in the colonial style. Four centuries after the facts, the décor is the same! Certain exceptional sites have been wonderfully restored, for example the monastery of San Francisco, on which work has been going on for some years. It commands respect. Built in 1534, it houses eight hundred paintings and three thousand books belonging to the Franciscans, all of which are in the process of being restored, while its Mannerist church is reminiscent of the Moorish period. And not only the churches, but the houses too, display the prestige of a colonial century. For example, there is the most extraordinary dwelling of Maria Gangotena Jijon de Mancheno, which takes pride of place in the San Francisco plaza, and enjoys the distinction of having belonged to the same family since its construction in the 16th century. This same colonial past can also be found in the streets of Cuenca. To begin with, its motto ("Most noble and most loyal city of Cuenca") sets the tone. This is a city of character, as was demonstrated when, in 1835, it decided to convert to working with straw. Driven by the redoubtable determination of Bartolomé Serrano, the provinces of Azuay and Cañar, which had been forced to take up weaving, outstripped Manabí province in a few years. Their production is now beyond possible comparison with that of Montecristi, and though the "cuenca" is, according to its reputation, less fine than the "montecristi", it is nonetheless of good quality.

At Cuenca, the artisanate of the straw hat has opted for quantity. They produce, they export, they win markets, in the knowledge of possessing the best raw material.

There are several thousand weavers in the Azuay and Cañar provinces. The majority of them are women. The hat is a part of their lives. It accompanies them throughout the day, even when they move around – it is not uncommon to see a weaver working on a hat during a bus ride. In sum, they are rarely separated from a hat.

Everything begins at the straw market. The "toquilla" for the "cuencas" generally comes by lorry from Manglar Alto. In the early morning, the straw-sellers spread out their merchandise in the markets of Biblián, Azogues and Sigsig. The best weavers are already awaiting their suppliers. They go round the different piles of straw, sizing up the calibre, the size and the colour. They look for the start of the shoot, measuring the elasticity and solidity, gauging the suppleness. As for the "montecristi", the calibre of the straw determines the type of hat for which it will be used. The thicker the fibre, the less close will be the weave. They make their choice according to their talent, the amount of time they have at their disposal and the orders

> The regional market remains one of the liveliest cross-roads of the panama trade.

Previous pages
Left : Straw drying in the wind.
Right : Straw market in Azogues.
Opposite page
The non-finished hat market, where middle-men buy hats from the weavers.
Following pages
1. Alberto Pulla's shop, where hard hats are made and repaired.
2. Homero Ortega, a wholesaler of panamas in Cuenca.
3. "Cuenca" panamas arranged by size and by quality of weave.

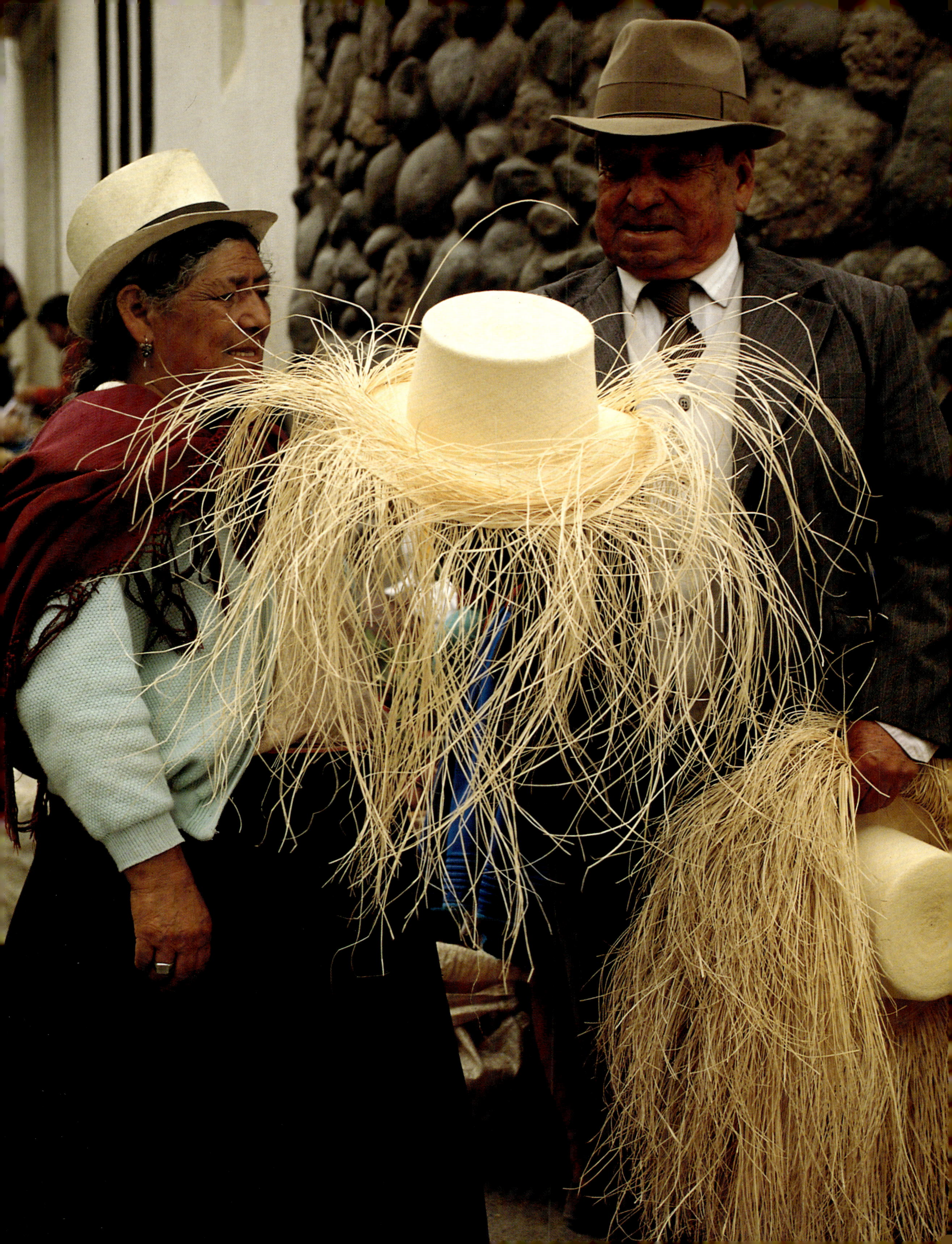

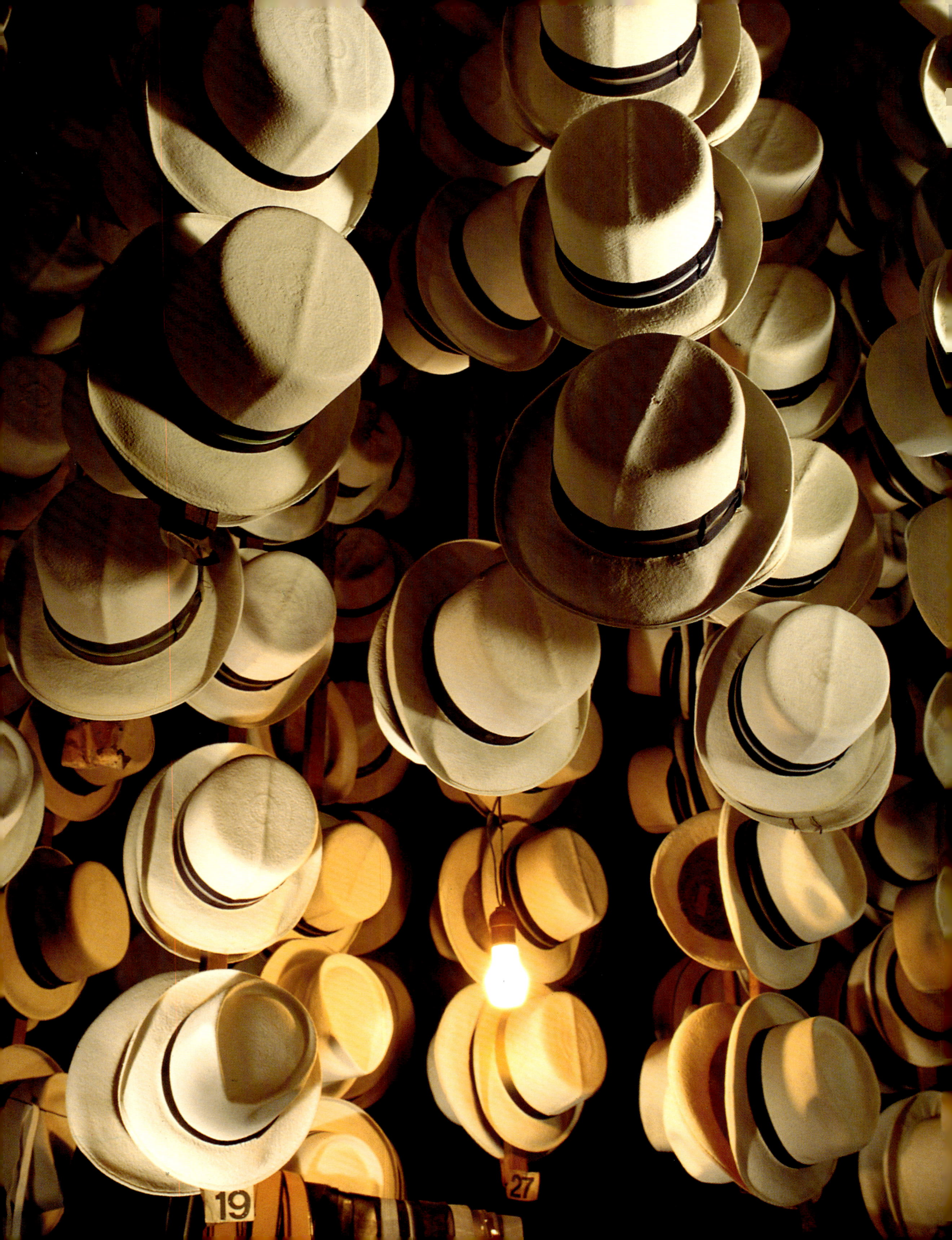
19
27

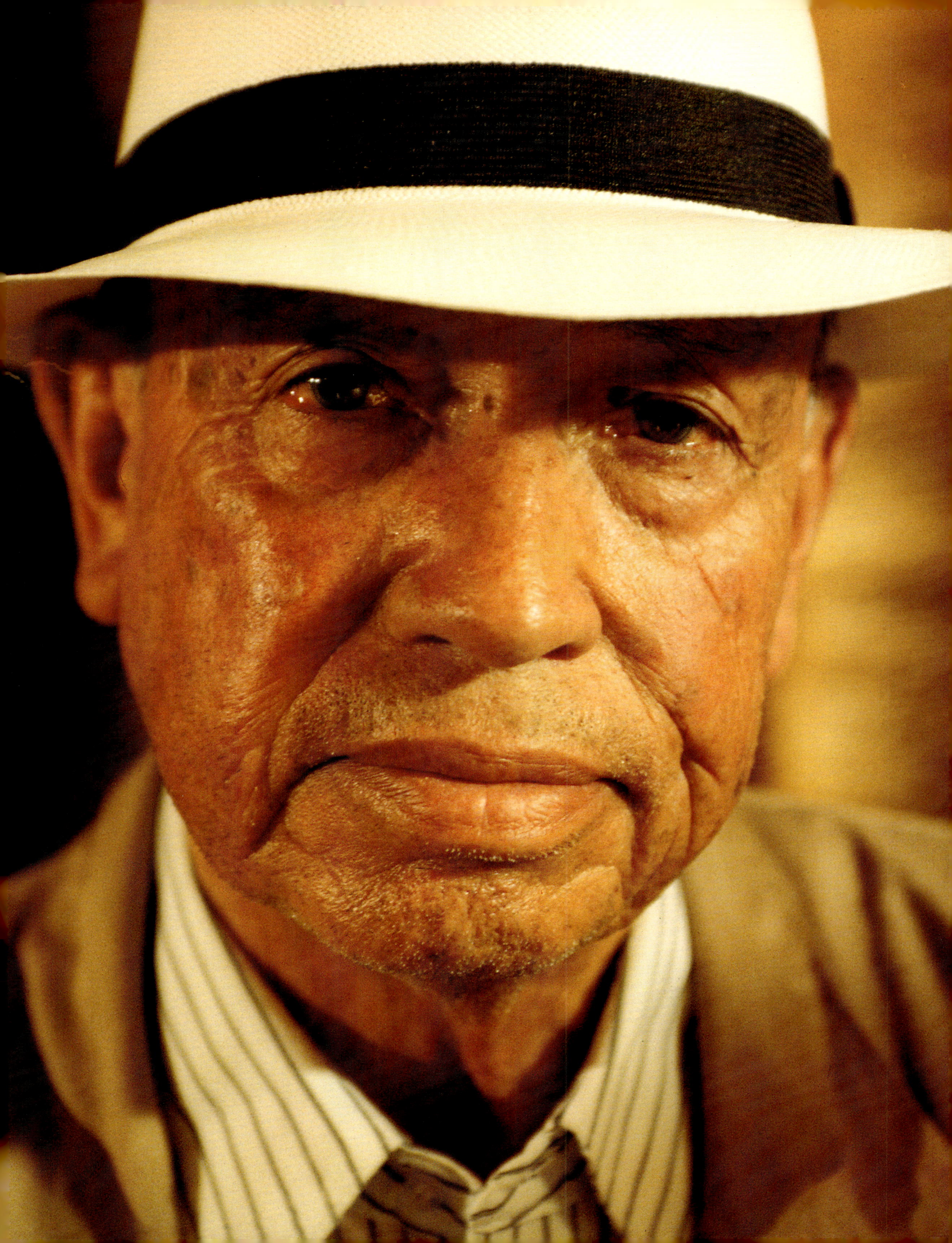

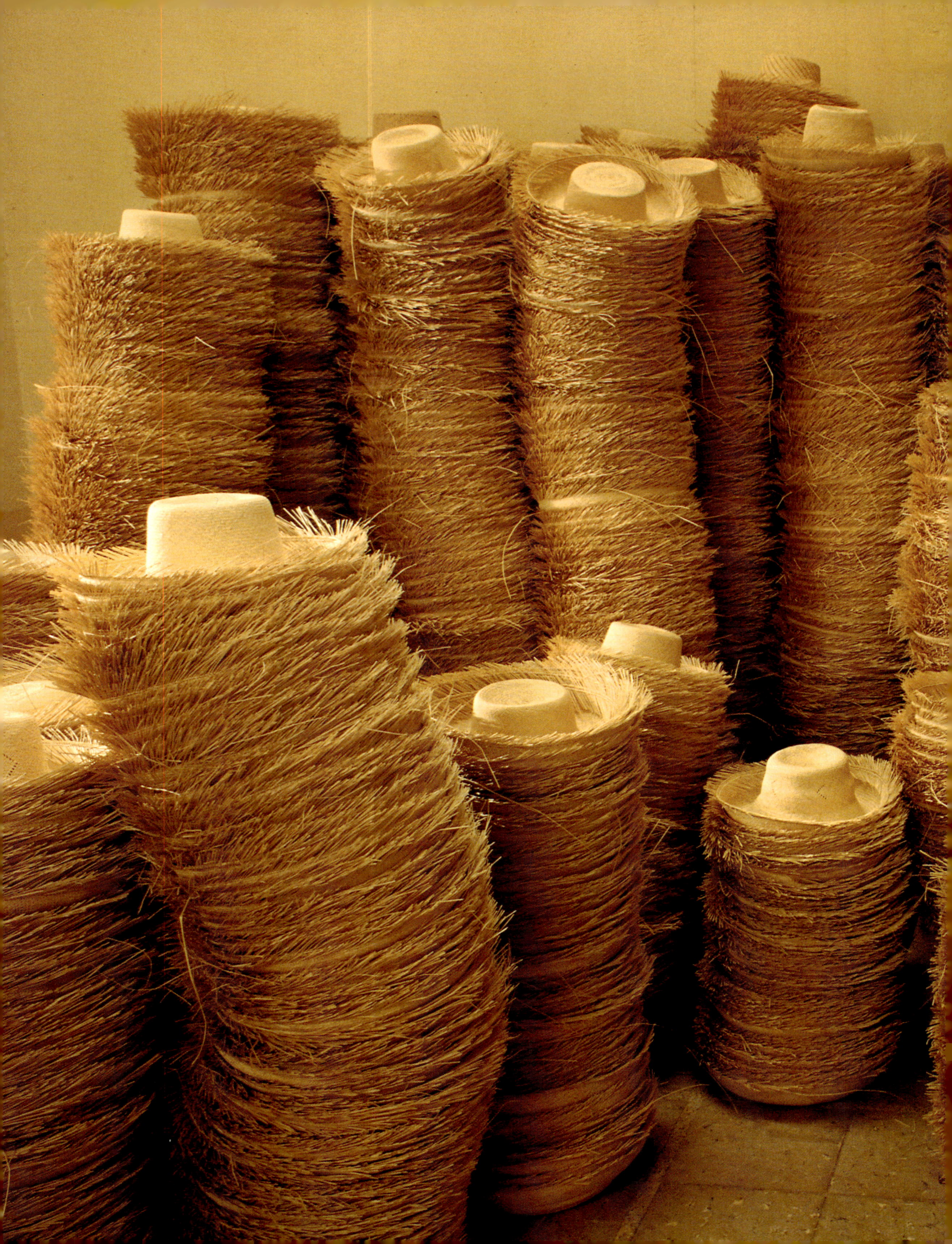

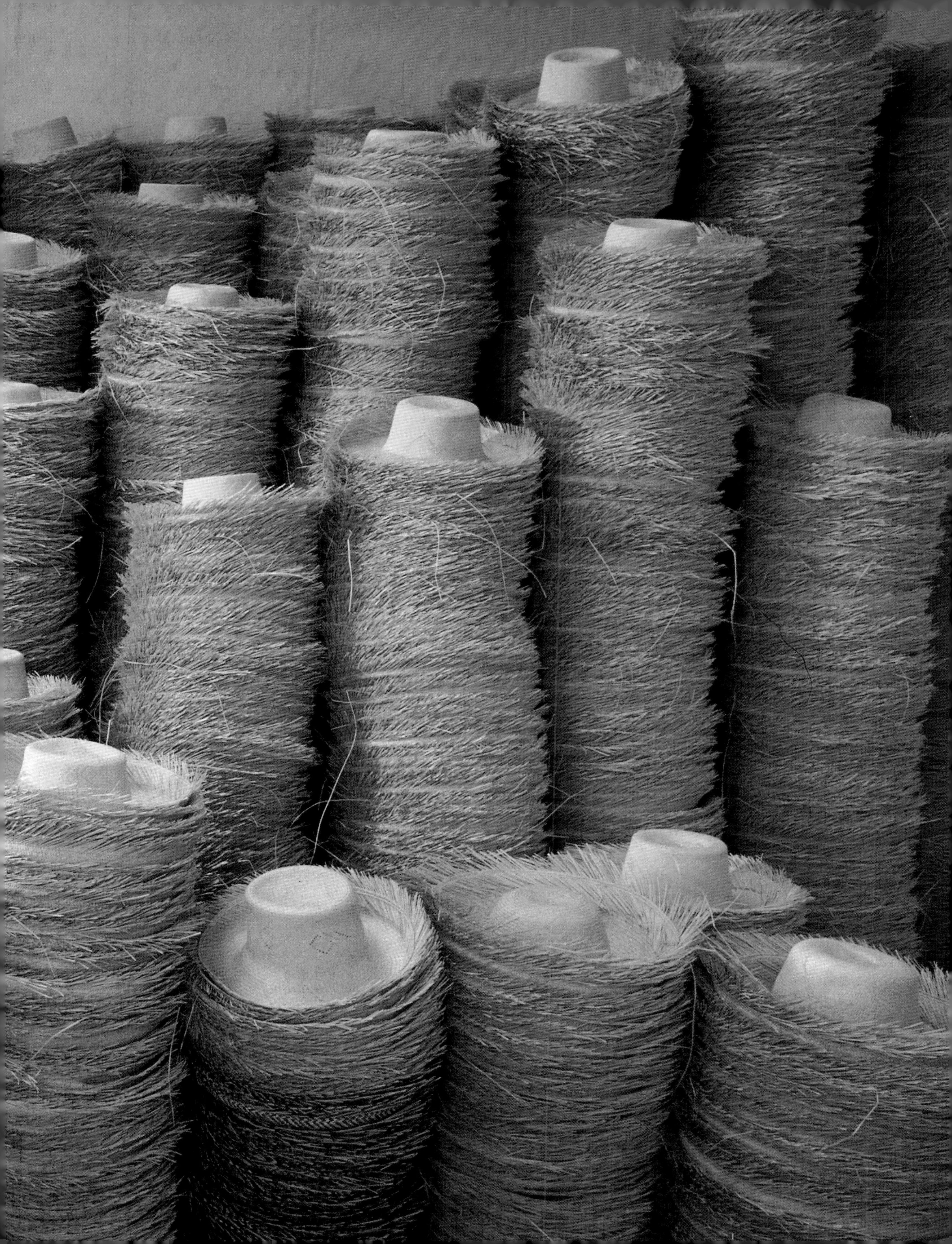

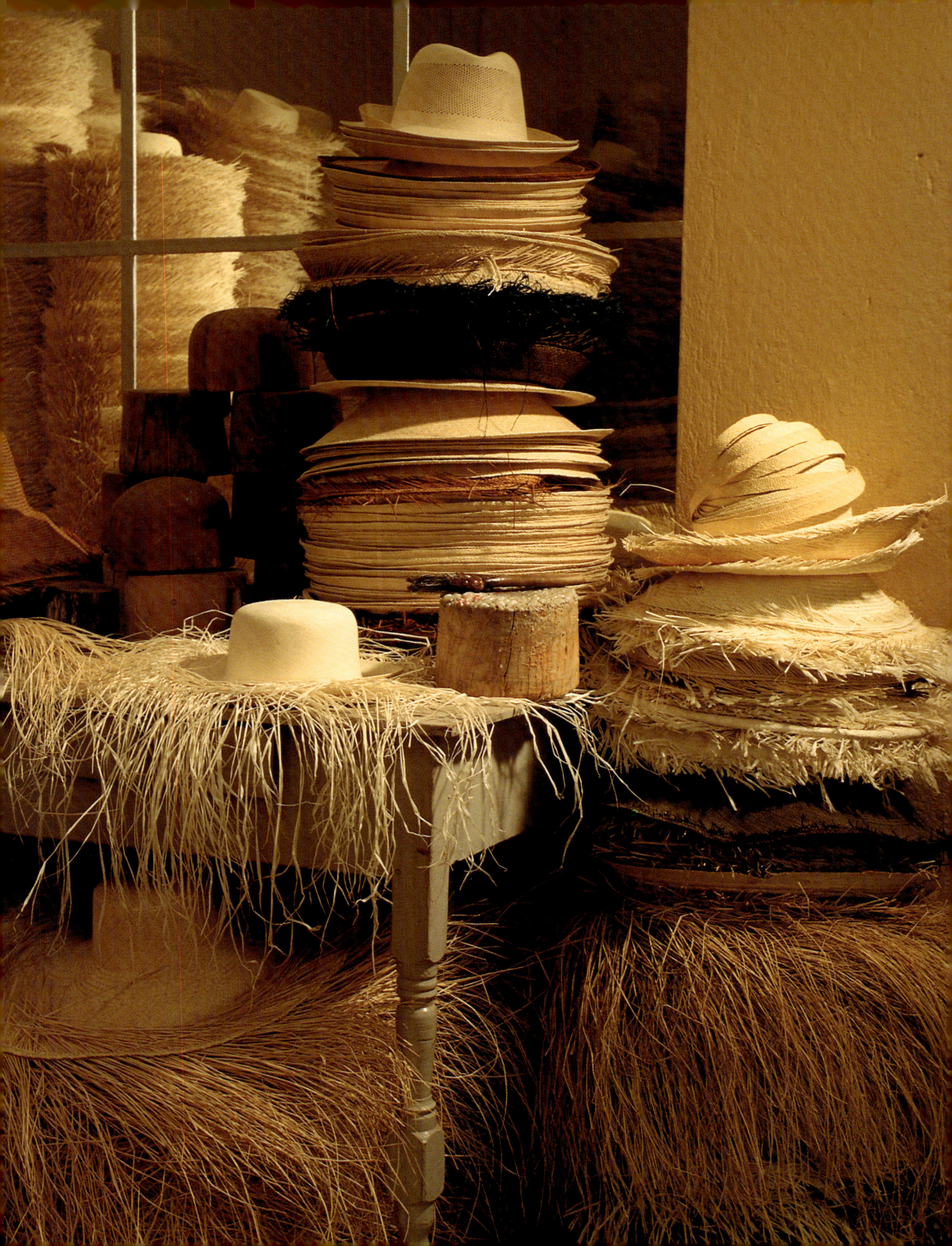

#2769
MAPI
BARRETOS S.P.
BRASIL
AWB 042-5685 62

#614
K.C.
YOKOHAMA
JAPON

#2441
PANAMA LIN
LONDON- ENGL
AWB 074-5928

#2443

they have been given. To soften the straw during the driest parts of the day, they dampen it with an ear of maize dipped in water.

The type of weave and the time taken is the factor which decides on a weaver's output. This can be anything from one to six a week, if she works all day, every day. But to make a fine "cuenca" can in fact take several weeks. The weave is judged by the "pulgada", an imaginary 1-inch square within which one counts the number of fibres woven in a given direction. The first degree corresponds to hats of modest quality, with thirteen fibres to the square; whereas the finest "cuencas" have at least twenty-five. When the weaving is finished, the weaver brings her "raw" article to a regional market and sells it to a middle-man. At this point, the hat still looks like a sort of "cloche", with a fringe all round its perimeter. The role of the middle-man is to select hats according to the orders that he has accumulated. These orders will generally come from abroad, via an exporter. Norberto Rodriguez, who has followed this profession for the last forty years, is one of these "peddlers" of hats who regularly visit the non-finished hat markets of the region. Rodriguez currently obtains the finest specimens in the Cañar province, where the weavers of Santa Marianita sell their wares.

In the different stages that the straw goes through, each one has its importance. At this stage, the middle-man has already raised the price of the hat by five percent. He most frequently works for a wholesaler who buys up and stores the articles for the exporters while waiting for orders. But he may also sell his products directly to the export houses. These firms do the finishing and marke-

Previous pages
*Left : "Cuencas" of different
weaves and styles in Kurt Dorfzaun's factory.
Right : The white cotton sacks
in which the panamas are transported are hand-sewn.
The means of transport
has not changed for more than a century.*
Opposite page
*A batch of "brisa" panamas
of the same weave drying in the sun before being finished.*

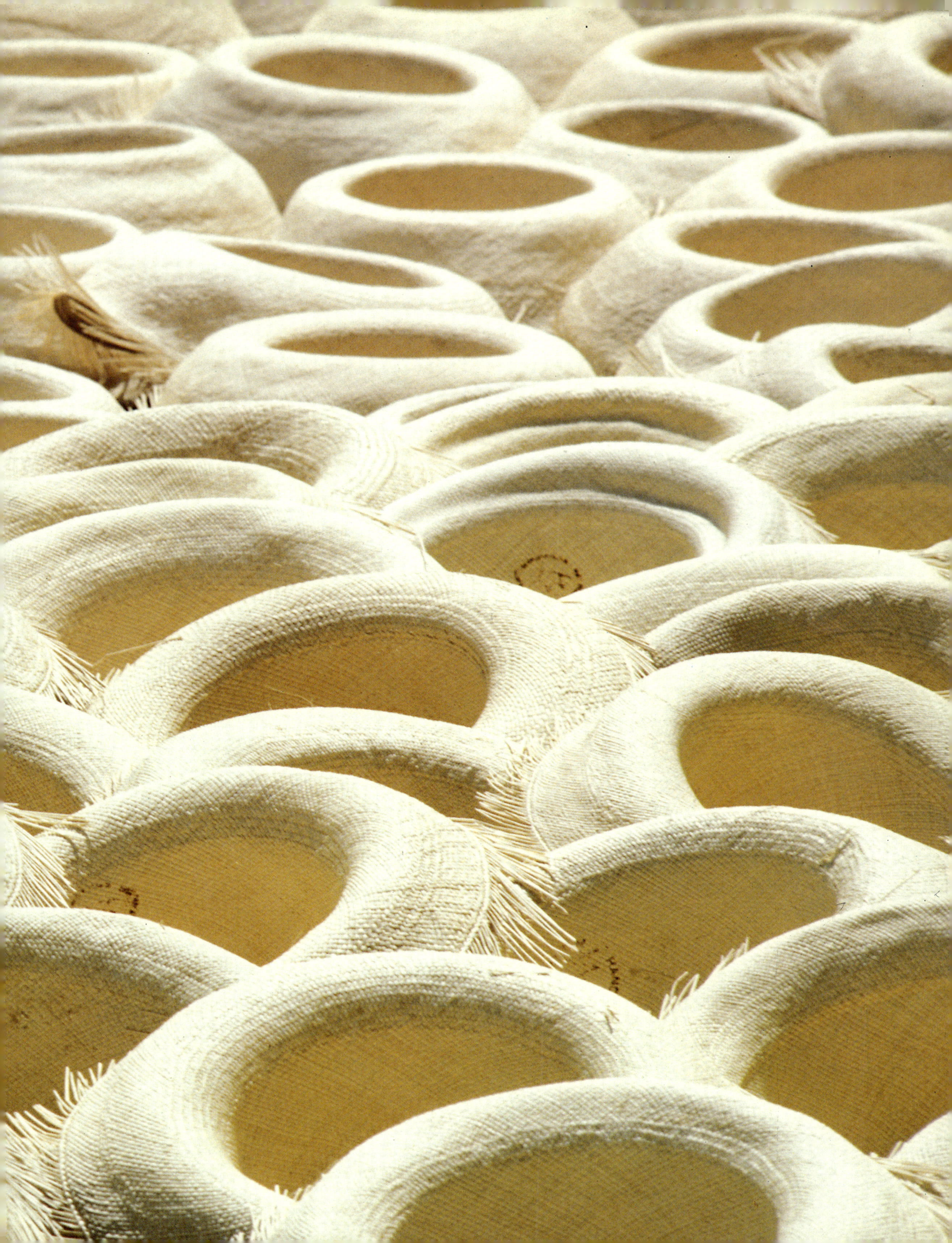

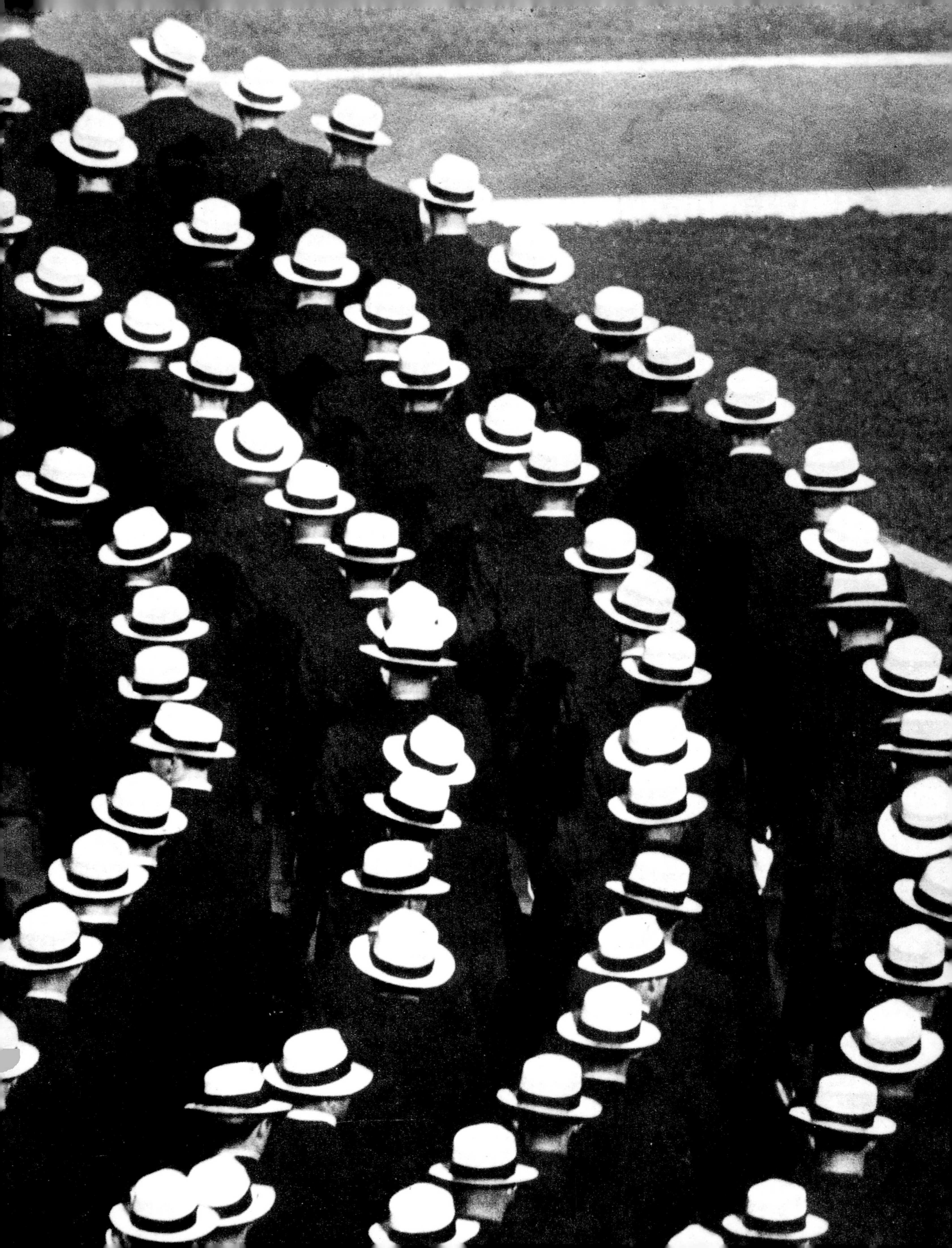

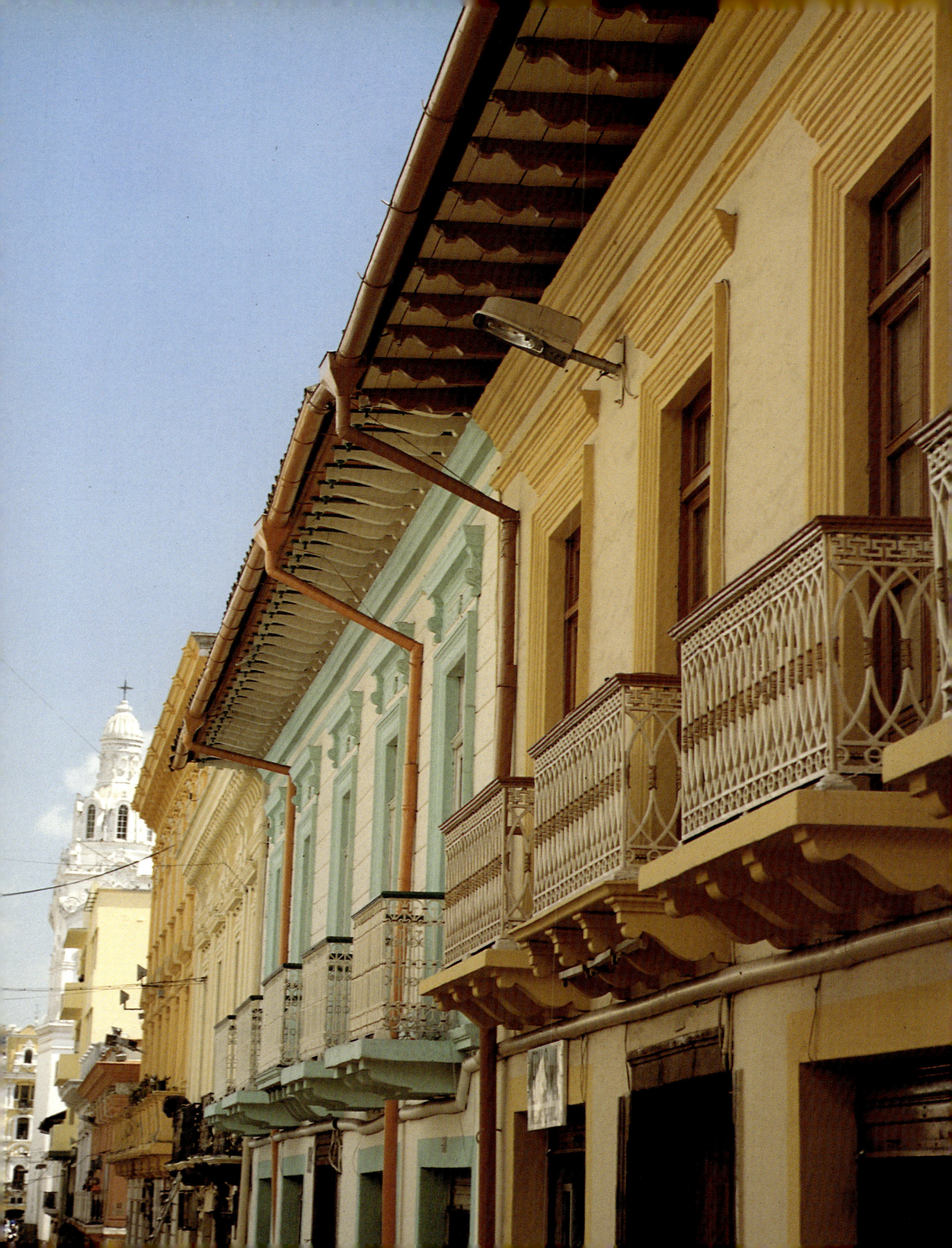

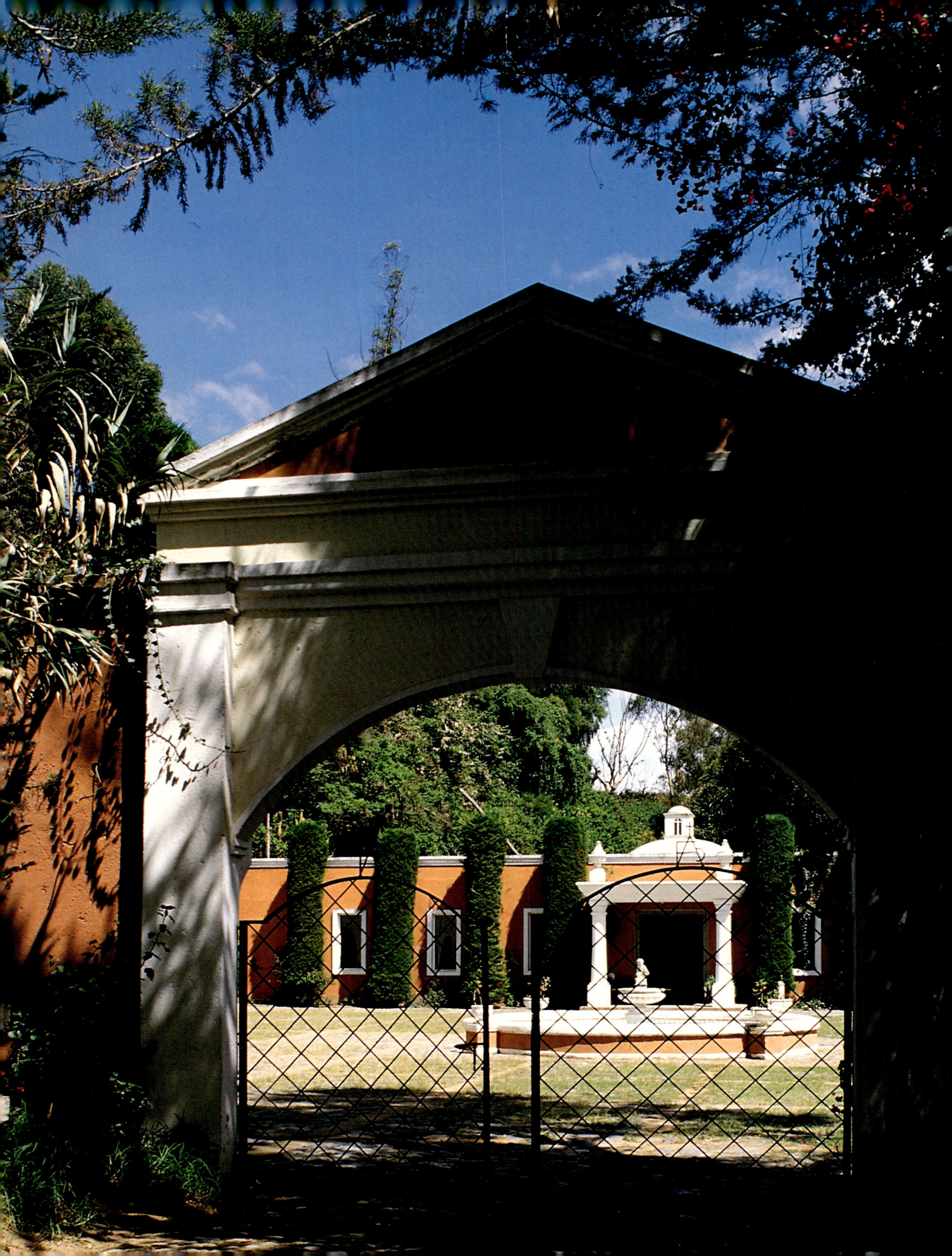

ting of the hats. They are full-scale factories, employing large numbers of people in the different phases of the finishing operation. Firstly, the long fringe of the panama is cut, then it is washed and left in a vat containing a bleaching solution so that it can take on a uniform colour. Contrary to what happens at Montecristi, where the sovereign among hats is given individual, unique treatment, the "cuenca" is worked in an industrial way, and batches of hats are put together into the same baths. Then comes the drying stage, which is carried out in the sun. At this point, the large courtyards are filled with orderly rows of "cloches". Next there is the process of fumigation in sulphur vapour, followed by a last washing, at which point some batches are given a colour bath, and in the courtyards, the red, yellow and turquoise baths make strange patterns.

At the beginning of this century, colourists were still using walnut bark and leaves in order to obtain a great variety of warm browns. But vegetal dyes have given way to the use of common anilines, which provide a greater choice of colours. Finally there comes the stage of forming the hat – borsalino, stetson, colonial, etc. An iron form is chosen, corresponding to the desired style and size, and the hat is subjected to the pressure of the machine, which is heated to 120 °C. Just a few years ago the procedure was different, since the machines did not yet exist. At that time, the hat was placed on a wooden stand, and the crown was softened with a mallet. Steam, and an oven, were used to give the hat the required shape, and it was finished by smoothing its brim with an iron heated in the embers of the fire. This method is now obsolete, and the wooden forms are used only as a measure of size.

Once finished, the hats are sorted by size, style, colour and destination. Packed in batches of twenty dozen in white cotton sacks, they are dispatched to the four corners of the world, via Guayaquil, which gives them the choice between the plane and the cargo ship. It often happens that orders come in for non-formed panamas, especially good-quality "cuencas". The hat must then await its final destination in order to be formed by a hat-maker, or according to a manufacturer's own styles. Between the straw and the hat, the number of actors in the story is what explains and justifies the multiplication by ten or twenty of the price paid to the weaver at the start of the chain.

> The panama has always travelled wrapped in hand-sewn cotton pouches.

China and Taiwan have now begun to compete with Ecuador, producing excellent imitations of panamas at extremely attractive prices. But the shantung, which is really a panama made of paper fibre, spoils very quickly due to the fact that it does not breathe. Natural straw, even though it is more expensive and a little less regular, is still the preference of the connoisseur.

Renowned for its raw material and its expertise, the town of Cuenca continues to be connected to every part of the world by its panamas. It is strange to see the extent to which this mountain town has made the hat a tradition. Here, all the Indians, men and women, wear

Previous pages
Left : The Australian delegation at the Olympic Games in 1964.
Right : A street in the centre of Quito, which has been listed as part of the world's cultural heritage by Unesco, and has been entirely repainted in its original colours.

Opposite page
Montelimar. A house near Quito.

Following pages
Left : Faena by Enrique Ponce in the bullring in Quito.
When the bullfight is a good one, it is common for people to throw their panamas into the ring!
Right : Panamas from Cuenca and Montecristi in the bullring in Quito.

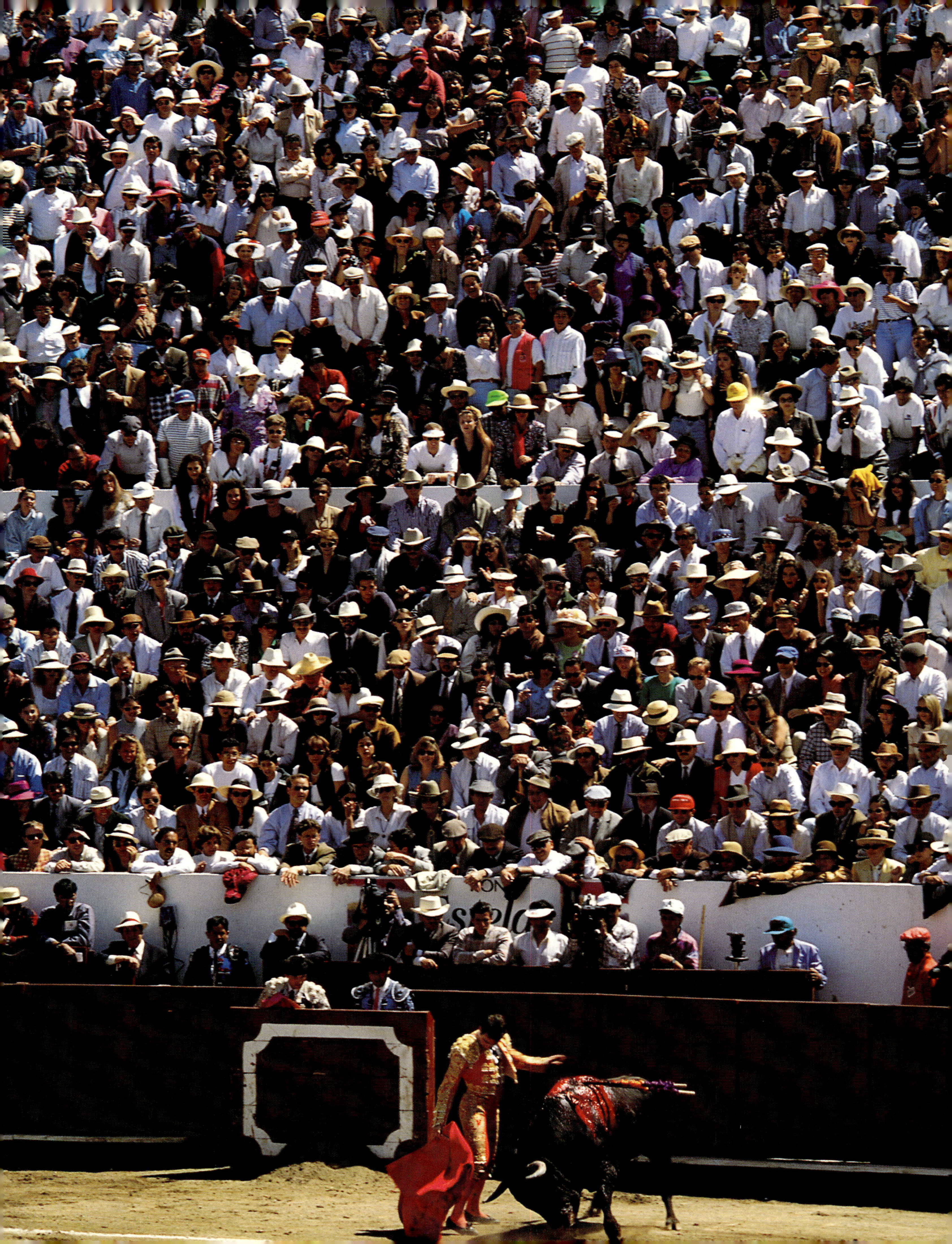

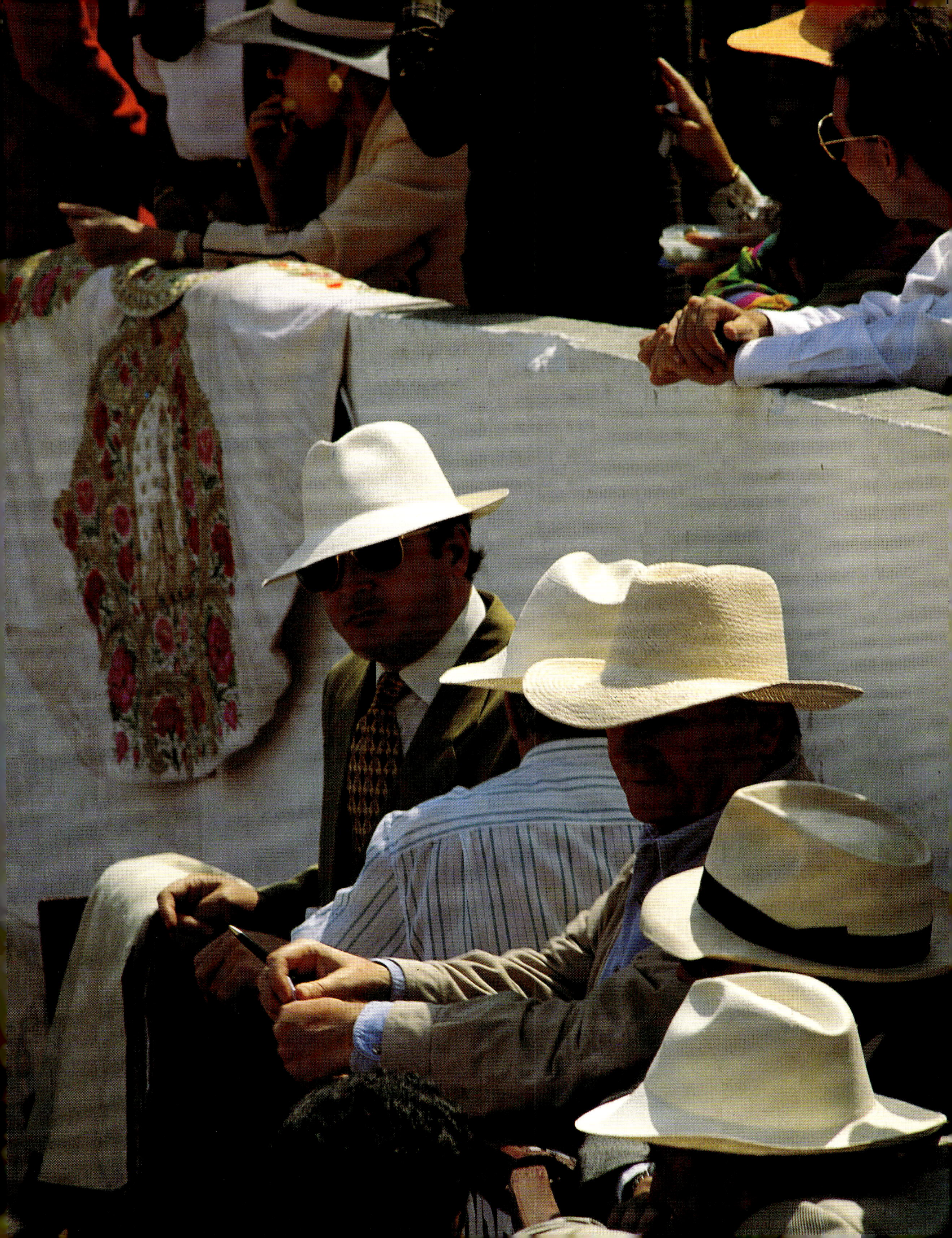

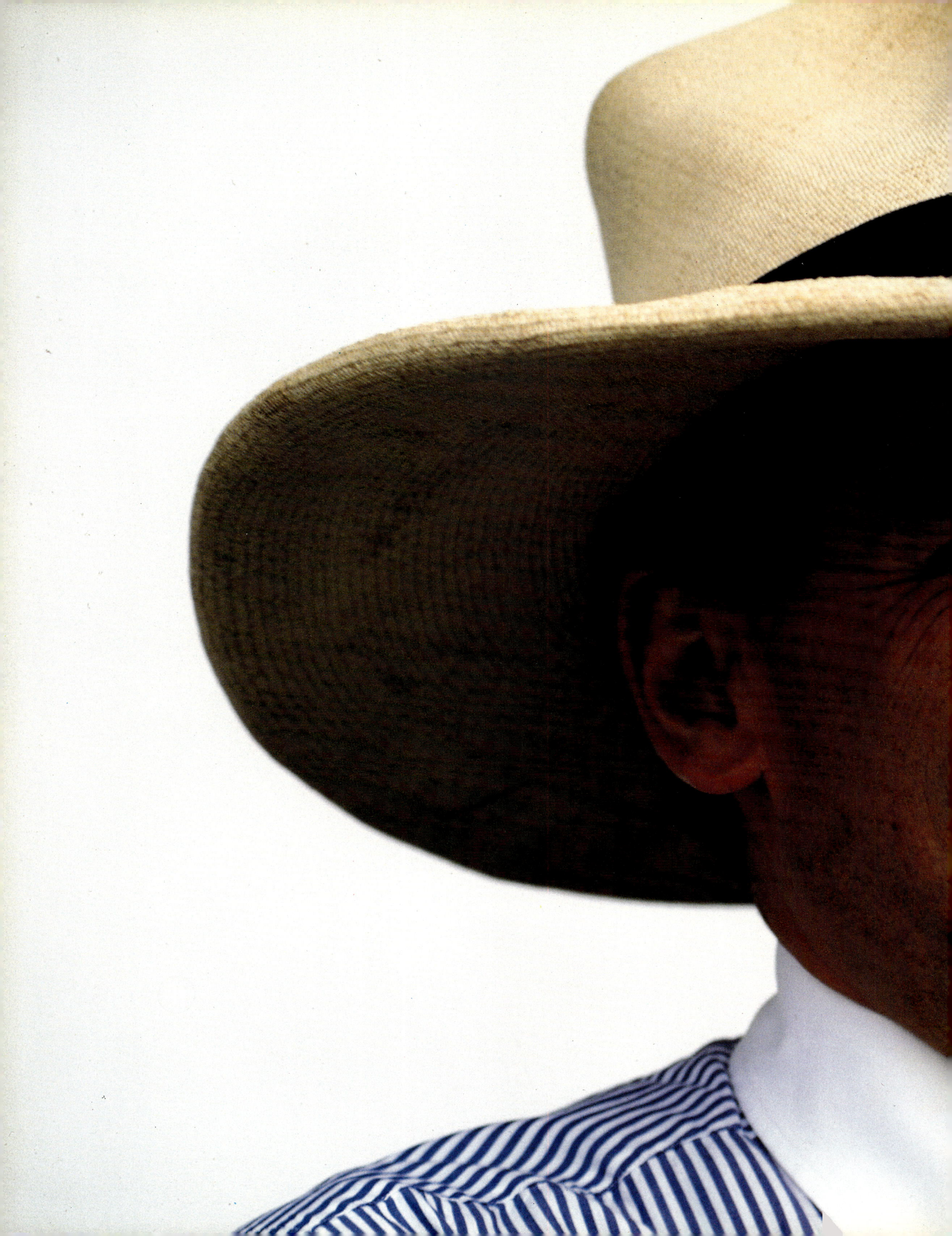

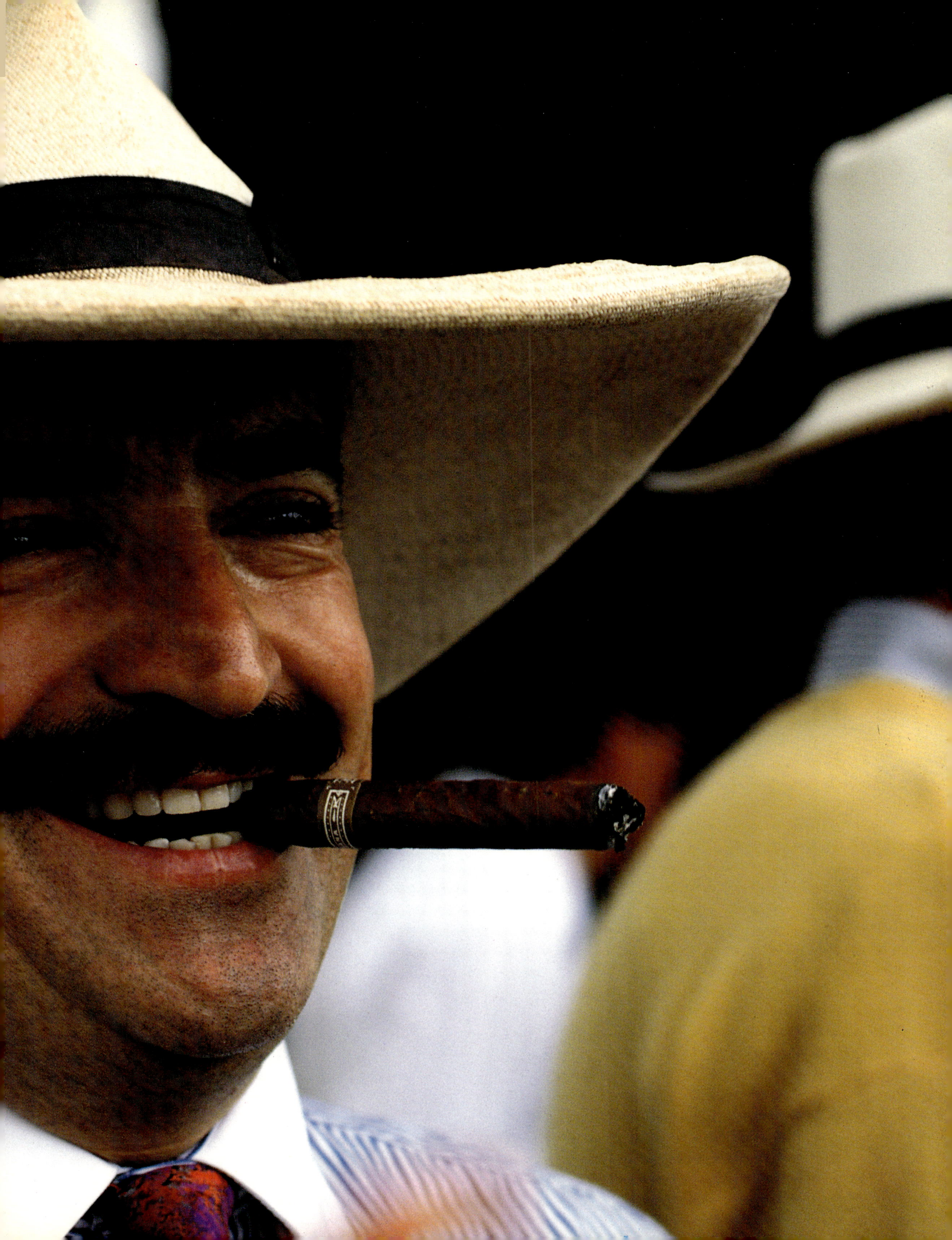

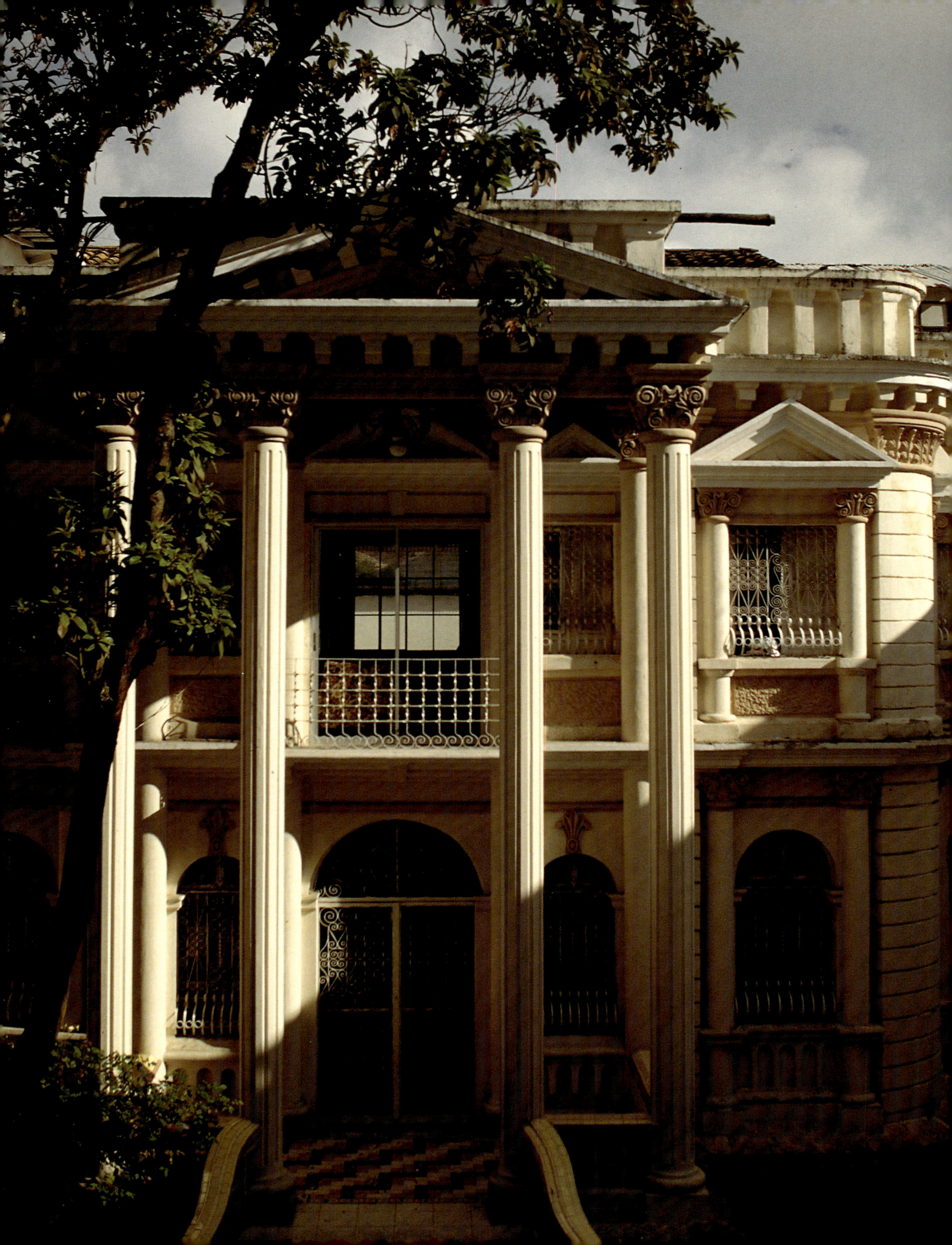

one. It is a mark of social status. Each Indian owns at least three, and, on Sunday, it is the custom to go to the market with a clean hat – the whiter the better. There are just two styles, one for men and one for women. The women's style is rather round, with a narrow brim, while the men's style, the "tango", resembles the borsalino. The people of the Andes prefer hard hats, and so the raw material is put through manufacturing processes which include successive treatments with sulphur vapour dissolved in water, which bleach and solidify the straw.

All the operations are done by hand, with the use of a brush. Thus "starched" and ironed, the hat is powdered with sulphur before the addition of its trimmings. This type of process makes the hat sensitive to rain and dust, which means that regular visits to the repairer become a necessity.

Alberto Pulla, a hat-maker in Tarqui Street, in Cuenca, has been making and repairing hats for more than forty years. The walls of his little shop are entirely covered with "tangos" and "azoguenos" of traditional design, each of which bears the name of its owner. They await repair or bleaching, in the knowledge of being the pride and joy of those who wear them. In Cuenca, as in the rest of the Andes, the hat remains a tradition, like the tradition which, each year, brings the Virgin of Quinche, wearing a hat, out onto the roads of Quiche l'Altiplano to lead a procession. She is known as the Virgin who voyages...

The legend of the panama hat, is naturally associated with an elegant and refined lifestyle.

Previous page
Panama and cigar in the bullring in Quito.
Opposite page
19th century colonial house in the centre of Cuenca.
Following pages
*Left : Chapel of the "La Cienega" hacienda.
Right : Galo Plaza Pallarés, the son
of President Galo Plaza, in his "Zuleta" hacienda.*

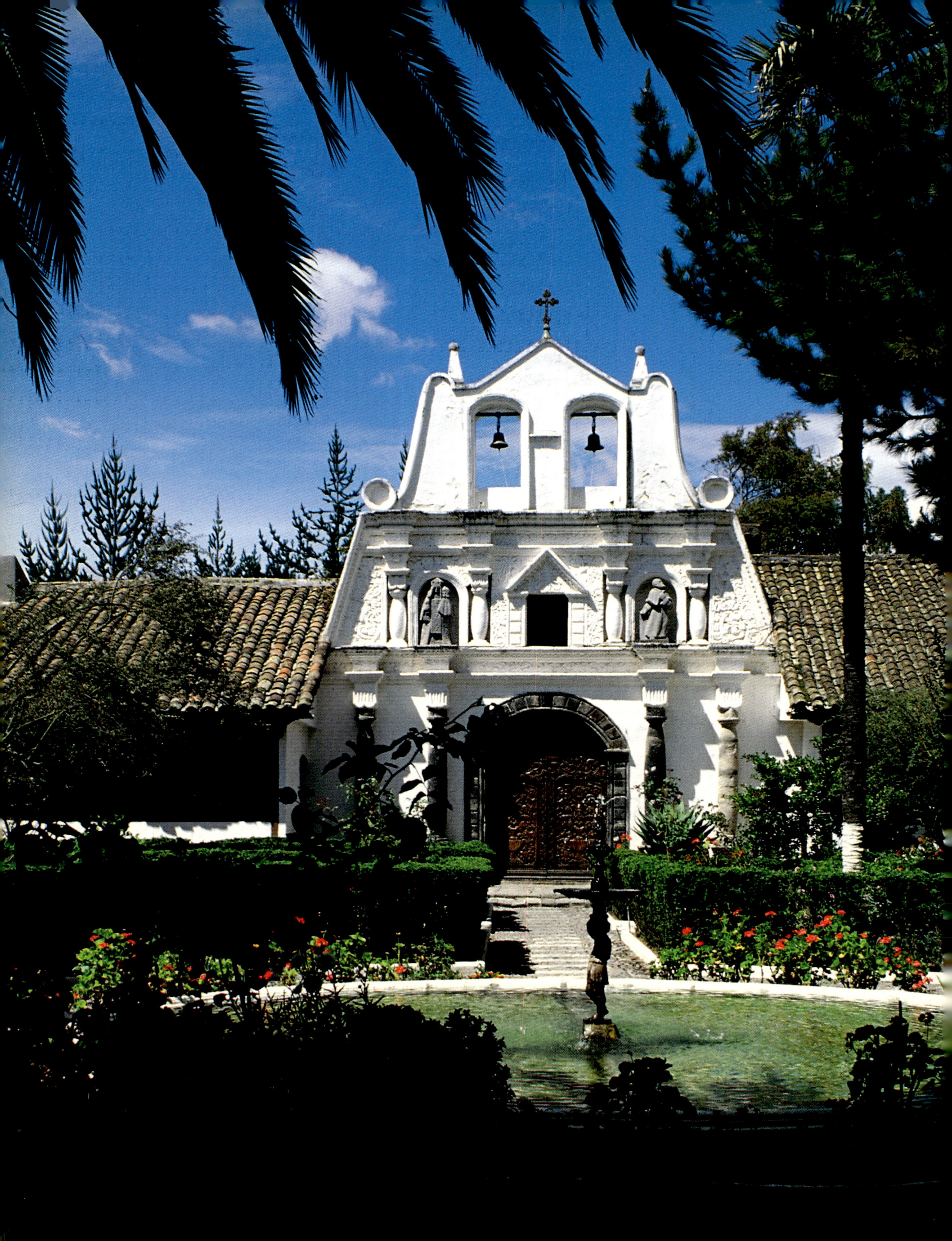

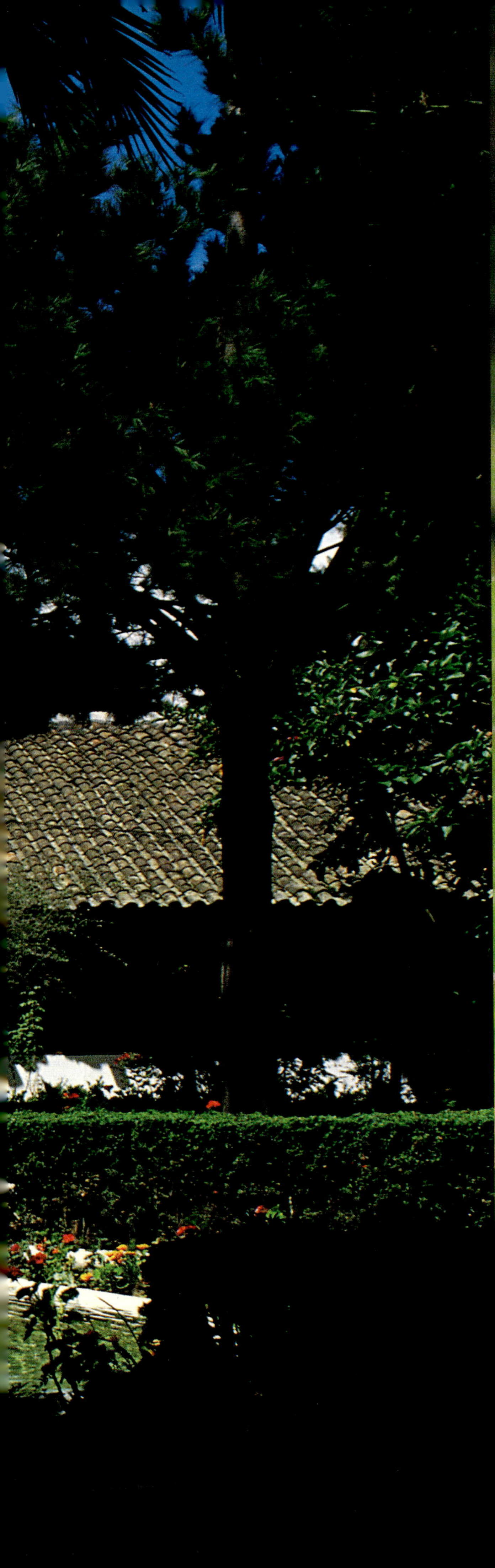

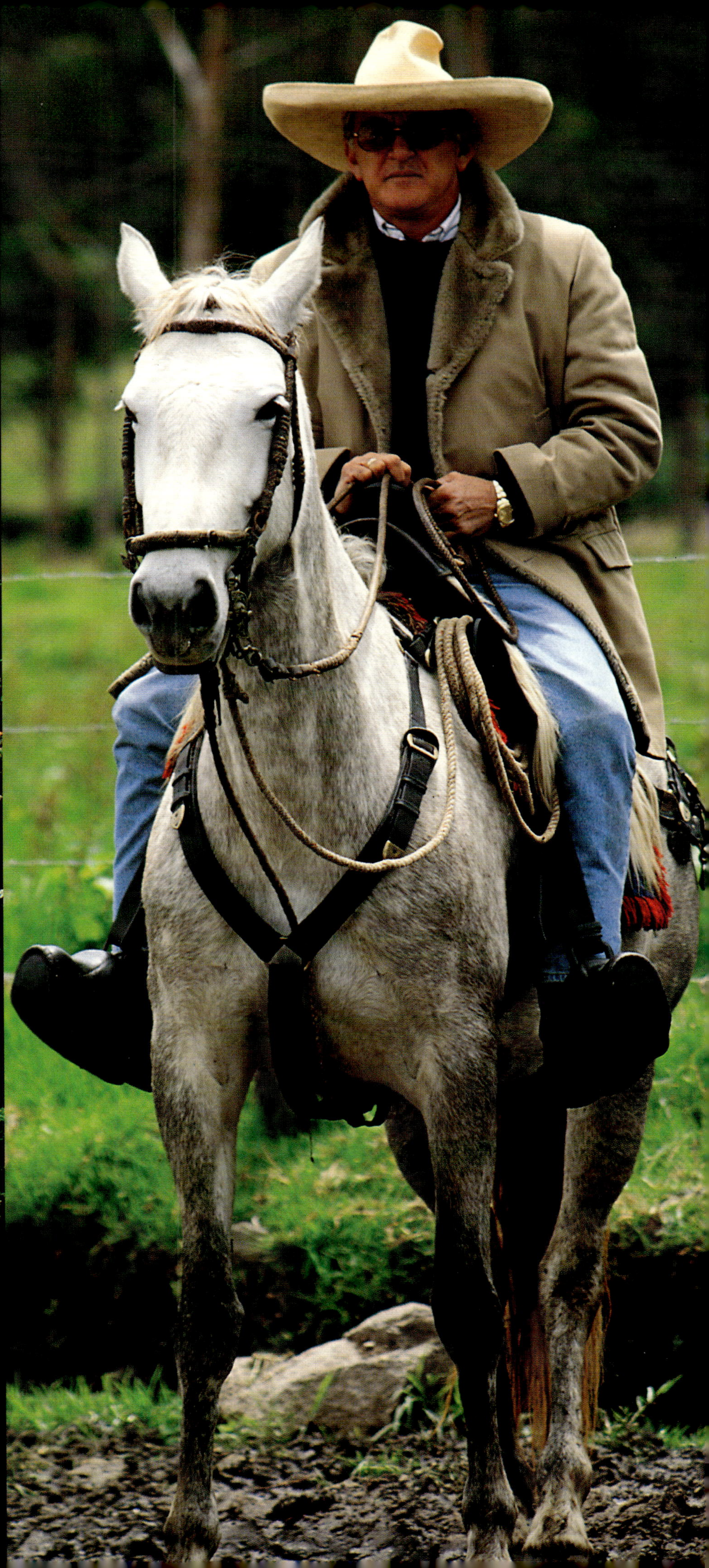

fer. vi. Parasceue.

Astiterunt

reges terrę,

principes conuenerunt

aduersus dominū,

et xpm eius. ps.

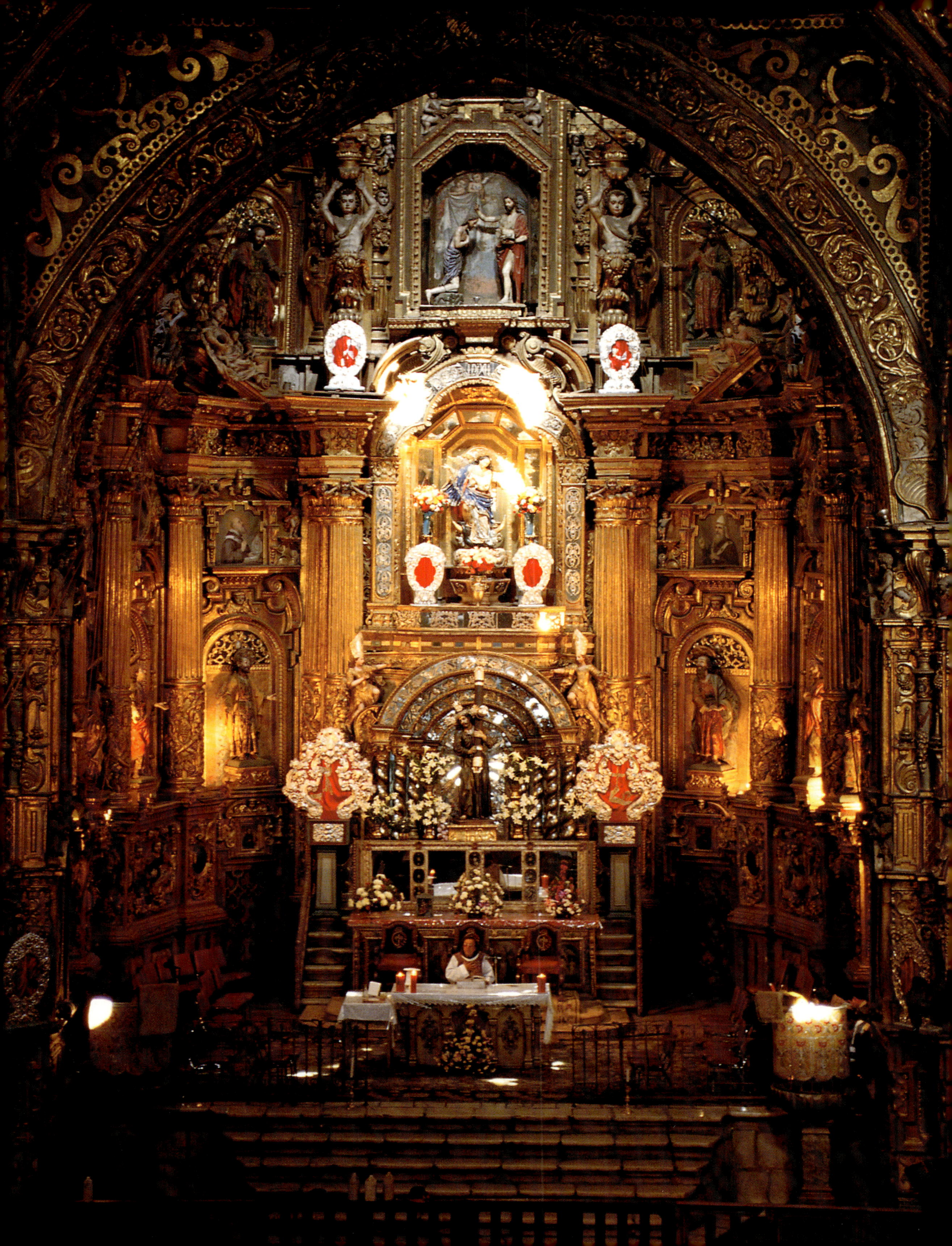

For centuries, Cuenca and Quito, cities of the Andes, have carried in them the history of the hat.

Previous pages
Left : A 15th century book of religious songs. Monastery of San Francisco.
Right : Church of San Francisco. The Virgin of Quito (centre) is always represented with wings.
Opposite page
"La Cienega" hacienda.
Following pages
1. A panama in the Andean sun.
2. The "Huagrawasi" hacienda. At the bottom of the volcano of Tungurahua.
3. A fighting bull farm. The "Huagrawasi" hacienda.

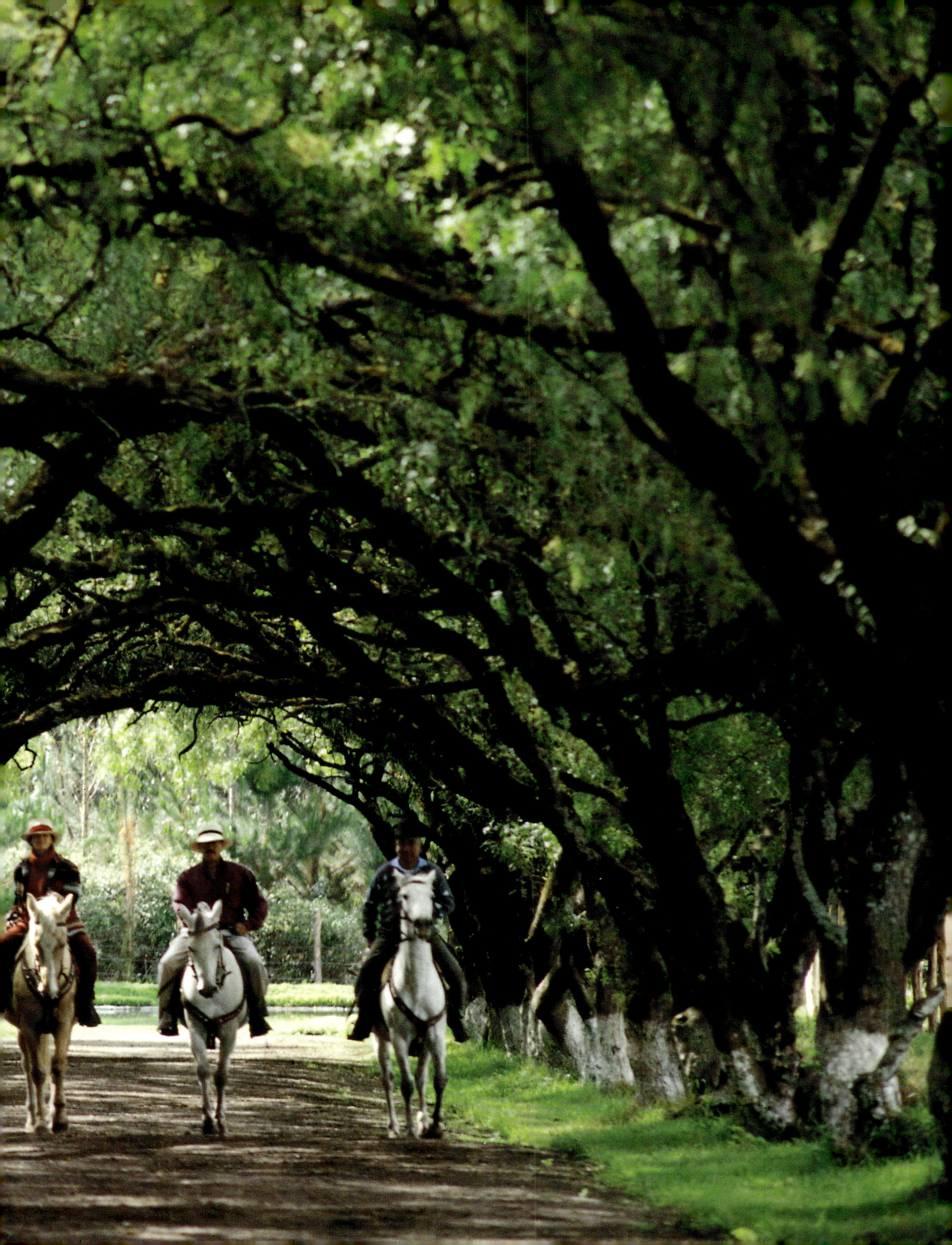

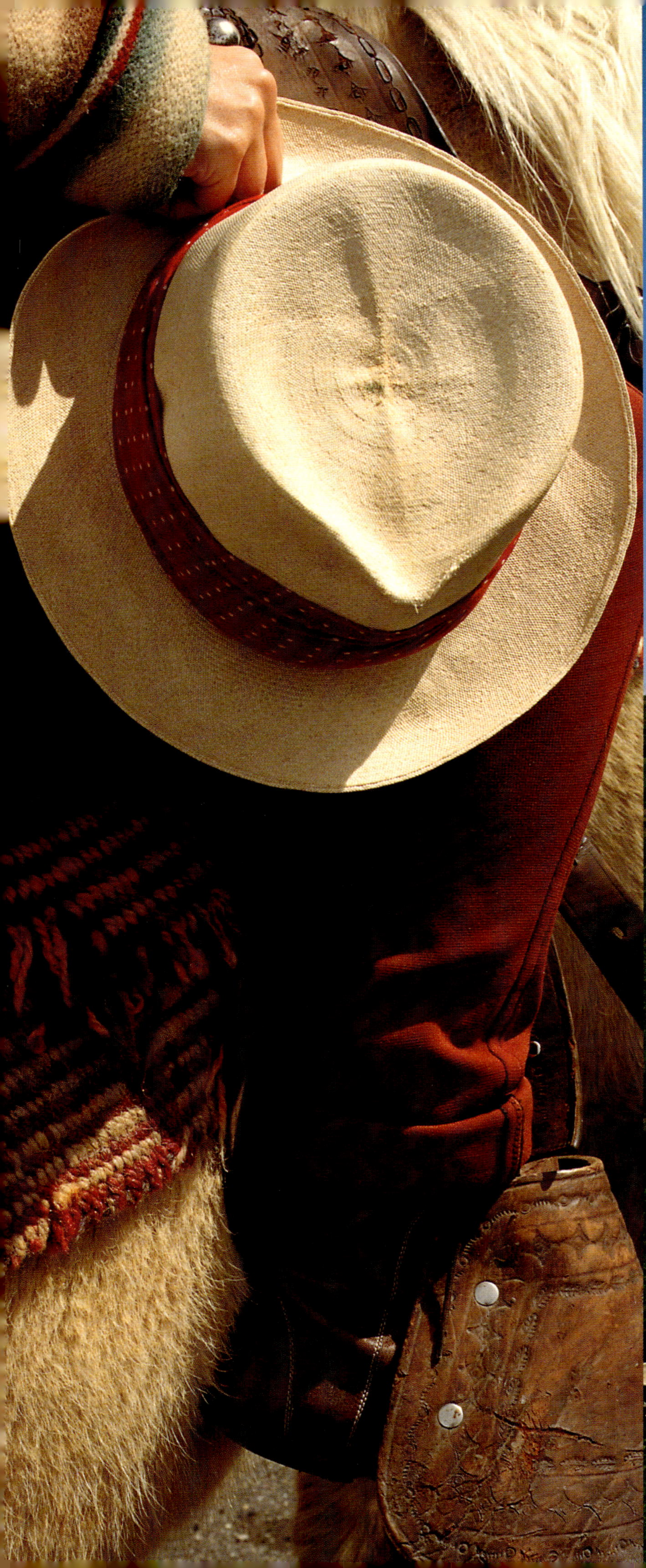

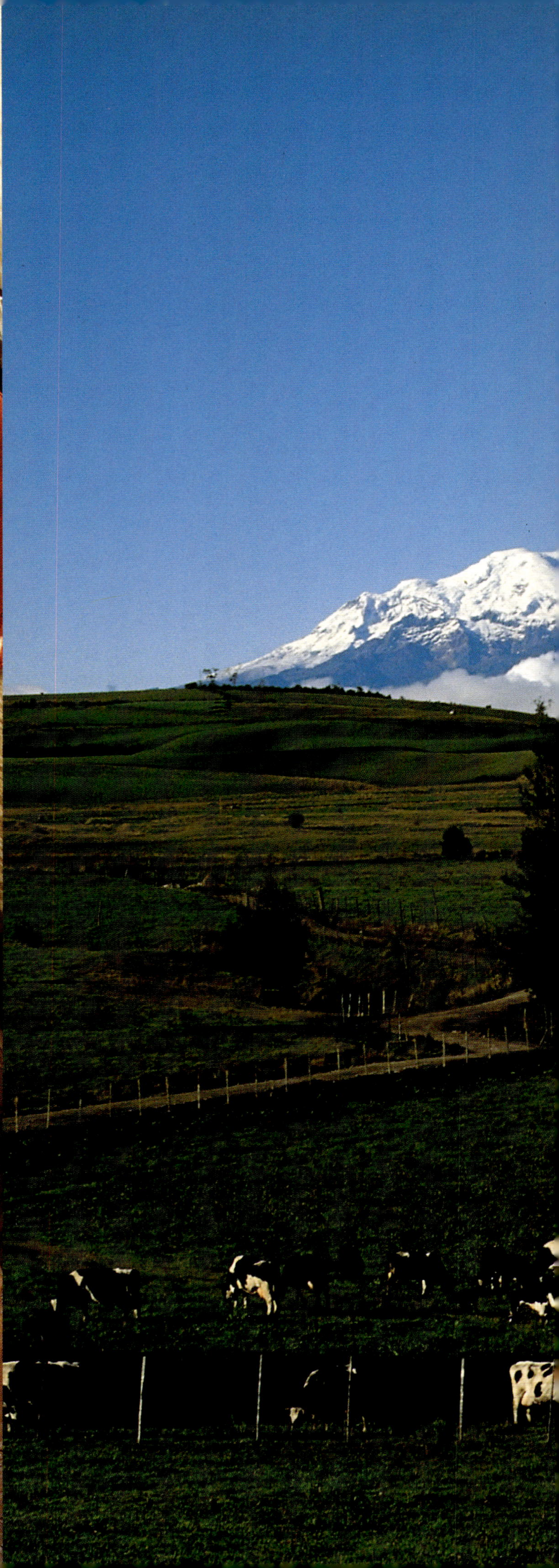

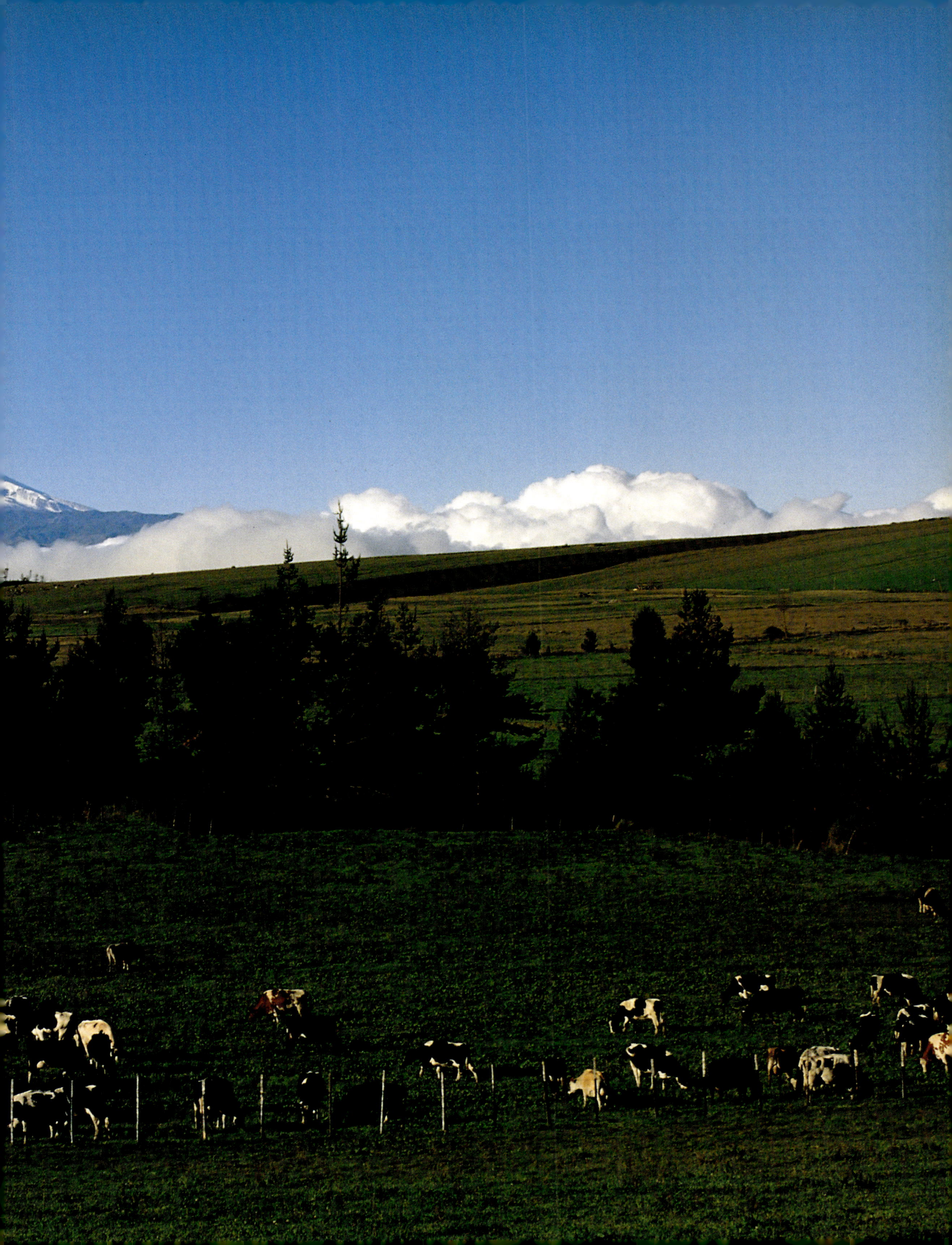

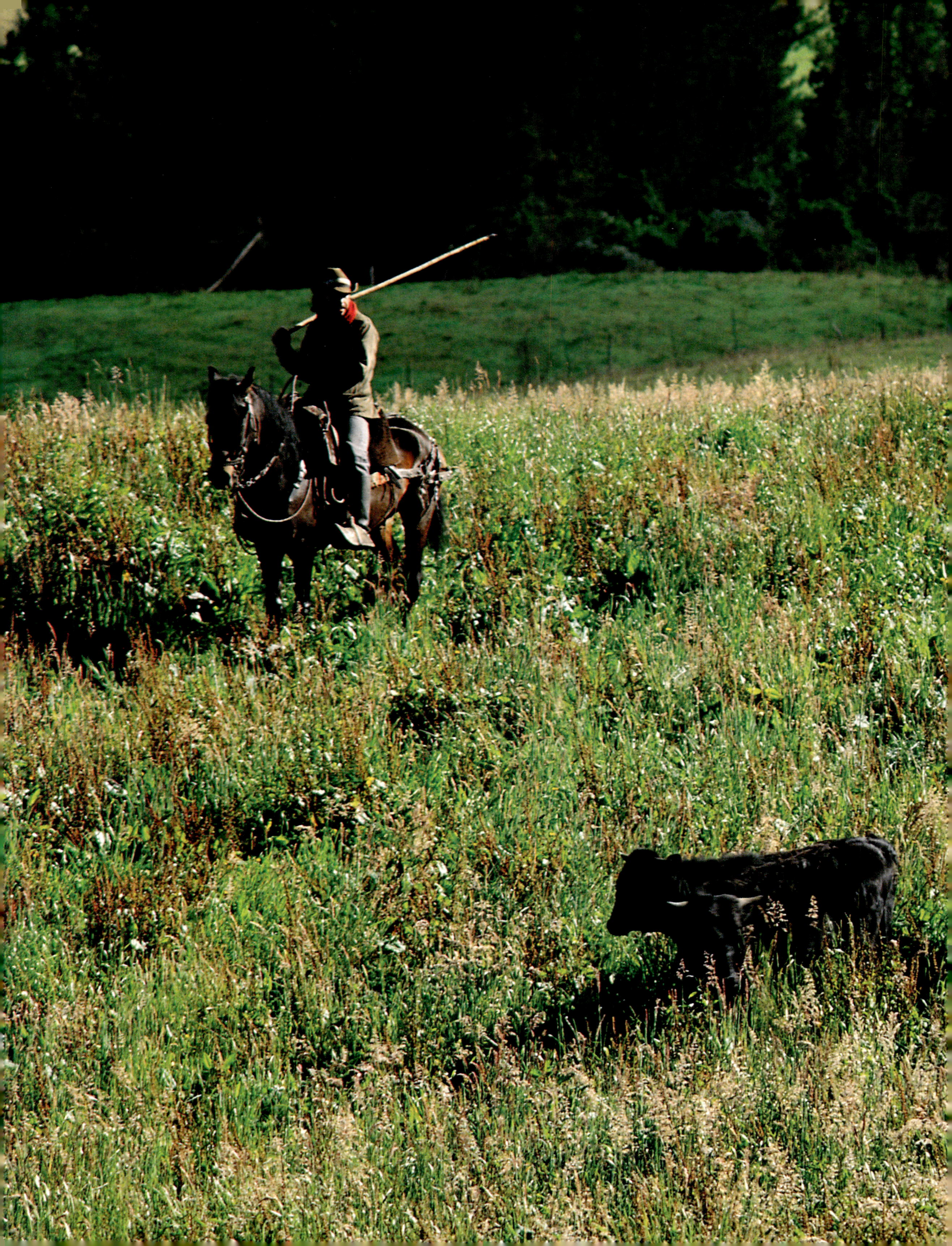

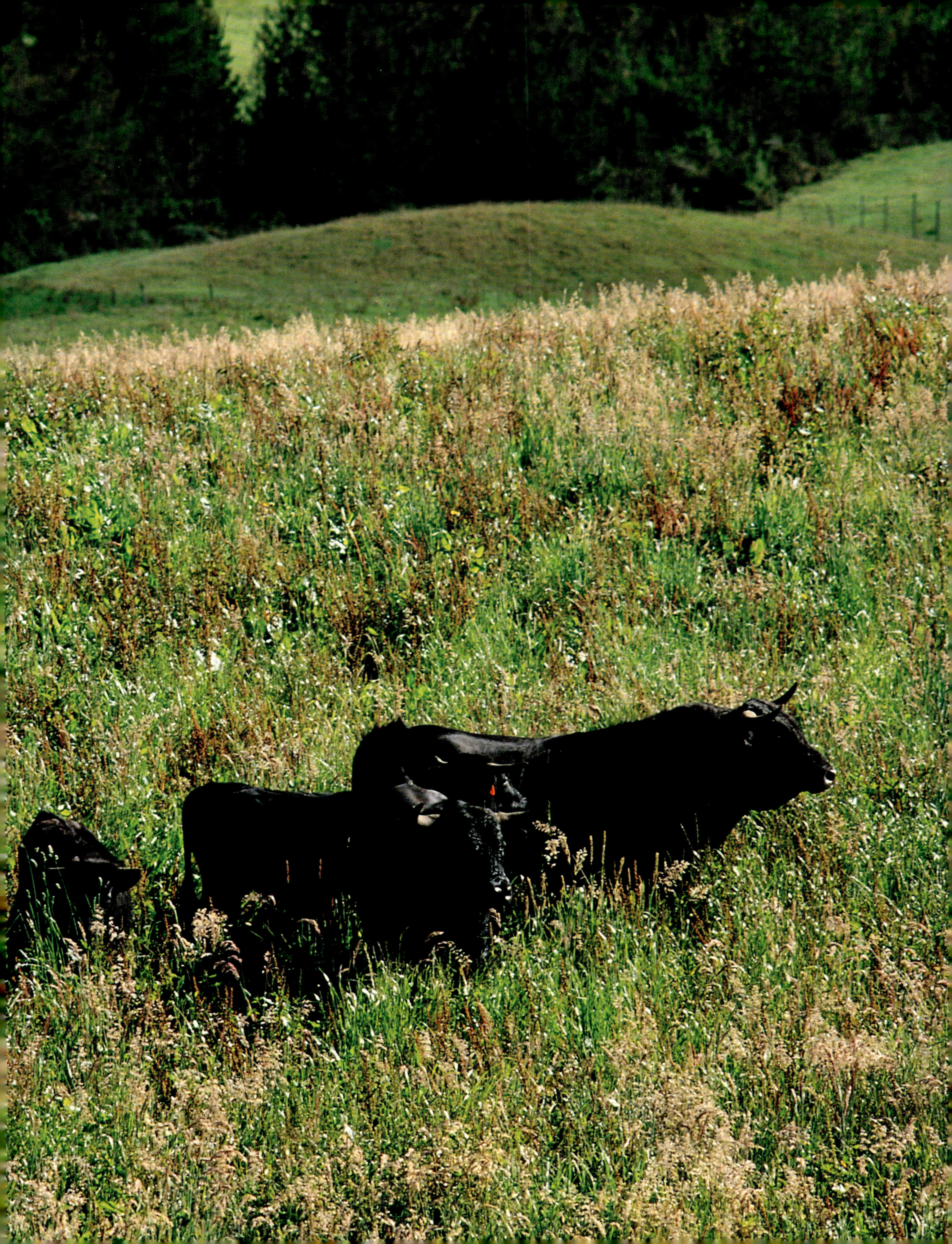

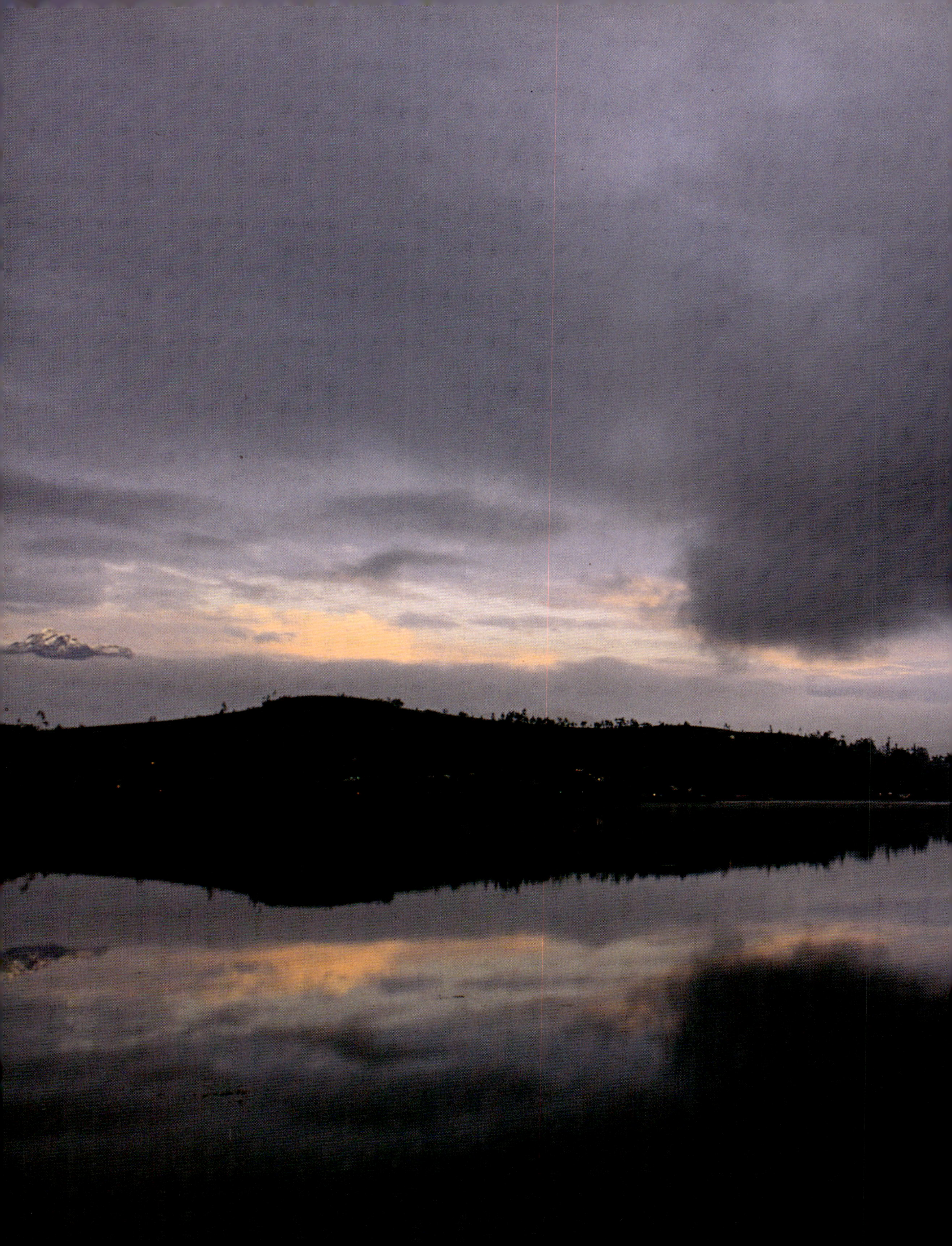

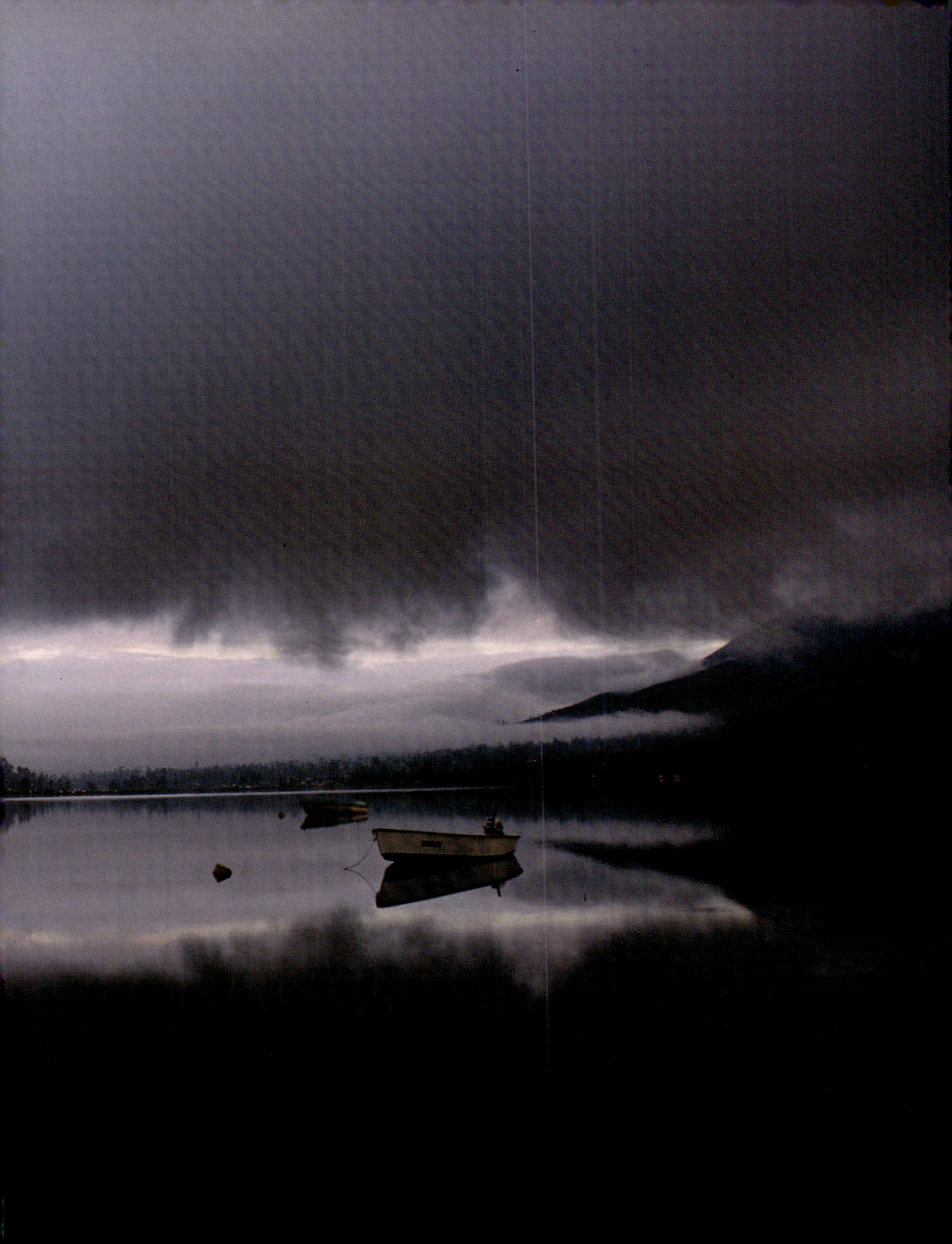

4

Guayaquil, the port of the panama

Since its foundation in 1535, the port of Guayaquil, situated on the immense estuary of its gulf, has seen the departure of many ships.
Having long been considered, from Alaska to Chili, as the shipyard of the Pacific, Guayaquil remains above all Ecuador's paramount centre of commerce. Merchandise and ideas have been passing through here since the 16th century. This hot, hazy, agitated town, constantly turned towards the outside world, has for long maintained very direct relations with the isthmus of Panama, which was the primary trading post for South America even before the building of the canal. The port of Guayaquil is the last stop in Ecuador: it is from here that the straw hats set out for Panama, which is where they were sold to the rest of the world. It is there that they were mis-named panamas. Over the course of time, history, trade and the universally-known name of a hat have created close relations between the two countries, and, even if these relations are today less intense than before, poetic images remain in the popular subconscious. Some of the old weavers of Montecristi, for example, when announcing the death of one of their number, say that he has gone to Panama, because, like the hat that has taken so long to make, he will never be seen again.

From Montecristi and Cuenca, the hats used to leave for Panama on the backs of mules, then by train or lorry. They passed through Guayaquil, continuing their journey in cargo ships. Today, it is often the Ecuadorian airline that takes over in Guayaquil.

When a hat does not leave for a long journey, it is generally because it ends up with Carlos Elias Barberan. For more than half a century, Barberan has been selling panamas of all categories in his shop in Guayaquil. His storehouse contain something like one hundred thousand hats of all prices and qualities. From the "ordinaries", at a few dollars, to the "superfinos" at several hundred dollars, through the "medium finos", generally already formed, borsalino-fashion, and the "finos", at prices that are extremely variable: the "cuencas" and the "montecristis" sit side by side in the specialist's storehouse.

Thus does one learn to distinguish materials and styles, placing them side by side. One can compare the weave of the "montecristis", which is extremely fine and regular, with that of the "cuencas", which is generally coarser. One discovers the "brisa" style, a Cuenca weaving style that is slightly flatter and more open. The "montecristi finos" can be compared to one another by counting the rows in their crown, and they can be recognised by their characteristic central ridge. Legend would have it that

Previous page
San Pablo lake in the cordillera of the Andes (Imbabura province).
Opposite page
*Colonial styles. On the left, a Cuenca panama, weave 14.
On the right, a "montecristi superfino".*

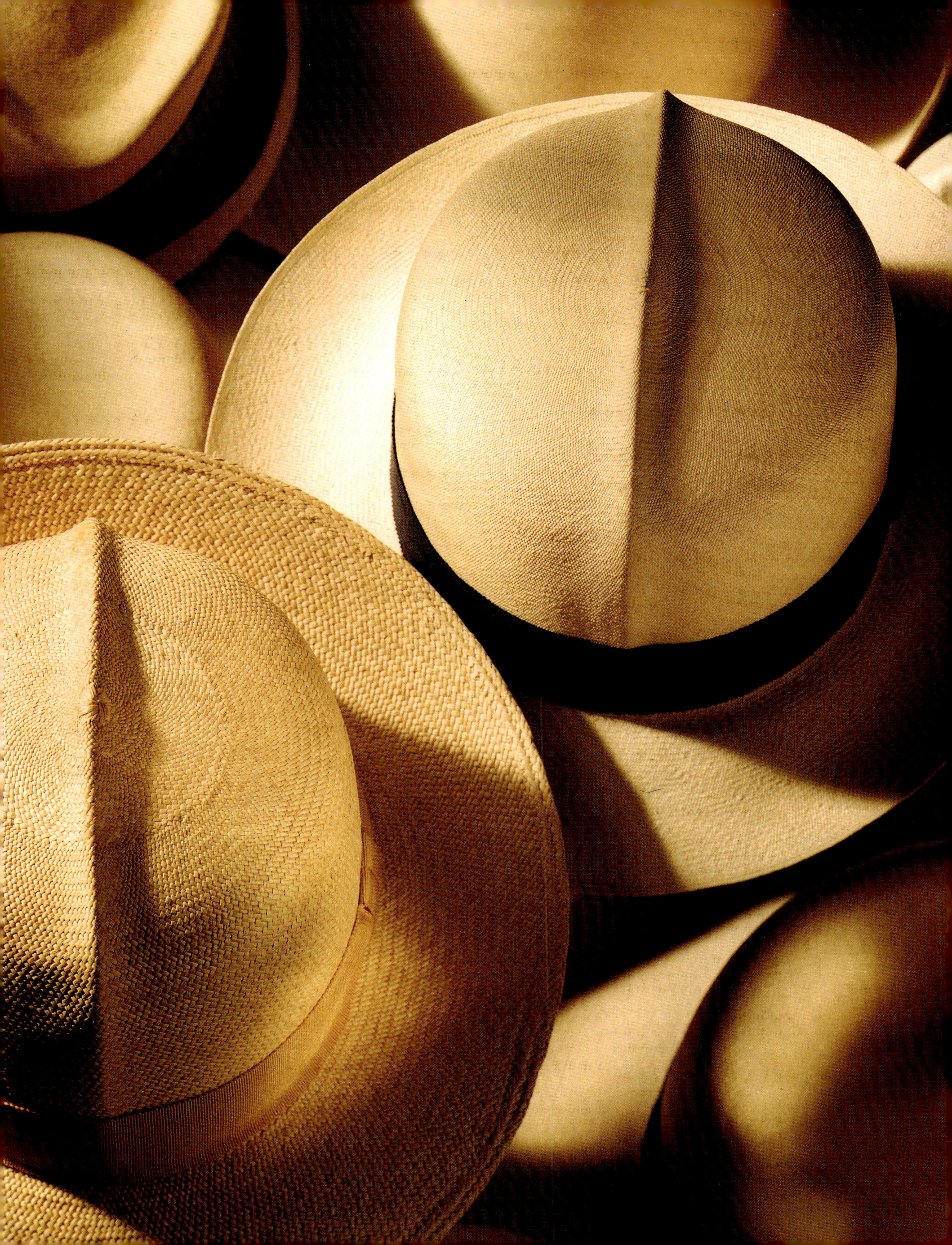

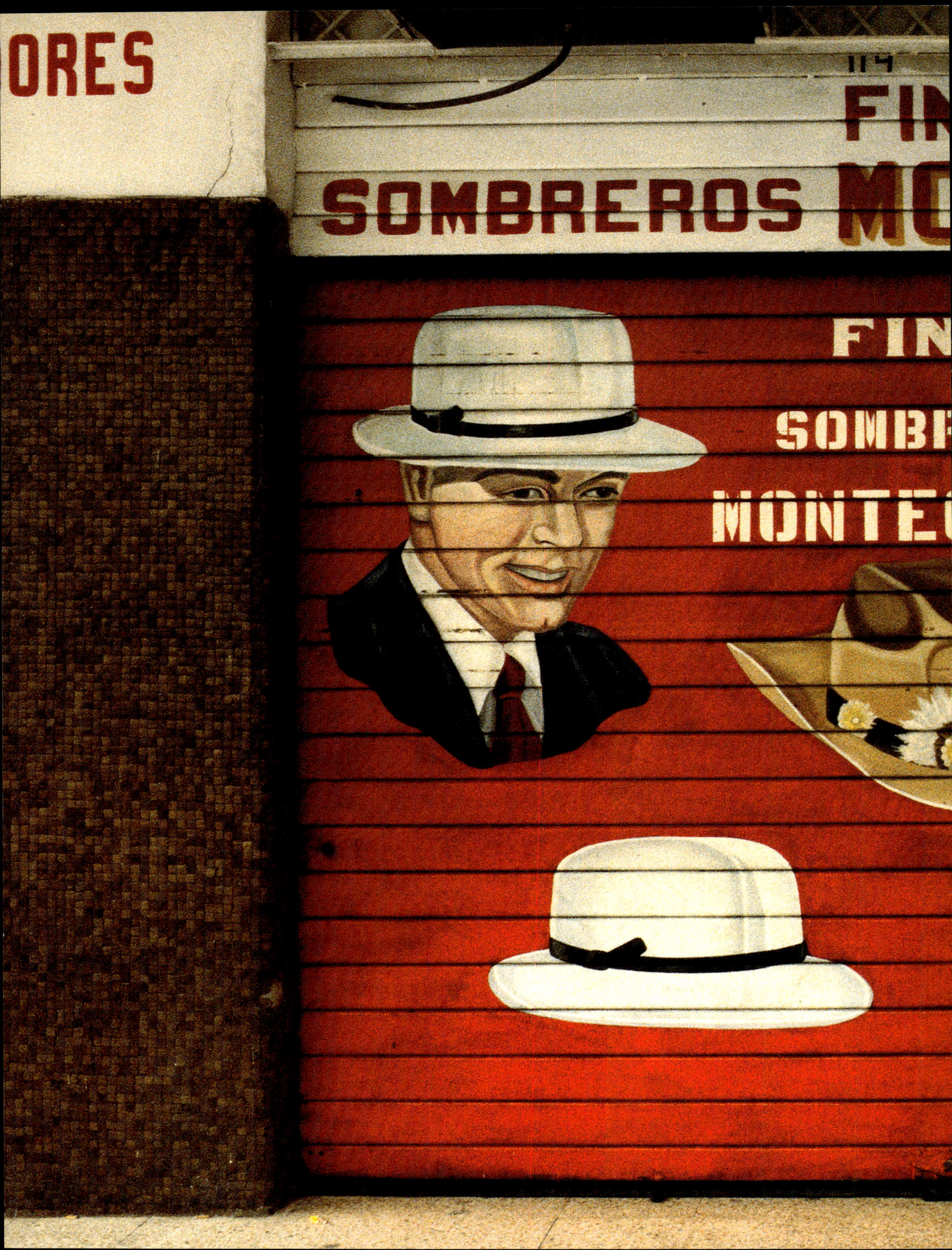
SOMBREROS

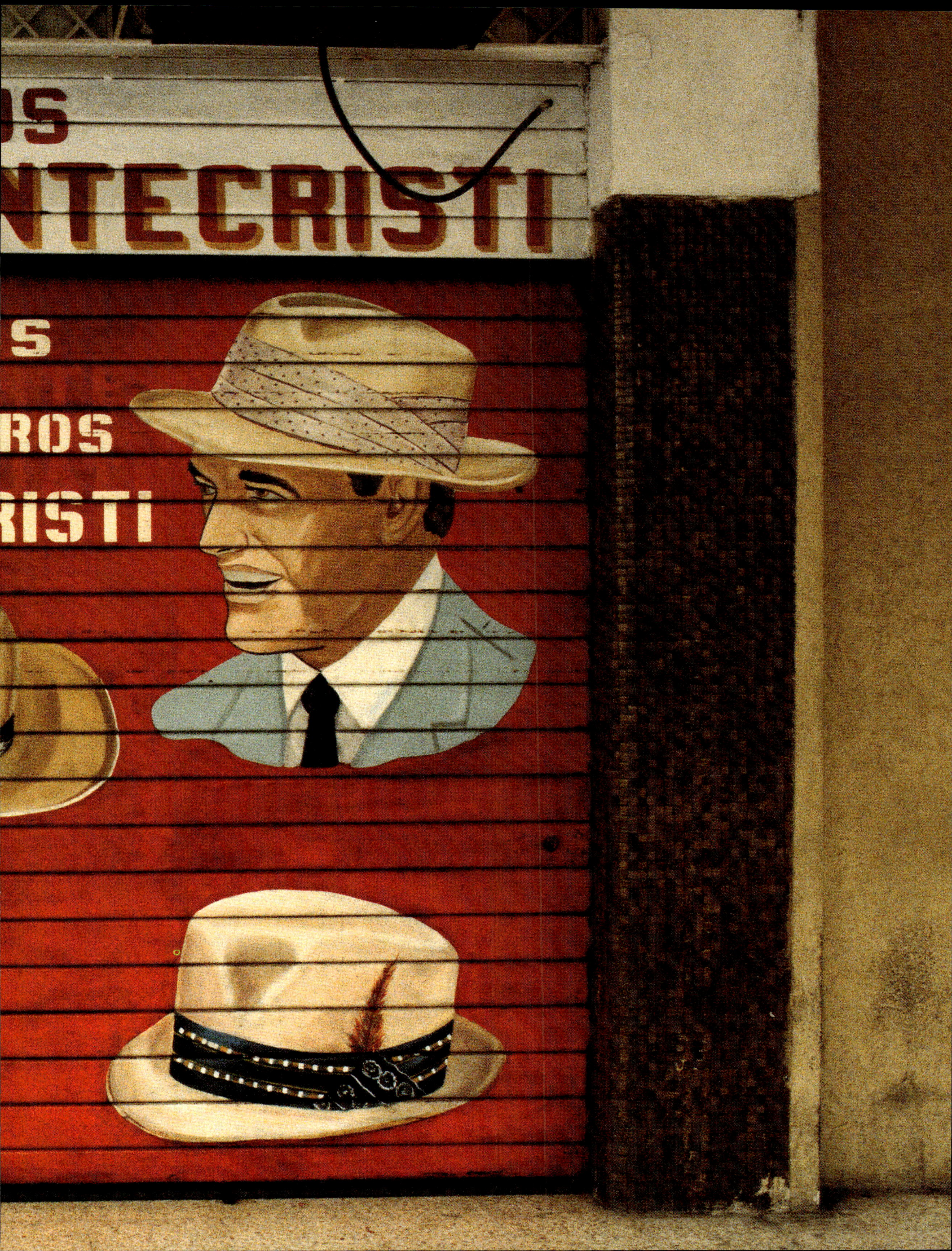
OS
NTECRISTI
S
ROS
RISTI

Ultimate port of call in Ecuador, Guayaquil sends the panamas off to conquer the world.

Previous pages
Carlo Elias Barberan's shop in Guayaquil.
Opposite page
Panamas in the tropics. Charlton Heston in The Naked Jungle.
Following pages
Left : Rodeo in Bucay (Guayas province). Right : Eduardo Blazero. Toquilla straw sombrero.

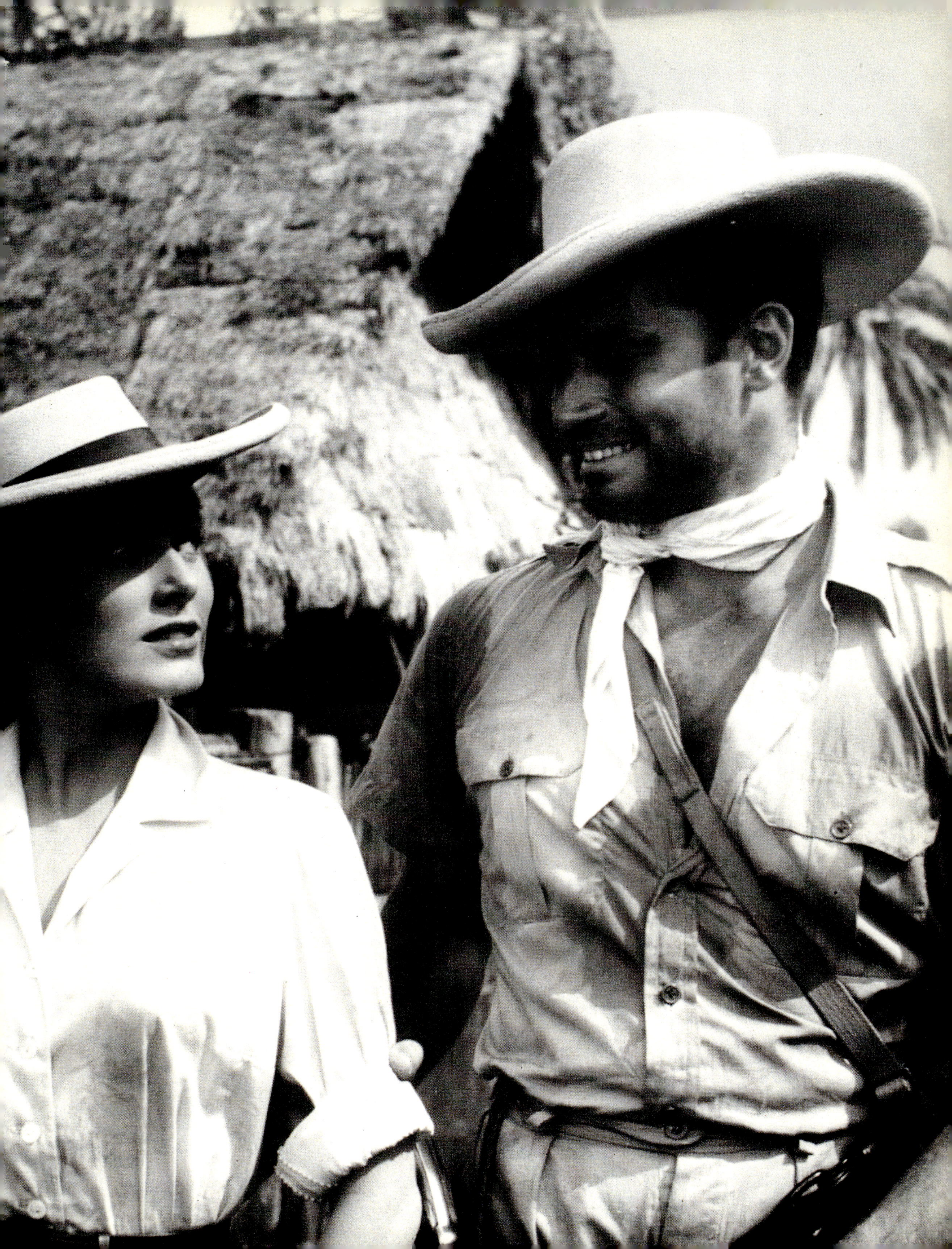

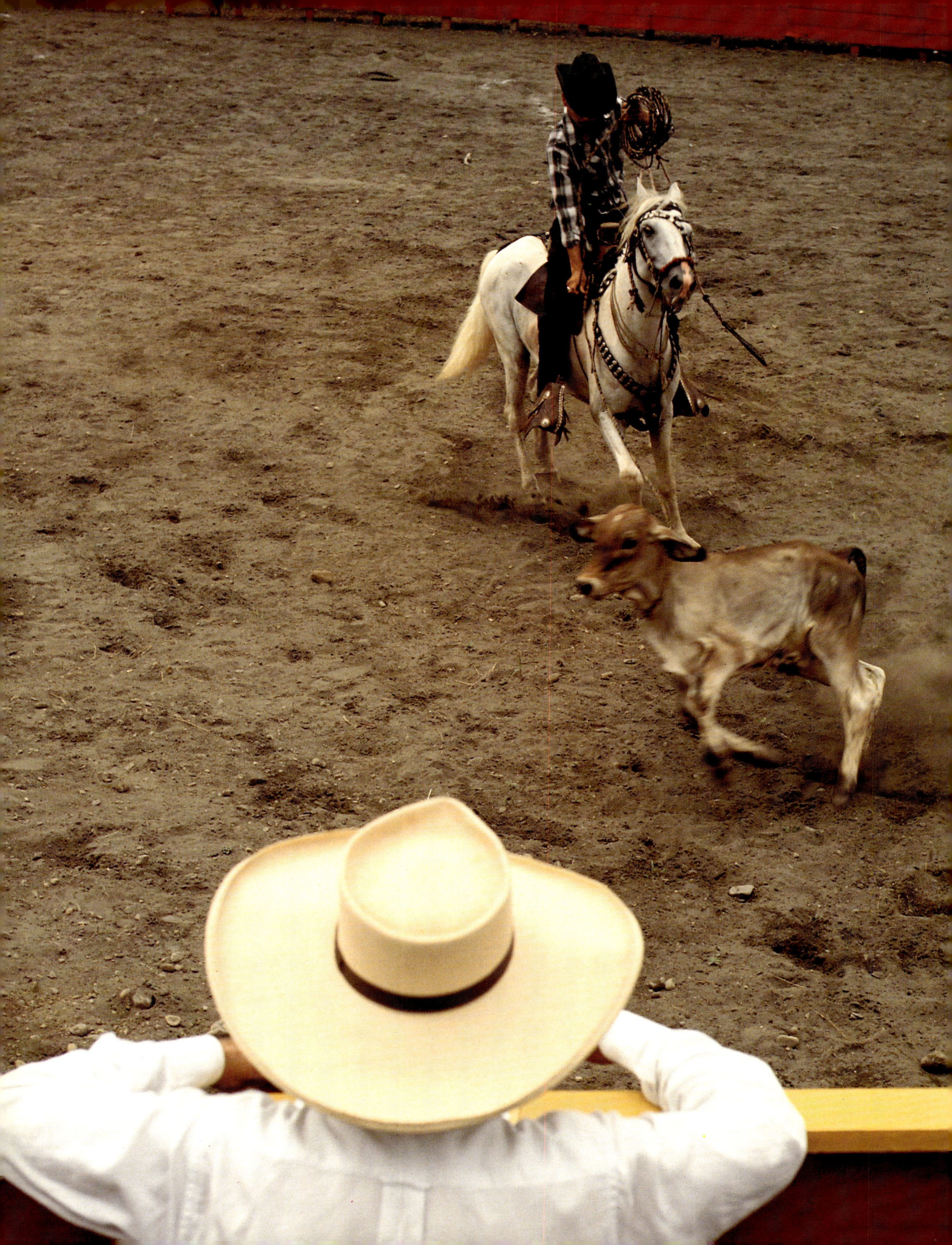

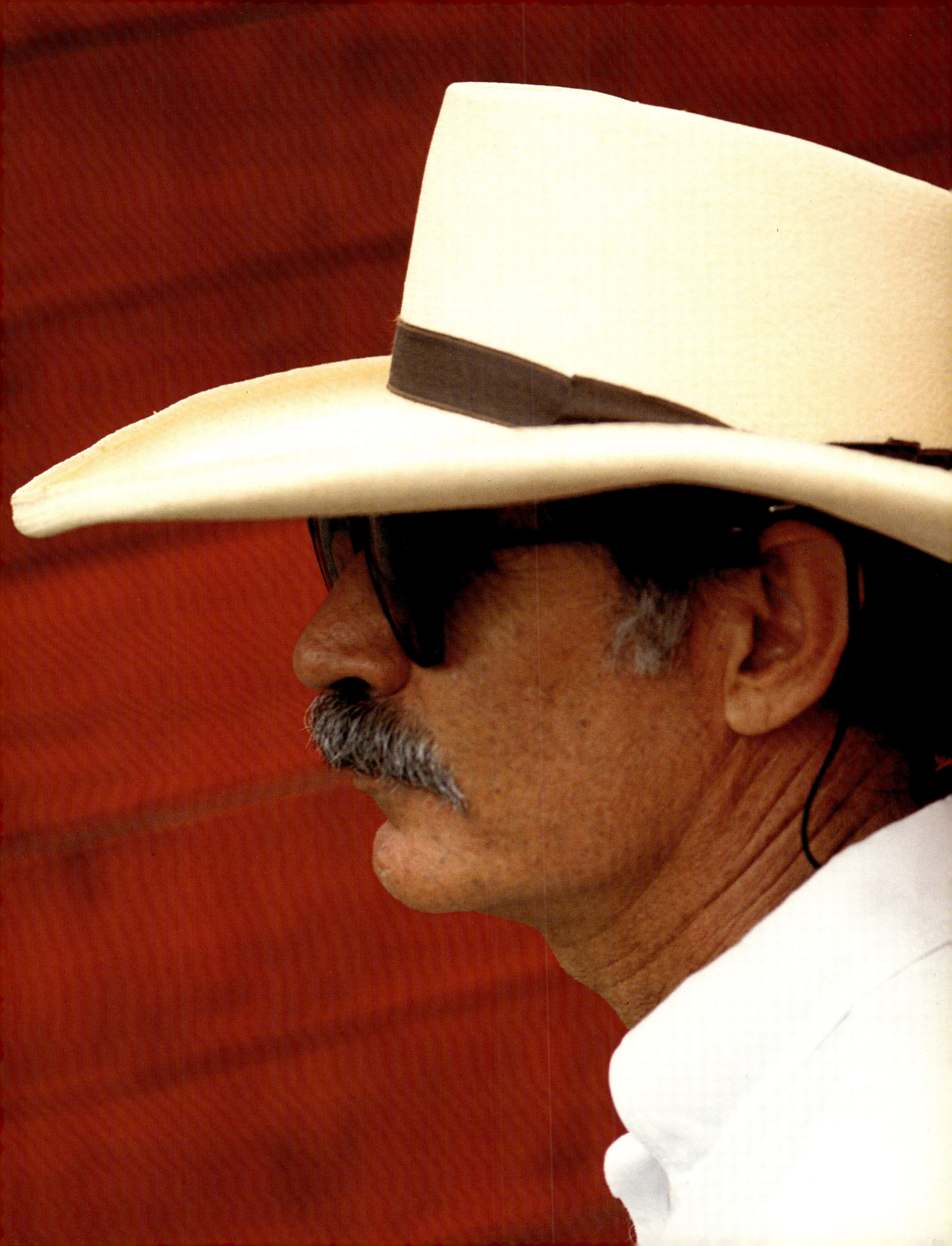

PANAMAS DELION

PROVENANCE DIRECTE

1ᴱᴿᴱ MARQUE

GUAYAQUIL

POUR DAMES ET MESSIEURS

the "fino" must be able to be folded, and this ridge, which makes it possible to roll up the hat and carry it around in a box or a jacket pocket, is always visible. And hence it has become a mark of quality! Unfolded, the "montecristi" recovers its initial shape, thanks to the suppleness of its straw and the quality of its weave. Without wishing to contradict the legend, it is however advisable not to over-use the pliability, especially in a dry climate. To conserve a "fino" of quality, it should be moistened regularly. This type of information is generally provided by the hatters who "deal" in the panamas. Such hatters are becoming increasingly rare, given that the great names of the profession search out the purity of the "montecristis", which are themselves hard to find. It is for this reason that a real "connoisseurs' circuit" has sprung up, starting with Don Rosendo in Montecristi and ending up with the prestigious international hat-makers: Gelot and Motsch in Paris, Lock and Herbert Johnson in London, J.J. Hat in New York, Newt at the Royal in Honolulu, Paul's Hat in San Francisco and Borsalino in Milan are among the addresses which are to be found in this select list. The finest "cuencas" and "montecristis" naturally find a home with hat-makers who admire beautiful materials and who produce, each in his own manner, the models that will satisfy their clients. In Guayaquil, Barberan keeps track of such a demand.

The borsalino of the 1940s is most certainly the great classic which seduces the urban Ecuadorians and the passing tourists. But demand for the stetson is increasing. This legendary hat with the broad brim is much in favour in the great plantations and numerous haciendas around the town. In particular the breeding farms such as the "Dolores y Changil" hacienda, where the cowboys raise fighting bulls and riding horses, those magnificent horses of long tradition which marry arrogance, style, beauty and gentleness – they are real works of art, and some people go as far as talk about them the way others talk about "montecristi superfinos" – with admiration and respect, in other words!

> Since the 19th century, the world's greatest hatters have been vying for increasingly scarce *montecristi finos*.

In New York and San Francisco, the amateurs of panamas tend to like highly-finished hats, while the European tendency is to prefer "natural" panamas that are lightly formed by hand. But there are many exceptions to the rule, like certain nostalgic Englishmen who wear the colonial style so well. In Rome, they go for the "capone", in the islands they prefer the planter. And there is also the "dandy", the "deauville", the "madagascar", the "malibu", and so on. There are even bowler-type panamas! The material is such that it invites hat-makers to create new styles, and they all enjoy the challenge of this inimitable straw.

By boat or plane, the white cotton sacks filled with panamas set out on the road to the celebrated shops. The names are written by hand on the cloth sacks, the same kind that were already setting out in the last century towards new worlds – sacks full of hats, and perhaps also dreams, like that of the character in Céline's novel, describing a panama: "It was one of a kind, a true masterpiece, the sombrero type; a gift from South America, a weave of the rarest! It would be impossible to replace… In simple terms, it was beyond price…"

Opposite page
Advertisement for panamas, 1912.

Panamas vary greatly in quality, according to the straw chosen, the expertise of the weaver and the time spent creating it.

Opposite page
Different weaves and qualities: upper left, a 2/3 "cuenca". Lower left, a 17/18 "montecristi". On the right, a 17/18 "cuenca".
Following page
"Montecristi superfino", colonial style.

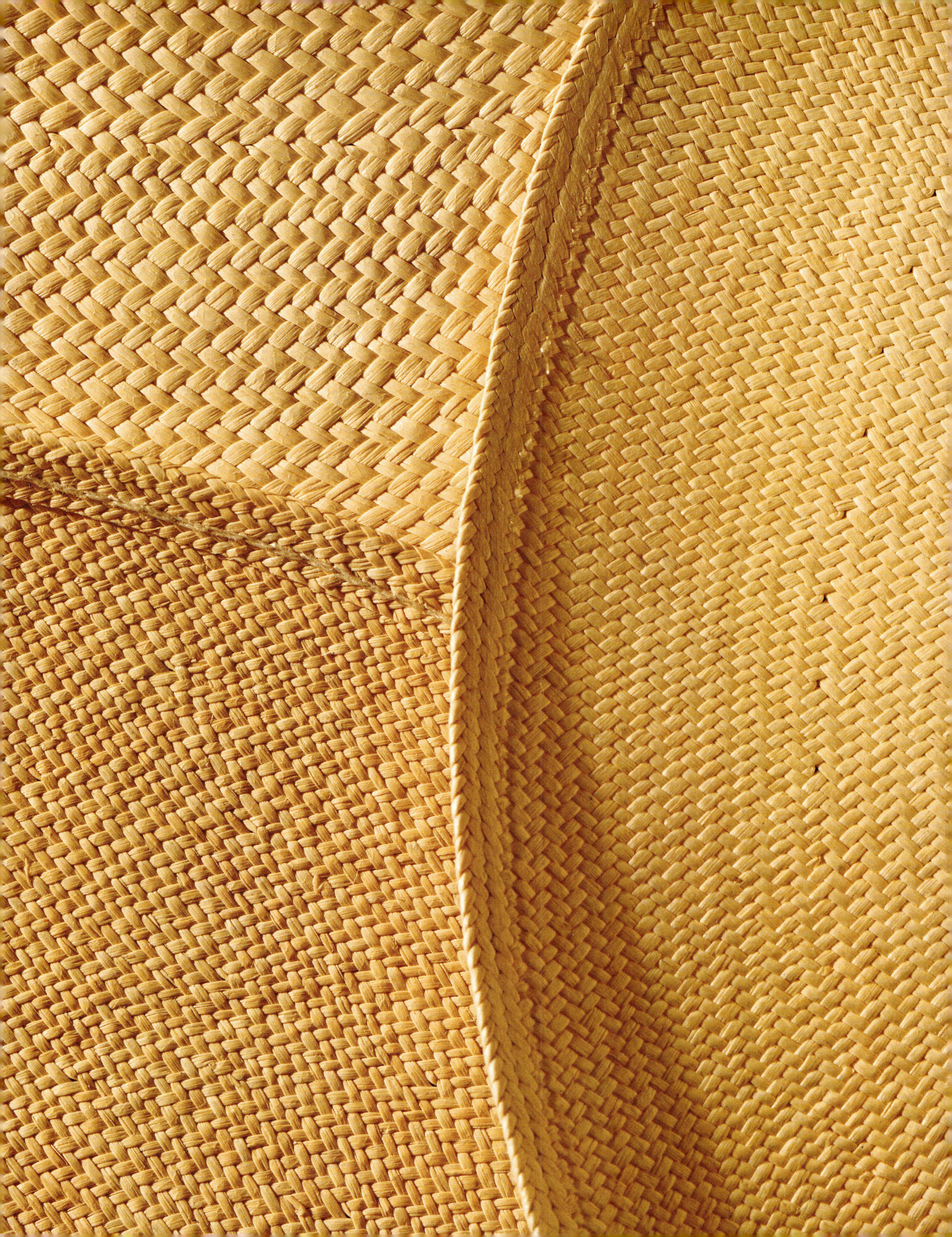

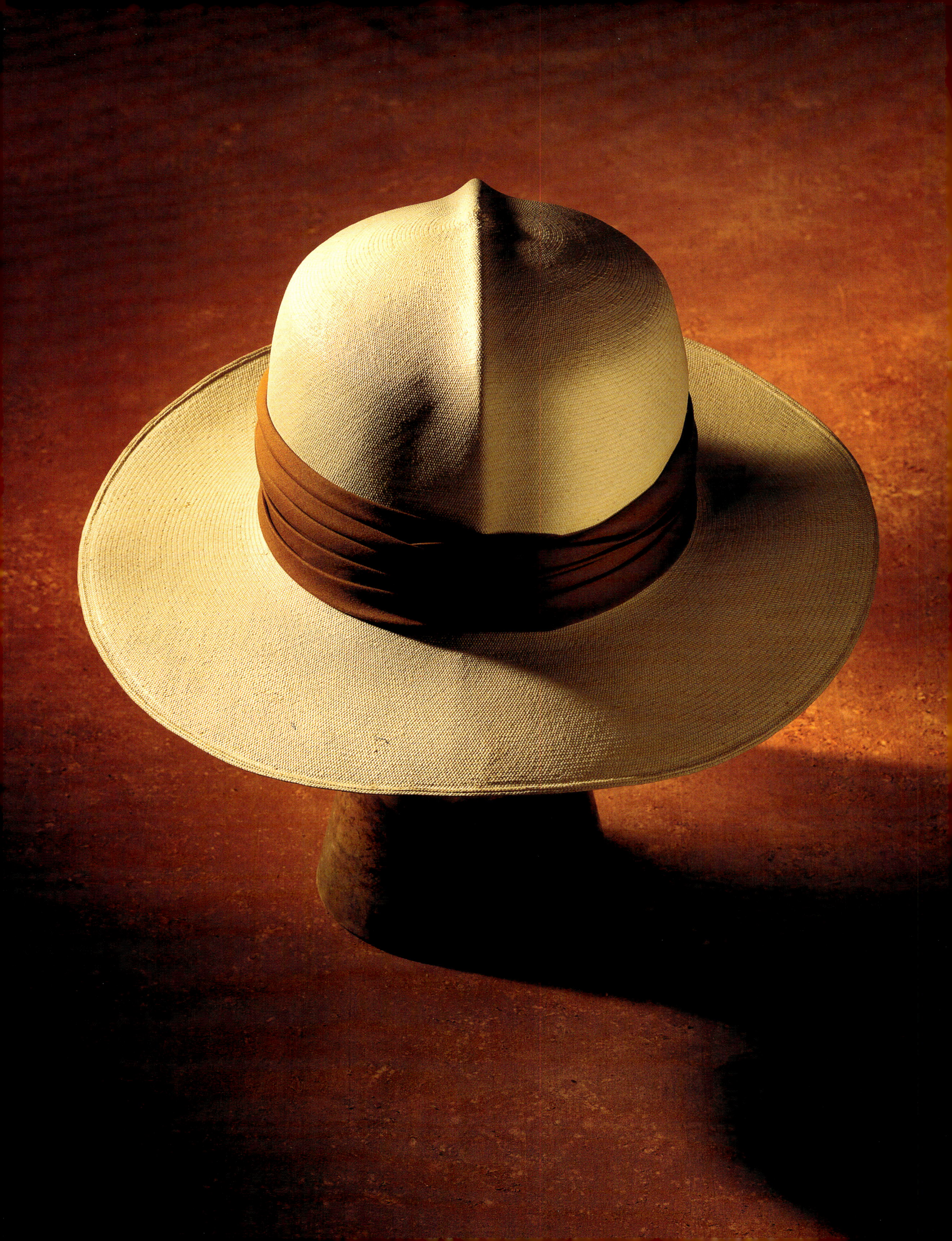

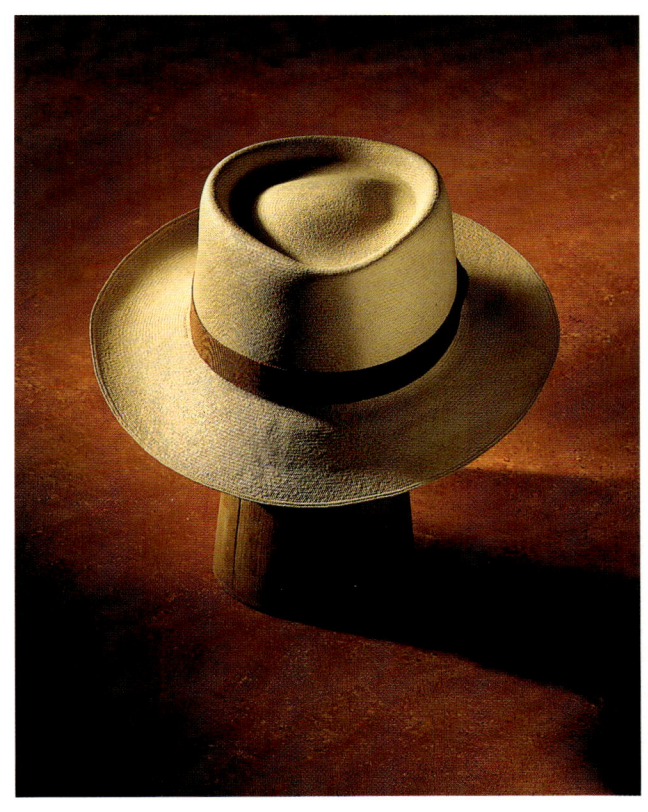

Borsalino style
Montecristi "fino"

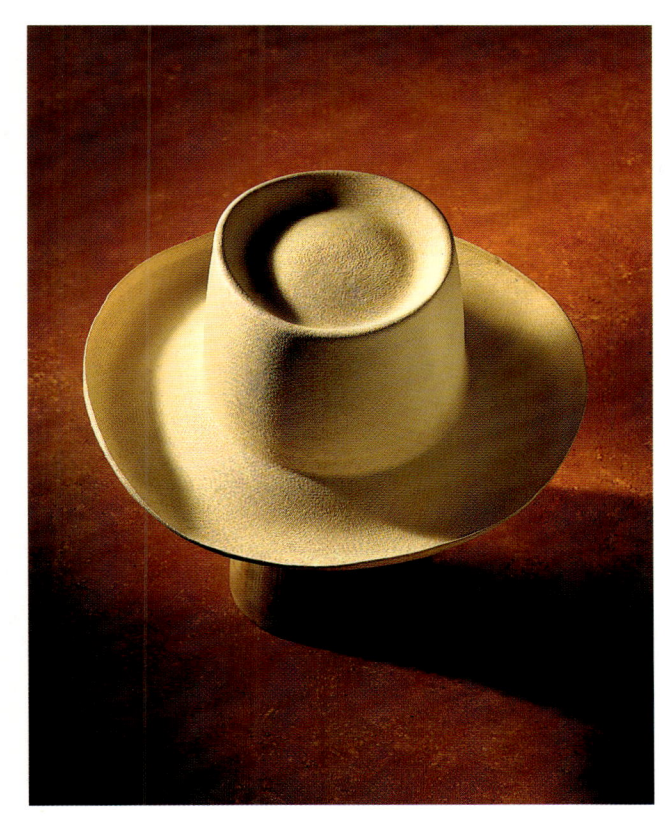

Planter style
Montecristi "superfino"

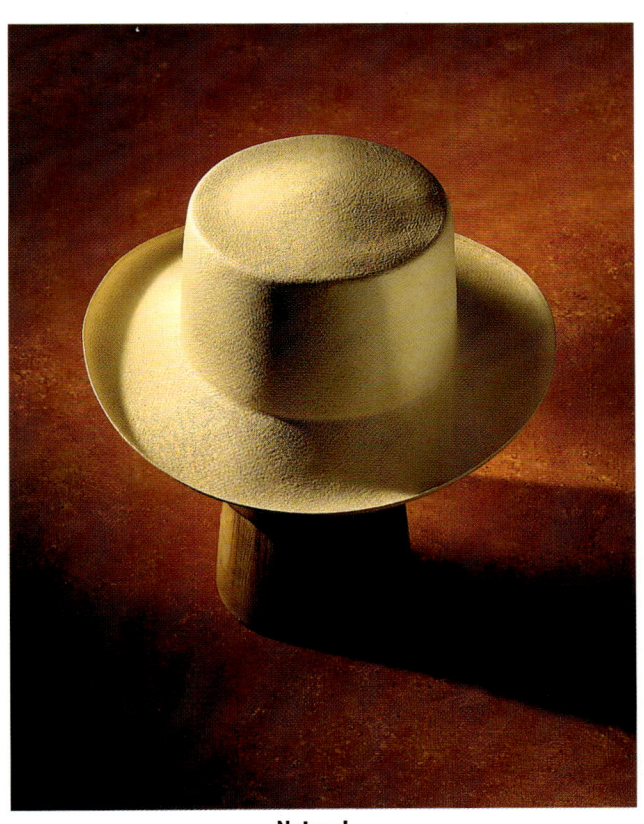

Natural
Montecristi "superfino"

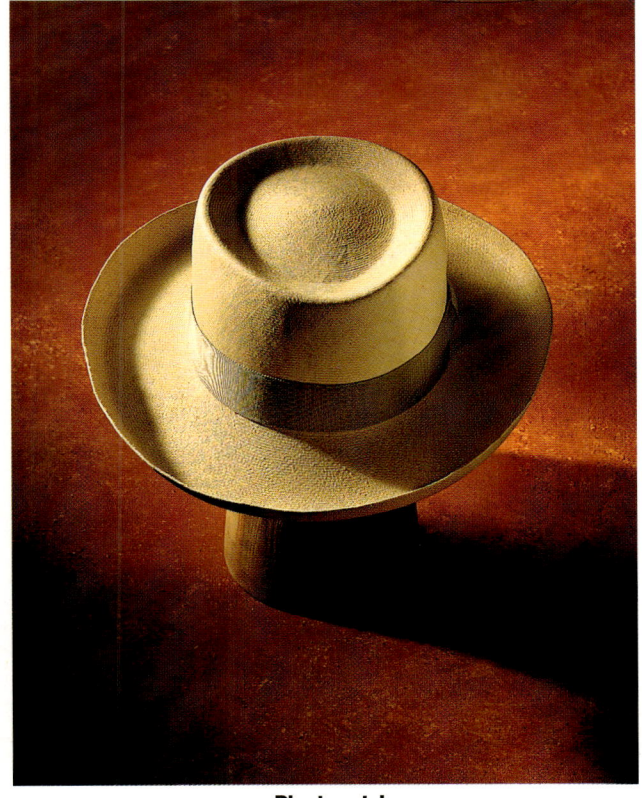

Planter style
Montecristi "superfino"

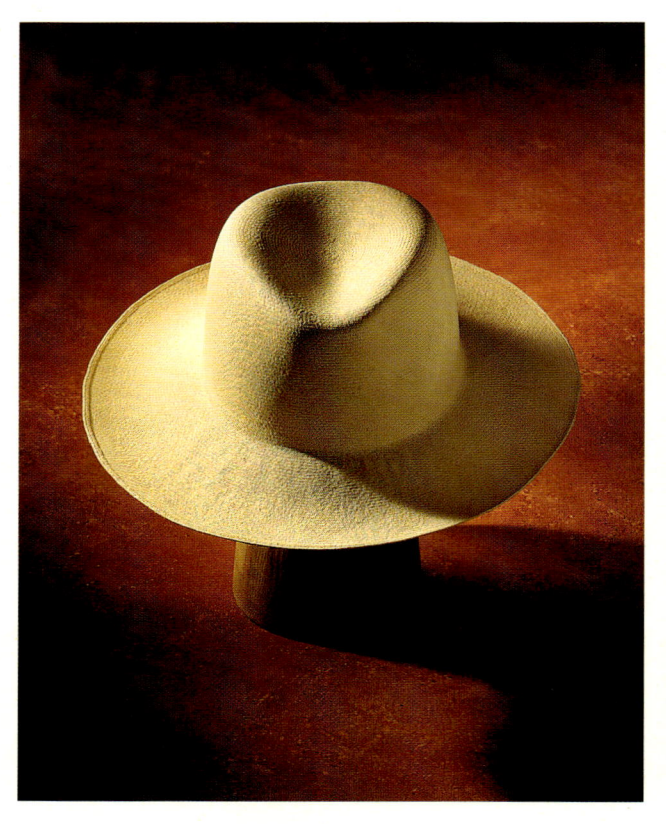

Borsalino style
Montecristi "fino"

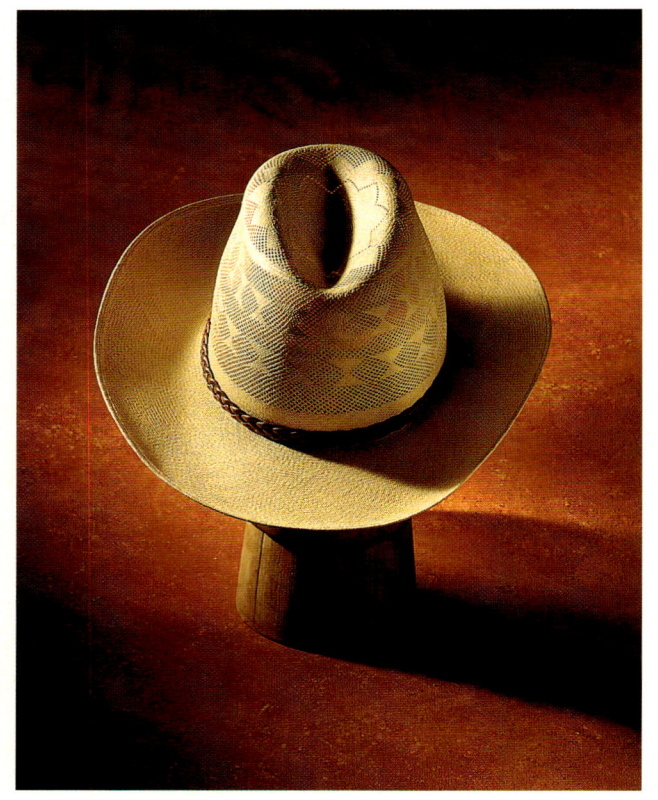

Stetson style
Montecristi "fino"

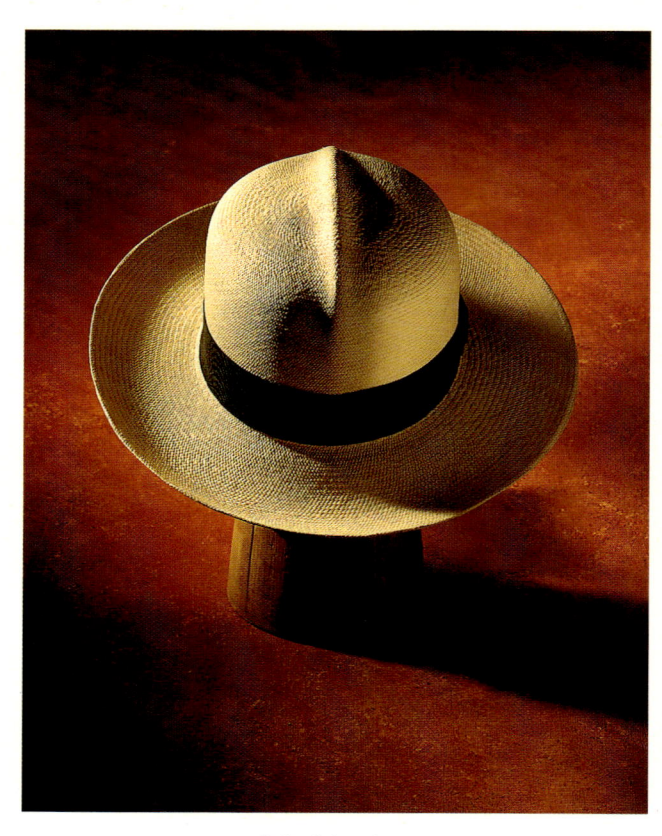

Colonial style
Cuenca 11/12

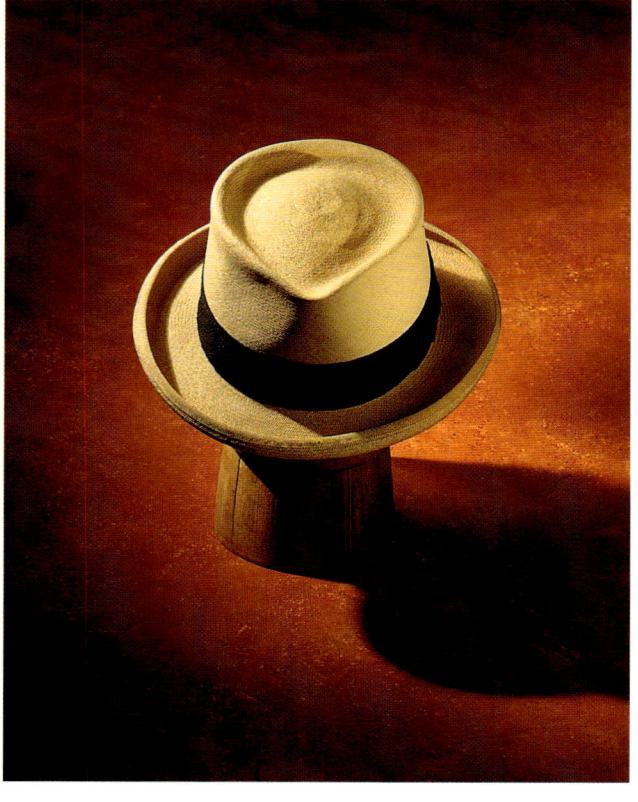

Dandy style
Cuenca, 15/16 weave

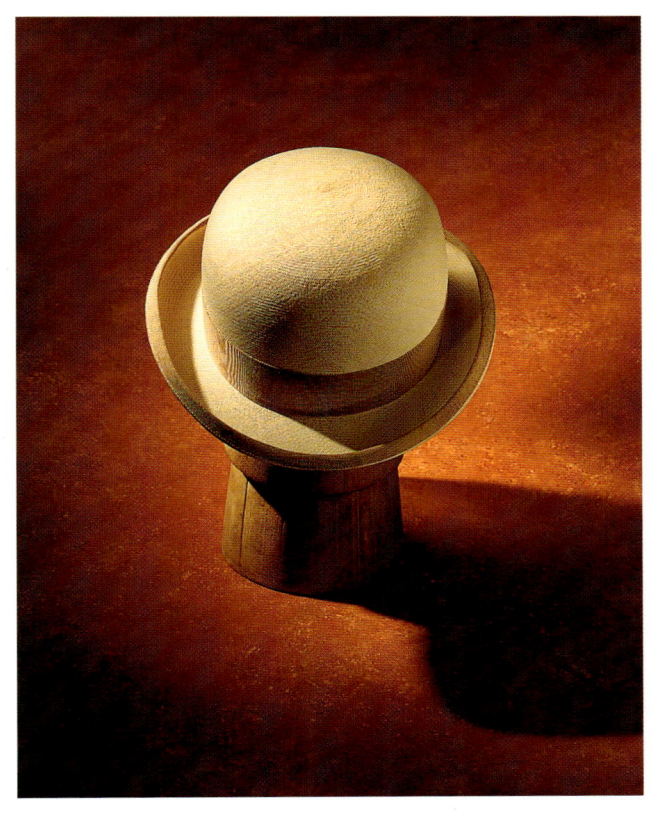

Bowler
Montecristi "superfino"

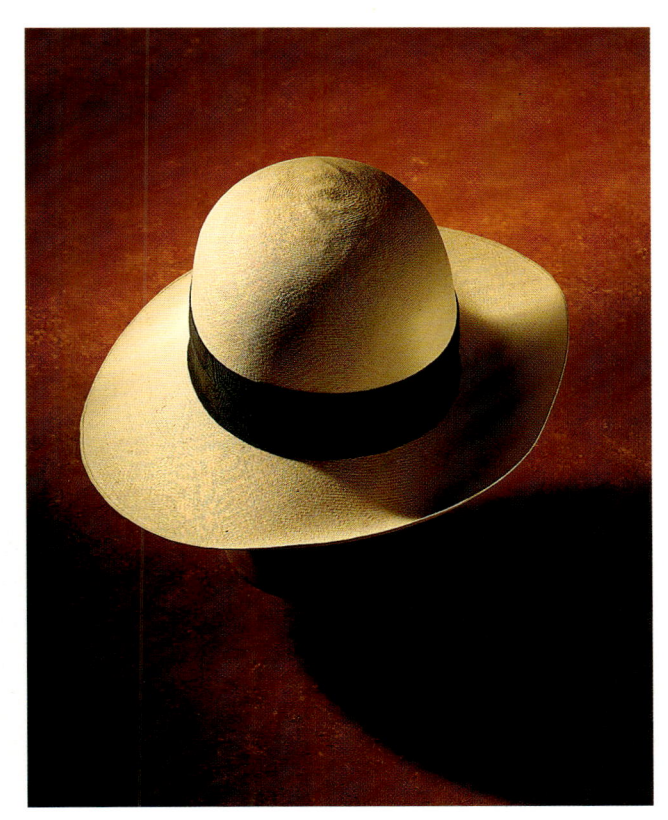

Etretat style
Montecristi "superfino"

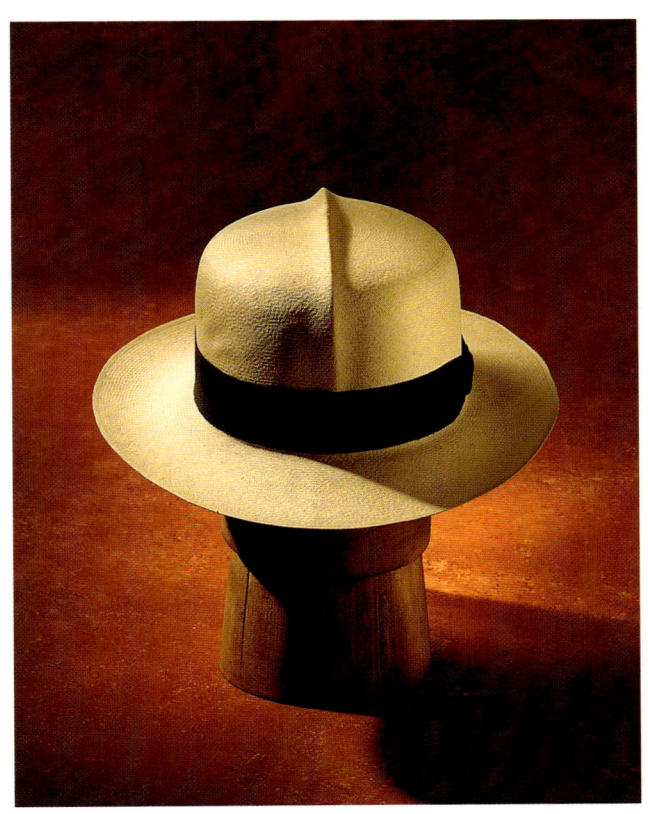

Colonial style
Montecristi "superfino"

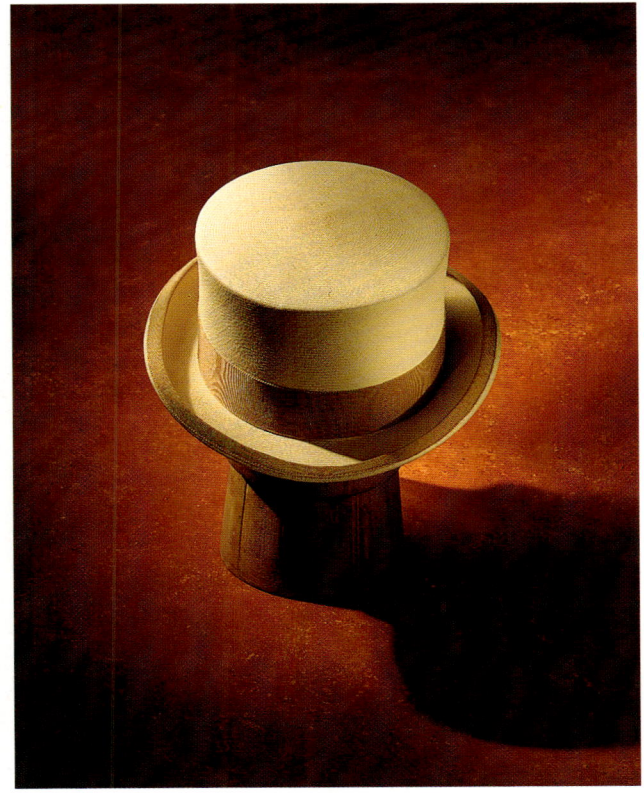

Top hat
Montecristi "superfino"

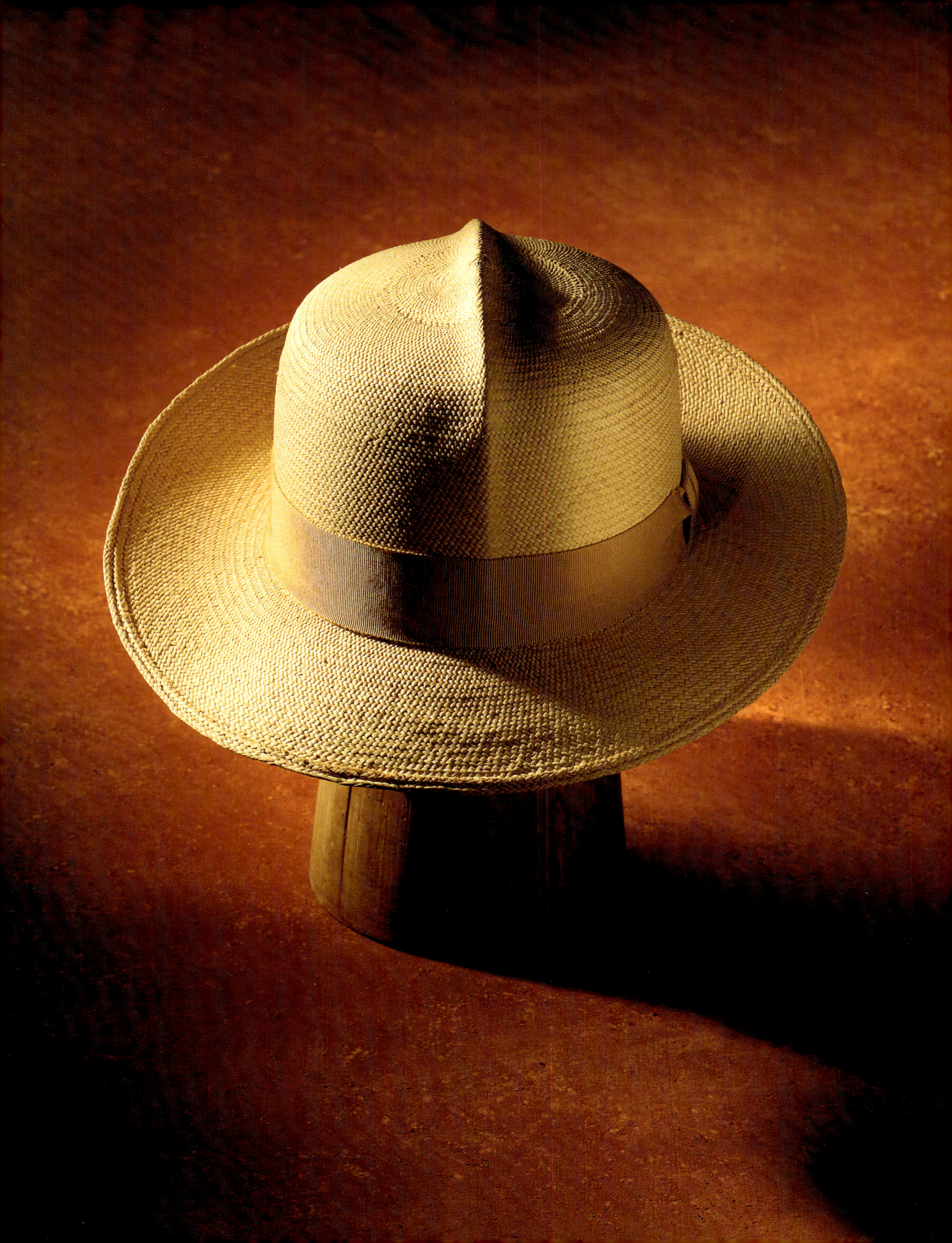

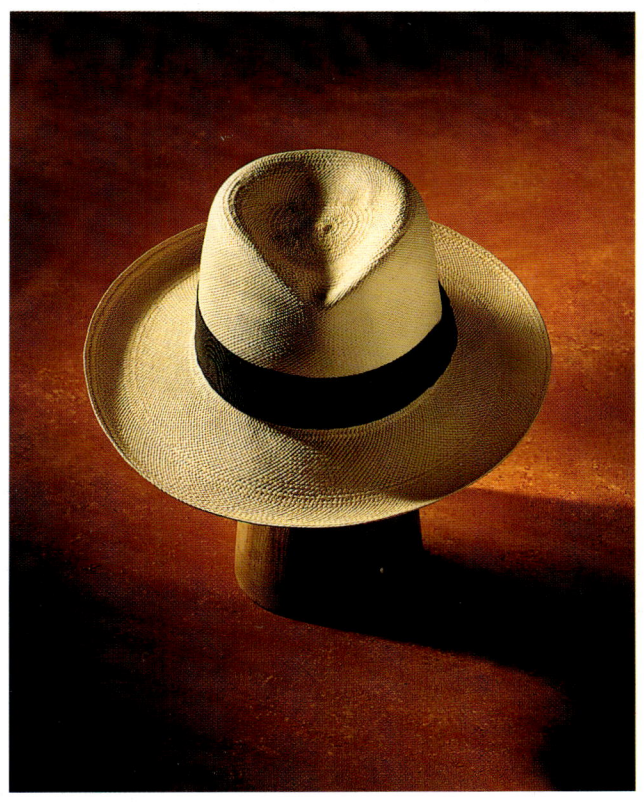

Borsalino style
Brisa, 2/3 weave

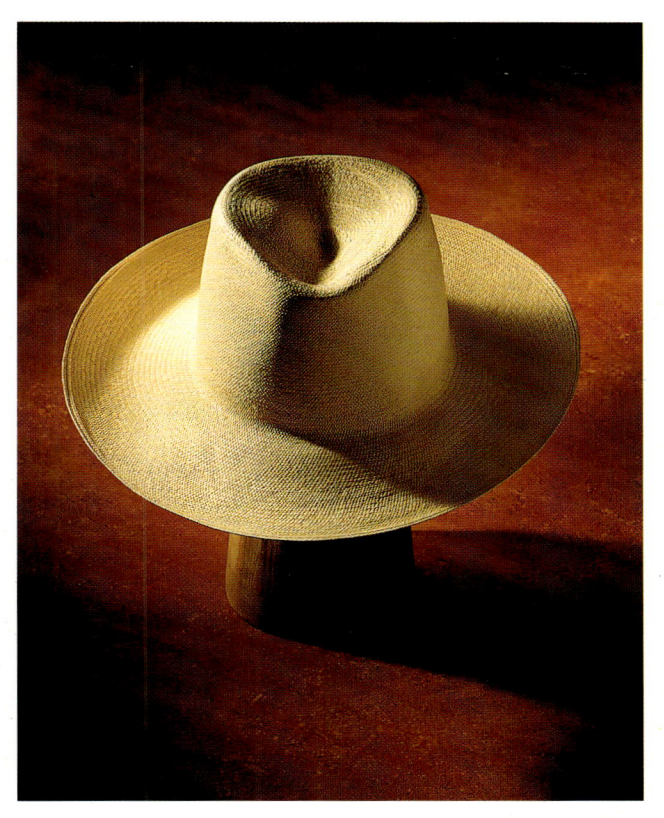

Borsalino style with wide brim
Cuenca, 15/16 weave

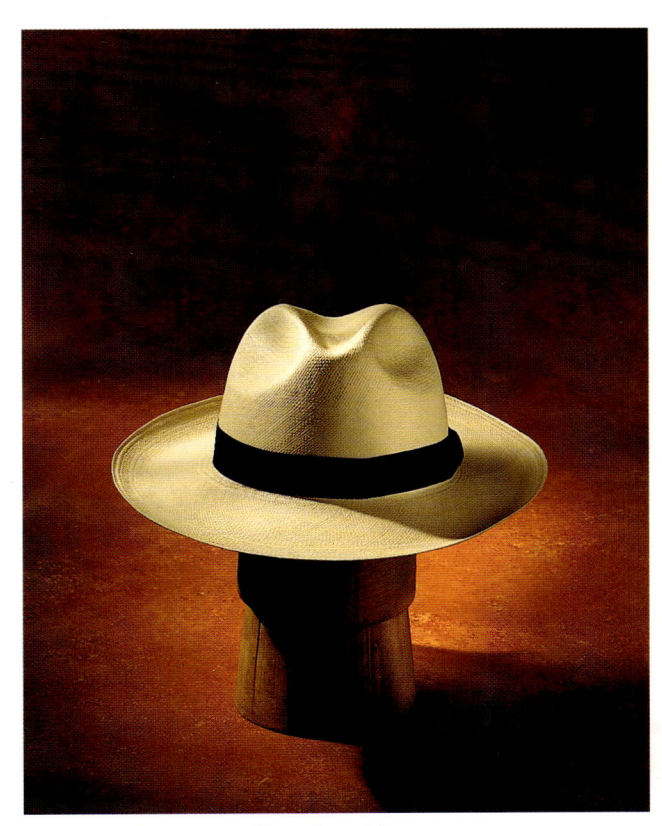

Borsalino style
Brisa, 5/6 weave

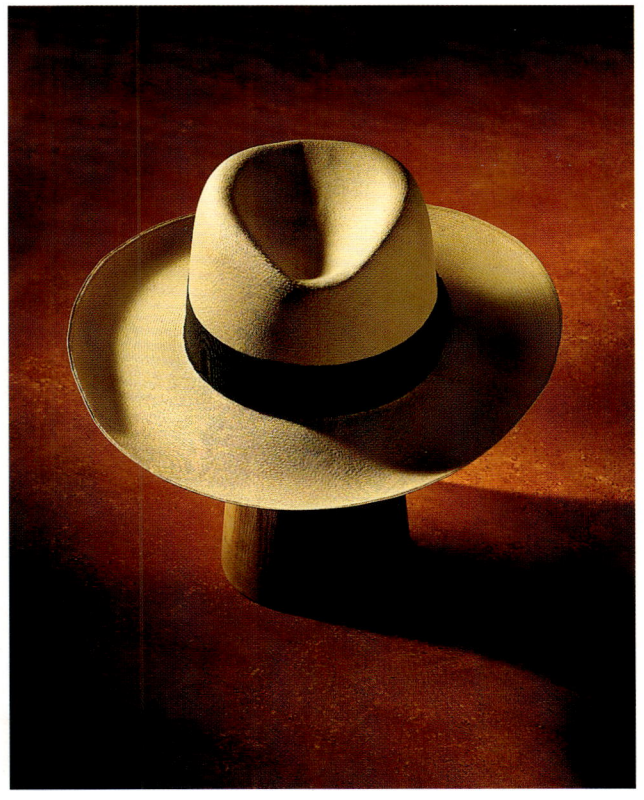

Borsalino style with wide brim
Montecristi "superfino"

Opposite page
Cuenca, 7/8 weave, colonial style.

The finest panamas in the world

France

GELOT - Founded in 1835
15, rue du Faubourg-Saint-Honoré
75008 Paris
Tel: 44 71 31 61
Fax: 44 71 31 77

MOTSCH - Founded in 1887
42, avenue George-V
75008 Paris
Tel: 47 23 79 22
Fax: 47 20 59 60

CHAPELLERIE BROSSON
Founded in 1890
43, rue d'Alsace-Lorraine
31000 Toulouse
Tel: 61 21 15 60

LOUIS SCIOLLA
2, boulevard des Moulins
98000 Monte-Carlo
Tel: 93 50 50 61
Fax: 92 16 75 38

PANAMA MONTECRISTI
(Importer to Europe)
19, rue de Vaugirard
92190 Meudon
Tel: 46 26 45 36
Fax: 46 23 92 52

England

HERBERT JOHNSON -
Founded in 1872
30 New Bond Street
London W1Y 9HD
Tel: 01 71 408 11 74
Fax: 09 33 41 01 06

LOCK & CIE - Founded in 1676
6 St James's Street
London SW1A IEF
Tel: 01 71 930 88 74 / 58 49
Fax: 01 71 976 19 08

HARROD'S
Knightsbridge
London SW1X 7XL
Tel: 01 71 730 12 34
Fax: 01 71 581 04 70

Italy

BORSALINO - Founded in 1857
Corso Vittorio Emanuele II, 5
Milan
Tel: 39 2 869 08 05

Switzerland

PORETTI SA
via Vegezzi 2
CH 6900 Lugano
Tel: 91 23 27 37
Fax: 91 23 83 16

Belgium

PIERRE DEGAND
415 avenue Louise B 1050
Brussels
Tel: 2 649 00 73
Fax: 2 640 03 06

Spain

BEL Y CIA
Paseo de Gracia 20
Barcelona 08007
Tel: 3 302 43 86
Fax: 3 317 20 24

United States

J.J. HAT CENTER - Founded in 1911
310 Fifth Avenue
New York NY 10001-3605
Tel: 212 239 43 68
Fax: 212 971 04 06
MAIL ORDER DEPT :
1 800 622 19 11

DAVIDOFF OF GENEVA
232 via Rodeo / N. Rodeo Dr.
Beverly Hills, CA
Tel: 310 278 88 84

NEWT AT THE ROYAL
ROYAL HAWAIIAN HOTEL
Honolulu, Hawaii
Tel: 808 922 0062

GEORGETOWN TOBACCO
3144 M Street N.W.
Washington, DC
Tel: 202 338 51 00

PAUL'S HAT WORKS
6128 Geary Blvd
San Francisco, CA
Tel: 415 221 53 32

MONTECRISTI CUSTOM HAT WORKS
118 Galisteo Street
Santa Fe, New Mexico
Tel: 505 983 95 98

PANAMA HATS COMPANY
OF THE PACIFIC
(Importer in the United States)
1164 Bishop Street,
Suite 124-109
Honolulu, Hawaii 96813
Tel: 808 262 28 90
Fax: 808 262 77 25

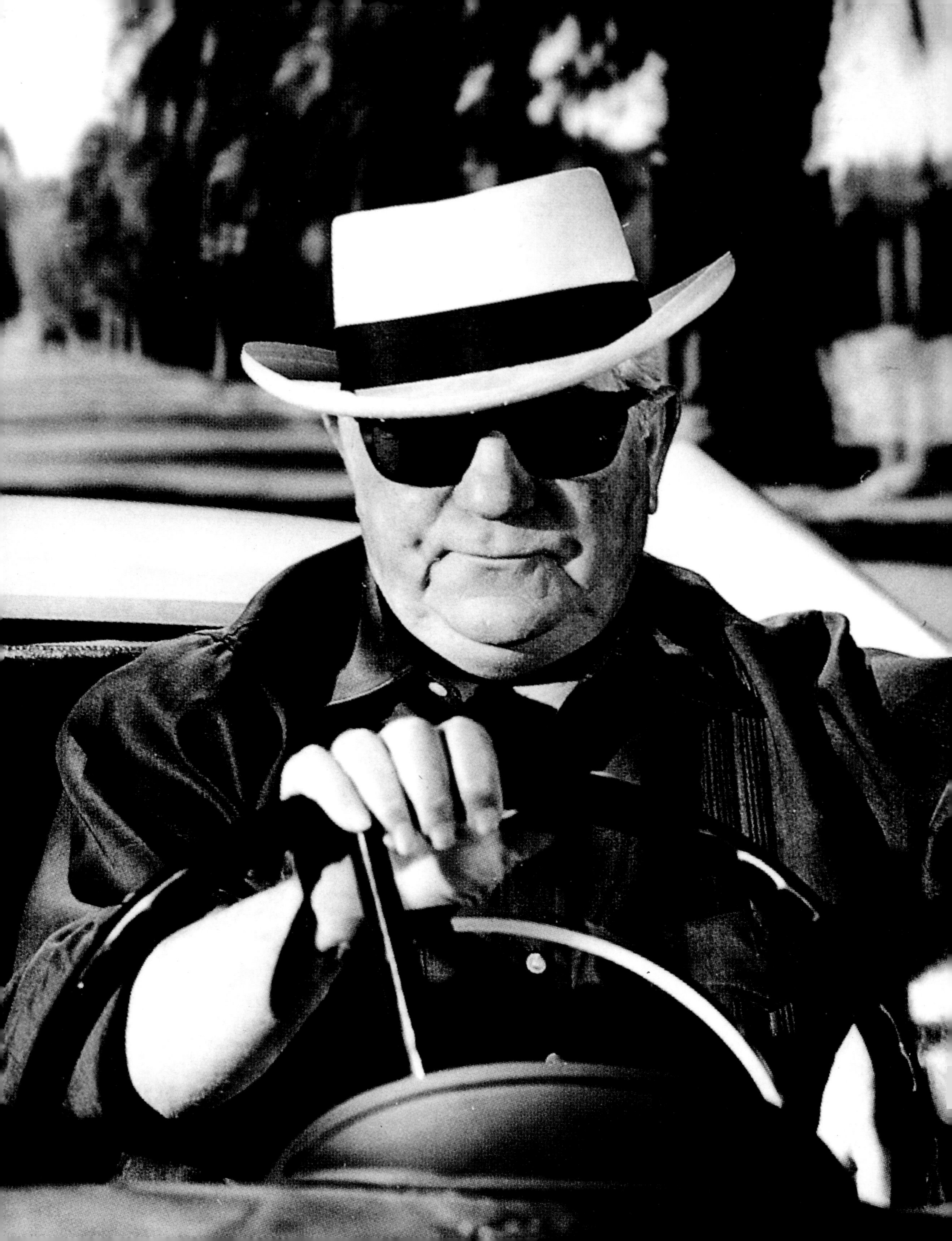

Acknowledgements

This book would not have existed without Nicole Fougeret, an importer of panamas into France, who was the originator of the idea, and whose knowledge of panamas is equalled only by her passion for them.

Thanks are due to Laziz Hamani and Philippe Sébirot, who contributed valiantly to the success of our journey to the land of the panama.

Thanks are due to Maria-Christina Pallarés, Cultural Attaché at the Ecuadorian Embassy in Paris, who was kind enough to accompany us to her country and to introduce us to her friends.
Thanks are due to her parents, who contributed in their own way to this quest for the panama.

Thanks are due to Metropolitan Touring Ecuador, who helped us to discover Ecuador, and to Mariano Proaño and Françoise de Tailly, who had faith in this project.

Thanks are due to Patrick Lifshitz, to whom we owe many wonderful meetings, and who introduced us to this unique hat.

Thanks are due to Brent Black, importer of panamas into the USA, for his participation in the production of this book.

Thanks are due to Oswaldo Viteri for having spoken to us of his country through his collections, and to his wife, who is a model of South American femininity.

Thanks are due to Chichi, Margarita, and Galo Plaza, for their friendly welcome to Zuleta, and their research into this dearly-loved past!

Thanks are due to José Miguel Orska Lasso, and to Marco Naranjo and Omar Tejada, the administrators of the La Cienega hacienda.

Thanks are due to Maria-Elena and Eduardo Balarezo: their warm welcome is in our memories.

Thanks are due to Mercedes Santiesteban de Noboa, and to Ricarda Hogaboom, Bernardo Manzano Torres and Bernard Jean Clement Manzano, who were our guides to the discovery of Guayaquil.

Thanks are due to Carla Mantilla de Albornoz and her husband, Fernando Albornoz Bueno, for having opened the beautiful gates of Montelimar with so much simplicity.

Thanks are due to Doris Cashmore de Mantilla for the very beautiful memory of the house which she carries within her. Very particular thanks go to Maria Gangotena Manchero for her great kindness.

Thanks are due to Javier Pesantes Garcia, to Jorge Haro, and to Jorge Valencia and Hugo Creamer, for their help during our travels in Ecuador.

Thanks are due to the Cobo family for having opened up to us the doors of the bullfighting world in Ecuador.

Thanks are due to Carlos Vera for his enthusiasm in getting people in his country to talk about the panama.
Thanks are due to Eloy Alvires Alfaro for his stories about his heroic grandfather.

Thanks are due to Wilson Hallio for his help and his knowledge of the Valdivia civilisation.

Thanks are due to Don Rosendo Delgado Garay, Maria Clothilde Lopez, Juana Isabel Lopez, Manuel Lopez Espinal, Sevovio Italo Espinal, Maria Lopez de Delgado and Jacqueline Simon de Munizaga for the time they gave us during our discovery of Montecristi and the province of Manabí.

Thanks are due to Mr and Mrs Kurt Dorfzaun, Homero Ortega, Gerardo Serrano, Klever and Alberto Pulla, and also Norberto and Raul Rodriguez, who helped us to arrive at a better comprehension of Cuenca and its region.

Thanks are due to Farid Chenoune, Philippe Mollins Martin, Jeanne Berna, Isaline de Mommeja, Hania Destelle, Christiane Sanguin de Livry, Linda Newton, Pierre Debard, Jean Pascal Billaud, David Ballu, Michel Assouline, Olivier Assouline, Florence Lemonde, Laure d'Abzac, Eliane Allain, Christian Chaboud, Olivier Buchet and Jean-Pierre Gaudot, as well as to the Fashion Institute of Technology in New York, for their help and advice in the writing of this book.

Thanks are due to the Musée du Chapeau in Chazelles for their kindness in loaning us documents.

Thanks are due to Jeremie Benoit, curator at the Musée de Malmaison, for the information he provided about the imperial legend.

Thanks are due to Isabelle Ducat for her role as art director. Thanks are also due to Daniel Delisle and the Studio Prunelle, and to the Laboratoire Publimod Photos, for their participation in the production of this work.

Thanks are due, finally, to the Bon Marché, and most particularly to Christine Delaroche, Laurence Desmousseaux and Séverine Merle, for their enthusiastic participation in spreading the word about the panama.

Bibliography

Chapeaux, 1750-1960. Paris : palais Galliéra, 1980.

Des modes et des hommes, Farid Chenoune. Editions Flammarion.

La Filière des panamas (the Panama Hat Trail), Tom Miller. Editions Actes Sud - 10/18.

Les Chapeaux - Une histoire de tête, Florence Müller et Lydia Kanitsis. Editions SIPAS.

Céline. *Mort à crédit*. Folio éditions Gallimard.

La garde-robe de Gabriele D'Annunzio.

L'élégance masculine, Abel Léger. 1912.

Fortune : de Rotschild à Rockefeller, Alexis Gregory. Éditions Assouline. 1993.

Napoléon chez lui, F. Masson, 1894.

La vie quotidienne de Napoléon à Sainte Hélène, Gilbert Martineau, 1966.

Napoléon raconté par l'image, Arnaud Dayot, 1902.

Resumen de Historia del Ecuador, Enrique Ayala Hora. Corporacion Editora Nacional.

El Montenero de Montecristi, Horacio Hidrovo Peñaherrera.

Tejiendo la vida... Maria Leonor Agnilar de Tamariz. CIDAP.

Notas de viaje-Manabí, Jose Alberto Donoso. Quito 1933.

Eloy Alfaro y Cuba. Emeterio S. Santovenia. La Habana. 1929. Imprenta del siglo XX.

Hats : a History of Fashion in Headwear, Hilda Amphlett, Chalfont St. Giles : Sadler, 1974.

Hats on Heads, Midred Anlezark, *The Art of Creative Millinery*. Rev. ed. Kenthurst, NSW : Kangaroo Press, 1990.

The Collector's Encyclopedia of Hatpins and Hatpin Holders, Lillian Baker, Paducah, KY : Collector Books, 1976.

Edwardian Hats, Anna Ben-Yusuf, *The Art of Millinery* (1909). Mendocino, CA : R.L. Shep, 1992.

Hats, Fiona Clark, London : B.T. Batsford, 1982.

The Hat Book, Alan Couldridge, London : Batsford, 1980.

Hatpins, E. Eckstein and J. Firkins, Princes Risborough, Buckinghamshire, UK : Shire Pub., 1992.

The hat Book, Annette Feldman, New York : Van Nostrand Reinhold, 1978.

Millinery in the Fashion History of the World, Paul Louis Victor de Giafferri, from 5300 B.C. to the Present Era. New York : The Illustrated Milliner, 1928.

The Hat : Trends and Traditions, Madeleine Ginsburg, Hauppauge, New York : Barron's, 1990.

The History of the Hat, Michael Harrison, London : Jenkins, 1960.

Hats, v. 1. (1876-). New York : Millinery Associates, 1876-. [Formely Millinery Trade Review. Library has v. 1 - 57 (1876-1932 ; 1943-1970).]

Hats in Vogue since 1910. New York : Abbeville Press, 1981.

A Pageant of Hats, Ancient and Modern, Ruth E. Kilgour, New York : Mc Bride, 1958.

Hats : Status, Style and Glamour, Colin Mc Dowell, New York : Rizzoli, 1992.

The Man in the Bowler Hat : His History and Iconography, Fred Miller Robinson, Chapel Hill : University of North Carolina Press, 1993.

Here's Your Hat, William Severn, New York : McKay, 1963.

Hats : A Stylish History and Collector's Guide, Jody Shields, 1st de. New York : Clarkson Potter, 1991.

The Mode in Hats and Headdress, Ruth Turner Wilcox, New York : Scribner, 1959.

Esquire's Encyclopedia of 20th Century Men's Fashions, O.E. Schoeffler, New York : Mc Graw-Hill, 1973.

Clothes and the Man, Alan Flusser. Editions Villard books.

Straw Hats. Their History and Manufacture, Harry Inwards. Londres 1922.

Photographic credits

P. 8: Bibliothèque nationale de France (Napoleon's hat), p. 10: Valdivia Foundation Collection, p. 14, 15, 18, 19, 22: Banco Central Archives, p. 24, 78-79 et 140: Star Films (*Death in Venice*, Sacha Guitry, Sailors), p. 34, 66: Archive Photo France – Catherine Terk (Winston Churchill, Kruschev…), p. 79: Roger Viollet (Santos Dumont), p. 96: Paris-Match p. 7, 11, 12, 13, 15, 16, 17, 20, 21, 31: private collection of Plaza family, p. 70: Hulton Deutsch (Signor Baizinni, 1905), p. 25: Musée du Chapeau de Chazelles (… extracts from *La Vie illustrée* N° 357), p. 22: Sygma (Theodore Roosevelt, 1910), p. 123: Cinestar (Charlton Heston), p. 29, 77: private collection archives of the SBM, p. 26: Bettman Archive, p. 118, 129: Nicole Fougeret's private collection.

CASA MIGUEL HEREDIA C. - Recepción a los Comisionados

CASA MIGUEL HEREDIA C. - Planchando Sombreros